THE PERSONS IN RELATION PERSPECTIVE

INTERNATIONAL ISSUES IN ADULT EDUCATION

Volume 9

Series Editor:

Peter Mayo, *University of Malta, Msida, Malta*

Scope:

This international book series attempts to do justice to adult education as an ever expanding field. It is intended to be internationally inclusive and attract writers and readers from different parts of the world. It also attempts to cover many of the areas that feature prominently in this amorphous field. It is a series that seeks to underline the global dimensions of adult education, covering a whole range of perspectives. In this regard, the series seeks to fill in an international void by providing a book series that complements the many journals, professional and academic, that exist in the area. The scope would be broad enough to comprise such issues as 'Adult Education in specific regional contexts', 'Adult Education in the Arab world', 'Participatory Action Research and Adult Education', 'Adult Education and Participatory Citizenship', 'Adult Education and the World Social Forum', 'Adult Education and Disability', 'Adult Education in Prisons', 'Adult Education, Work and Livelihoods', 'Adult Education and Migration', 'The Education of Older Adults', 'Southern Perspectives on Adult Education', 'Adult Education and Progressive Social Movements', 'Popular Education in Latin America and Beyond', 'Eastern European perspectives on Adult Education', 'An anti-Racist Agenda in Adult Education', 'Postcolonial perspectives on Adult Education', 'Adult Education and Indigenous Movements', 'Adult Education and Small States'. There is also room for single country studies of Adult Education provided that a market for such a study is guaranteed.

Editorial Advisory Board:

Paula Allman, Research Fellow, University of Nottingham, England

Stephen Brookfield, University of St Thomas, Minnesota, USA

Phyllis Cunningham, University of Illinois, Urbana Champagne, USA

Waguida El Bakary, American University in Cairo, Egypt

Budd L. Hall, University of Victoria, BC, Canada

Astrid Von Kotze, University of Natal, South Africa

Alberto Melo, University of the Algarve, Portugal

Lidia Puigvert-Mallart, CREA-University of Barcelona, Spain

Daniel Schugurensky, OISE/University of Toronto, Canada

Joyce Stalker, University of Waikato, Hamilton, New Zealand/ Aotearoa

Juha Suoranta, University of Tampere, Finland

The Persons in Relation Perspective

In Counselling, Psychotherapy and Community Adult Learning

By

Colin Kirkwood

With an Introduction by Judith Fewell, an Afterword by Tom Steele, and
contributions by Emilio Lucio-Villegas, Anna Other and David Tait

SENSE PUBLISHERS
ROTTERDAM / BOSTON / TAIPEI

A C.I.P. record for this book is available from the Library of Congress.

ISBN 978-94-6091-907-7 (paperback)
ISBN 978-94-6091-908-4 (hardback)
ISBN 978-94-6091-909-1 (e-book)

Published by: Sense Publishers,
P.O. Box 21858, 3001 AW Rotterdam, The Netherlands
https://www.sensepublishers.com/

Printed on acid-free paper

To Gerri, with love and gratitude

CONTENTS

SECTION V: APPLYING THE PERSONS IN RELATION PERSPECTIVE IN ADULT EDUCATION AND ADULT LEARNING

ACKNOWLEDGEMENTS

The title of the present book is adapted from John Macmurray's *Persons in Relation*, first published by Faber and Faber in 1961 as the second volume of his Gifford Lectures on *The Form of the Personal*. The first volume, *The Self as Agent*, was originally published in 1957. The extent of the influence of John Macmurray's life and work on my own will become apparent in the first chapter, in which his ideas are discussed and applied. In this connection I acknowledge with gratitude the contribution of John E. Costello, on whose *John Macmurray: A Biography* (Floris Books, 2002) I have drawn extensively. I have been influenced also by the writings of Macmurray scholars David Fergusson and Michael Fielding. To Ronald Turnbull I owe a special debt of gratitude, because it was Ronnie who reawakened my interest in Scottish philosophy in the late 1980s, first by drawing my attention to the work of Alasdair MacIntyre, then to John Macmurray and finally to Alexander Broadie. In the penultimate chapter of Broadie's *A History of Scottish Philosophy*, in which he discusses twentieth century contributions, he gives pride of place to Macmurray's work, illustrating it with reference to his influence in the fields of psychotherapy and interpersonal relations in the work of Ian Suttie, Ronald Fairbairn, John D. Sutherland and R.D. Laing, with the first three of whom my own contribution is concerned.

The Persons in Relation Perspective aims to articulate, in a new synthesis, the ideas that underlie my own practice and that of many others in the fields of counselling, psychotherapy and psychoanalysis, adult education, community development and community action. In doing so, it touches on many overlapping fields of theory and practice, including theology and religion, psychiatry, psychology and nursing, health and well-being, politics and sociology, social work and social care, education, literature and social geography.

The linking ideas are personalism and the practice of dialogue; and the best known personalists of the 20th century were John Macmurray, Martin Buber, Emmanuel Mounier and Paulo Freire. The influence of Paulo Freire on my work and that of many adult educators is discussed, with appropriate acknowledgements, in *Living Adult Education: Freire in Scotland* (second edition) (2011), by Gerri Kirkwood and myself. The Freirean dimension of my synthesis is explored in the last two chapters of the present book. Chapter 11 contains a Freirean bibliography.

It is usually the case that acknowledgements at the beginning of books such as this one are concerned with intellectual sources, and make reference to authors and their published books and papers. But ideas expressed in writing, however vital, are not the only source of illumination. What I have in mind, in terms of influences to be acknowledged with gratitude, is the profound impact the many women with whom I have collaborated have had on my orientation and practice. This influence has entered me directly through their personalities, their presence, their ways of being, doing and relating, and their resourcefulness and inventiveness in carrying out the work. They include my wife, Gerri Kirkwood, through our marriage, our work together in Barrowfield and Castlemilk in Glasgow in the 1970s, in the Adult Learning Project in Gorgie-Dalry in Edinburgh from 1979, and in our lives as parents and grandparents. I acknowledge with gratitude the influence of Margaret Jarvie in counselling and counselling training, through what I have learned from her and her husband David of their involvement in the Iona Community and the Gorbals Group, and through our work together in Shetland. I am grateful for the long collaboration I have enjoyed with Judith Fewell in a variety of projects and settings also related to counselling and counselling training. I remember with appreciation how much I have received from working with Mary Walker, Tom Frank, Mhairi Macmillan, Jo Burns, Alison Shoemark, Dave Mearns, Andrina Tulloch, David Morgan, Siobhan Canavan, John McLeod, Gabrielle Syme, Liz Bondi and Jo Hilton.

From my apprentice years as a psychotherapist at Wellspring, I acknowledge with thanks the influence of Di Bates (Dr Diana Bates, Director of Wellspring and daughter of Winifred Rushforth, founder of the Davidson Clinic). Di's personal being and relating spoke more deeply to those of us who worked with her than a ton of words could ever do.

In my counselling and psychoanalytic psychotherapy training at the Scottish Institute of Human Relations, I am grateful for what I learned in many different ways from Alan Harrow, Mona Macdonald, Judith Brearley, John Evans, Una Armour, Cathy Smyth, Bobbie Fraser and Neville Singh. I am grateful, also, for the help and support of Chris Holland, Penny Holland and Norah Smith. Gerri and I will never forget the strength we drew from the support of Janet Hassan. I express my appreciation of everything I have read by Colwyn Trevarthen.

In the latter part of the 1980s I was fortunate to work with the Scottish Association for Counselling in their collaboration with the Scottish Health Education Group, and benefitted from lasting collegial and friendship relations with Ronald Beasley and Ian Thompson, and with Bill and Ingsay Balfour. In the later 1990s and the first decade of the new century, I have appreciated working with Stewart Wilson, Marilyn Cunningham and Brian Magee of COSCA, the professional body for counselling and psychotherapy in Scotland, with Gabrielle Syme, Elsa Bell and Craig McDevitt of the British Association for Counselling and Psychotherapy, with Malcolm Allen of the British Psychoanalytic Council and with Mika Haritos-Fatouros of the European Association for Counselling.

After retiring from the University of Edinburgh I did a five year stint as psychotherapist at the Huntercombe Edinburgh Hospital, working with women and girls with severe eating disorders. I learned an enormous amount from our patients and my fellow members of staff, for which I am very grateful. Selection is invidious, but I must mention with special gratitude the hospital's first Medical Director, David Tait, its manager, Diane Whiteoak, and my psychotherapeutic colleagues Michelle Conway and Laura Thomson. It was an inspiring and challenging experience.

Turning now to the contents of the book itself:

For her generous Introduction, I thank Judith Fewell, Honorary Fellow of the University of Edinburgh, and for his insightful Afterword, I thank Tom Steele, Senior Research Fellow of the University of Glasgow.

Chapter 1 was first published in *Counselling and Psychotherapy Research*, Volume 3, Number 3, September 2003. A few minor modifications have been introduced in the present version. My thanks to John McLeod, then editor of CPR and now Professor of Counselling at the University of Abertay Dundee.

Chapter 2 was first published in its full form in *The Legacy of Fairbairn and Sutherland: Psychotherapeutic Applications* (Routledge, 2005), edited by Jill Savege Scharff and David E. Scharff, Co-Directors of the International Psychotherapy Institute and Teaching Analysts at the Washington Psychoanalytic Institute. (My thanks to Jill and David are expressed more fully in the introduction to Chapter 8.) The version included here has been shortened, excluding a section on the work of John Macmurray, and modified in various other ways.

Chapter 3 is a modified version of a keynote presentation given in Athens in the spring of 2006, at an international conference entitled *Counselling in Europe: Theory, Research, Practice and Training* organised by Panteion University of Social and Political Sciences, the Greek Association for Counselling and the European Association for Counselling. Special thanks are due to Professor Mika Haritos-Fatouros of the conference organising committee and then President of the EAC.

Chapter 4 was first written for the Counselling Studies Team at Moray House School of Education in the University of Edinburgh, and first published in the Spring 2002 issue of the COSCA Journal, *Counselling in Scotland*. It is published here in a modified version. My thanks to my fellow team members and to Brian Magee, Chief Executive of COSCA.

Chapter 5 was written as a follow-up to the paper that became Chapter 4, again for the members of the Counselling Studies Team. It has been revised and expanded several times, and was first published in the Spring/Summer 2004 issue of the COSCA Journal, *Counselling in Scotland*. The version published here is significantly different from the 2004 version. Once again, I thank the team and Brian Magee.

Chapter 6 has a complex history. Some of the material was first presented at a meeting of the Scottish Institute of Human Relations Tayside Group, in Perth in 2007. A longer version was given at a meeting of the Scottish Association for Psychodynamic Counselling in Glasgow in 2010. It became possible to write the present version when I rediscovered the three letters sent to me by the patient with whom I had worked. I made contact with her again and sought her permission to include a selection of my reflective process notes on our work, together with her letters, all suitably anonymised. She was happy to agree. I then invited Dr David Tait, in his capacity as Medical Director of the Huntercombe Edinburgh Hospital when the work was being done, to write a Reflection on it from his own point of view, and he did so. This is possibly the first time that a verbatim account of an intensive psychotherapeutic relationship from three points of view has been published. I should add that I also asked David Tait and the patient (Anna Other) to go through the text carefully and propose alterations to anything with which they disagreed or which misrepresented the work of the Hospital and its staff. They did so. I express my deep gratitude to both Anna and David for their collaboration. I believe this chapter is worthy of the description A Dialogical Narrative, and that it makes a strong case for restoring psychotherapy to the place it formerly occupied in in-patient psychiatric treatment. I thank Tom Leonard for his permission to reproduce a line from his poem *This Island Now*. (Poems, Dublin, 1973)

Chapter 7 was first given as a paper at a conference held in Edinburgh in June 2003, organised by the Counselling and Society Research Team of the University of Edinburgh. I thank Professor Liz Bondi and our colleagues Judith Fewell and Arnar Arnason. The paper, which has not previously been published, has been significantly modified. Again, I thank Tom Leonard for permission to quote from his poem *This Island Now,* referred to above.

Chapter 8 is the most recent piece of writing in the present book. Full acknowledgement of the key contributions is given in the text of the chapter and in the bibliography, so I will not repeat them here. The chapter originated out of an initiative taken in 2007 following the publication of Jill Savege Scharff's selection of papers by Jock Sutherland in her book *The Psychodynamic Image: John D. Sutherland on Self in Society* (Routledge, 2007). The Sutherland Trust, of which I was then co-convenor, the Scottish Institute of Human Relations and the Centre for Counselling and Psychotherapeutic Studies of the University of Edinburgh combined to run a successful course introducing younger people to Sutherland's work. This chapter brings together two of my own contributions to that course.

Chapter 9 was delivered as the Immortal Memory of Robert Burns at the Moray House School of Education Burns Supper in January 2000, and first published in the November 2000 issue of Psychodynamic Counselling. The text here is almost identical to the previously published version. I acknowledge with thanks the contributions of my old school and University friend, the Burns scholar Kenneth Simpson, drawn from his book *Burns Now* (Canongate, 1994).

Chapter 10 was given as a contribution to the conference Scotland as a Learning Society: Issues of Culture and Identity held at the University of Edinburgh in February 1995. It was first published as Occasional Paper No. 9 by the Centre for Continuing Education, University of Edinburgh, 1996. I thank Tom Leonard for permission to quote from his poem *Tea Time* (Outside the Narrative, Etruscan Books/Word Power Books, 2009).

Chapter 11 was first published in The Scottish Journal of Community Work and Development, Volume 3, Spring 1998, both as a memoir of a conference in honour of the 70th birthday of Paulo Freire held in New York in 1991, and as a reflection upon Freire's life and work following his death in 1997.

Chapter 12 was first published in *Citizenship as Politics* (Sense Publishers, 2009) edited by Emilio Lucio-Villegas. It is the text of an interview by Emilio with myself, and I express my gratitude to him for his permission to reproduce it here.

In conclusion, I am deeply grateful to Jill Savege Scharff, Ian Martin, David Tait, Tom Steele and Judith Fewell for taking the time to read the whole text of the book in draft, and for giving me honest and helpful responses to it. Many of their comments have been incorporated into the final text. But the responsibility for its form, style and inadequacies is my own.

I thank John Shemilt and John McLeod for their appreciative endorsements of the book.

And finally, without the help of Jane-Ann Purdy of Geordie Mac, my struggle with wordprocessing and formatting would have failed utterly. She is responsible for extracting from the mind and index finger of a technically challenged interlocutor a document that now appears, at least to its author, very satisfactory indeed. Many thanks, Jane-Ann.

Colin Kirkwood
Edinburgh, Scotland
May 2012

INTRODUCTION

In 1986 I sat in a room with twenty-four other participants at the Scottish Institute of Human Relations (SIHR) in Edinburgh anticipating the start of the Human Relations and Counselling Course. Looking round the room I noticed that there were few men, four I think. One stood out, although now looking back across the years I'm not sure why I was drawn to him, perhaps it was his deep laughter, his friendly beard or the warmth that exuded from him. Whatever it was we ended up being both adversaries and lifelong friends and colleagues for the next 25 years of our working lives.

I was a Jewish Glaswegian radical feminist immersed in a PhD on gender and education with a growing interest in psychodynamic theory and counselling practice. He was a Scottish Nationalist, with Presbyterian Northern Irish parentage, a community activist and adult educationalist. Throughout the two years of the course we discussed, debated and fought intensely. He was one of the most interesting, stimulating and infuriating people I had encountered. Little did I know then that we were about to enter a working relationship that would dramatically change the shape, direction and nature of my working life. But my task in this introduction is not to write about the profound influence that Colin Kirkwood has had upon the way in which I think and my creativity but rather to try and offer up the flavour of the man which is so evidenced on every page of this book and to say something about his significant contribution to the world of counselling and psychotherapy in Scotland in all its different forms throughout these last 25 years.

Counselling in Scotland in the mid-80s was just about to blossom. There was no accreditation, no regulation, little training, few stakeholders, not many private practitioners, little research, hardly any competition and no randomised controlled trials (RCTs). The professionalisation of counselling had barely been considered. There was much freedom and many spaces into which a person with vision and creativity could insert himself.

However there was a lot of pent up demand for practical and theoretical frameworks to make sense of relationships of all kinds, with our selves, family, friends and intimate partners, colleagues and groups, and our relationships with our communities and the wider social and cultural contexts in which we were embedded. From 1986, Colin Kirkwood spearheaded many of the subsequent developments: researching and writing a directory of the provision of counselling services and counselling training in Scotland for the Scottish Health Education Group (SHEG) and the Scottish Association for Counselling (SAC); developing and delivering, with me, training courses in counselling skills for the Scottish Council of Voluntary Organisations (SCVO) across Scotland, and for the social work department of Lothian Regional Council; taking counselling training to

Shetland; supporting the development of therapeutic services at Wellspring, one of the oldest centres of therapeutic practice in Scotland; and helping the core organisation representing counselling in Scotland, COSCA, through its growth towards maturity, as its chair for four years.

All this time he was honing his craft, practising as a counsellor, starting at the counselling service of the Edinburgh Association of Mental Health, then as a couple counsellor at Lothian Marriage Counselling Service, now Couple Counselling Lothian, and then as a psychotherapist at Wellspring. At the same time all this was going on Colin and I were involved in the intensive training to become psychoanalytic psychotherapists at the Scottish Institute of Human Relations.

Eventually he joined Moray House Institute of Education in Edinburgh, in 1994, as Senior Lecturer in Counselling, a new post where he established the Centre for Counselling Studies in which I joined him a year later. Together we developed the postgraduate Certificate in the Counselling Approach and the postgraduate Diploma in Counselling, which was to become one of the premier professional trainings for counsellors in Scotland at that time.

I shared many of Colin Kirkwood's endeavours and I have been witness to his thinking and action. In my view these found their fullest expression in the philosophical framework Colin developed which informed and underpinned the courses and relationships at the Centre for Counselling Studies: see especially Chapters 4 and 5.

We were presented with a dilemma. How were we to honour the richness of ideas and practices in the trainings already on offer at Moray House under the creative leadership of Margaret Jarvie, whom Colin succeeded, whilst finding a place for what we too could offer? And how were we to respond to the academic requirements of postgraduate work at university level which seemed to some antipathetic to the values of counselling? This became especially important when Moray House merged with the University of Edinburgh.

The notion of dialogue gradually emerged out of many discussions. At its most obvious, a dialogue between two historically antagonistic theoretical and therapeutic practice frameworks, the humanistic tradition of the person-centred approach on the one hand, and psychoanalytic perspectives on the other. This notion of dialogue was about being able to have meaningful conversations about and around profound differences and values, the very different ways of understanding what it meant to be human and how to be in relationship with oneself and others. These were questions that Colin had been pondering for many years, from his undergraduate studies of English Language and Literature through his work in working class communities in Glasgow and in adult education at the Workers Educational Association (WEA) in Edinburgh. The learning from all these different sites of action and thought came to fruition in the Centre for Counselling Studies. Colin was also explicit in his understanding that his engagement and deep interest in dialogue came from experiences of sectarianism in Northern Ireland and Scotland, and the many attempts to find ways to bridge what at times seemed the unbridgeable.

If we were to fully live dialogue in our relationships, our internal worlds and external realities, in our interactions and teaching, then we had to find ways to talk, explore and reflect across the divides of position-taking and defensive investments in identifications. Colin had the vision (an overused word but apposite here): he led the way, always inviting, encouraging, interested, always challenging the other to experience, to think, to explain, to elaborate. At times this could be very trying and tiring especially when I just wanted a cup of tea and not to have to think or feel or reflect. But this was also and always exciting and at times exhilarating as we walked down the corridor together on our way to the cafeteria, Colin telling me what he had been reading and thinking the night before, continuing the conversation we had yesterday, continuing the conversation as we sat down, Colin involving and inviting other colleagues to join in and later on the next day or the day after, Colin letting me know that he had reached a kind of synthesis of the disparate ideas and conversations. Dialogue was not just a theoretical premise upon which to hang some interesting ideas, for him (and for me) it was a daily, lived experience.

Nor was this dialogue restricted to theoretical debates in the corridors, cafeteria and classroom. It informed every encounter, with student, colleague and practitioner; how we conceptualised the learning/teaching environment and even how we approached assessment. It informed how we thought about and structured each learning experience to maximise 'knowledge of' rather than 'knowledge about' (see Chapter 1). Here Colin was able to draw upon his extensive engagement with Paulo Freire's work, always starting from the students' experiences and their views of the world. We sat in circles, we didn't give lectures, we offered inputs where the students' contributions were encouraged, we moved from experience through reflection to theory and practice. We engaged in the assessment process as if we were in a continuing dialogue with the student. Colin's spontaneous, ongoing and extensive comments on the text of a student's essay as if he were having a lively conversation with her exemplified this. And his students loved him for this, for the time, attention and respect he gave to them and especially their written work.

When Colin discovered John Macmurray's writing it was as if he recognised that what he had been involved in creating was a living embodiment of Macmurray's thinking about persons in relation, as he discusses in Chapter 1. This chapter and the following two in the section 'Defining the persons in relation perspective', on Suttie and Fairbairn, exemplify that quality of Colin's thinking and writing which is about how to embrace an idea, a conceptual framework, interrogate it, turn it this way and that, work out his understanding and his response, making it his own. I remember talking with Colin about how he studied for his English degree at Glasgow University. He said that he wanted to discover how he felt and what he thought about the text he was reading first, before he read any commentaries or critiques of it, be it poem or novel or play.

This independence of mind and capacity for originality as well as an underlying commitment to persons in relation can be found in every chapter of this book. I want to comment on a couple that capture for me the depth and breadth of Colin's passionate interests.

Therapeutic accounts of working with a client where the client's voice is given parity with the therapist's are rare in the psychotherapeutic literature for a variety of reasons, not least because of issues to do with confidentiality and ethical practice, since the therapeutic work is for the benefit of the client. Making clinical material available in the public domain is problematic. Having said this, to read accounts of therapeutic work in practice from both the perspective of the client and the practitioner is always illuminating. We can learn a lot through reading these kinds of accounts. Their rarity makes the ones that do become available even more valuable

In Chapter 6, Colin offers us one such account. Here he puts together a narrative of how he and Anna worked to try and make sense of her anorexia. Whilst the storyteller is the therapist, the voice of the client is given equal place in the story that they, client and therapist, construct together. What emerges is not a story of triumph, or of getting better, or even of failure but rather one of time being taken, of what we might call internal continuity where the therapist has been taken in as an empathic, deeply interested listener. This has a real impact over time even after the therapist is no longer present in the client's external life. Thus after leaving the hospital and leaving her therapist, Anna was still making use of her internal experience of him. He is internally present in her search for meaning and in her story making. And what an extraordinary story she has to tell of her relationship with anorexia. What is so moving about this is that Anna feels able to return to Colin, in the form of a letter and, I would suggest, in her continuing dialogue with him, the next chapter of her story. This is an extraordinary gift from Anna to Colin. As therapists we rarely get to hear what happens next. I think that Anna felt able to let Colin know because of the particular kind of therapeutic relationship Colin was able to offer her, one that deeply embodied his persons in relation perspective, one where her story of control and survival and her struggle to have an intact sense of self was witnessed and honoured as having validity however painful and life threatening it might be. This chapter alone makes two important contributions, to the literature on anorexia and the literature on what goes on in the consulting room between therapist and client because it offers us the voices of the client and therapist in dialogue together.

The other chapter I wish to touch on is Chapter 9, *Robert Burns in the counsellor's chair: a psycho-socio-cultural analysis of the Burns myth*, but rather than write about it I want to explore the memories it brought to mind which I hope will illustrate something of Colin's literary sensibilities amongst other things.

When we were attending the required seminars for the adult psychoanalytic psychotherapy training at the SIHR there was one evening when we were trying to really understand the emotional experiences of jealousy and envy and the psychoanalytic theories that attempted to explain them. Quietly from Colin came this quote:

For sweetest things turn sourest by their deeds:
Lilies that fester smell far worse than weeds.
(William Shakespeare, Sonnet no. 94)

Later in the pub Colin quoted the whole sonnet. I was to have this experience with him over and over again especially when we were teaching together. There might be a moment's confusion in the room with the students, or one of silence or of non-comprehension, and then out of his reverie Colin would quote a line or more of poetry. This was not a party trick or Colin being clever. Rather it was evidence of the extent to which Colin had taken in, absorbed and understood the writings of others that had moved him, had meant something to him, that he had studied and internalised, so that 35 or 40 years later this poem, that quotation, was still available to him and therefore to us.

Judith Fewell
Psychoanalytic Psychotherapist
Honorary Fellow
University of Edinburgh

SECTION I

DEFINING THE PERSONS IN RELATION
PERSPECTIVE

CHAPTER 1

THE PERSONS IN RELATION PERSPECTIVE

Towards a Philosophy for Counselling and Psychotherapy in Society

Key words and themes: personalism, persons in relation, the self as agent, knowledge of, knowledge about, the good other, friendship in community.

This paper is the first in a planned series which aims to articulate and synthesise the persons in relation perspective in counselling and psychotherapy, drawing together the contributions of the philosopher John Macmurray (1891–1976), the psychotherapist Ian Suttie (1889–1935), and the psychoanalyst Ronald Fairbairn (1889–1965). The present paper introduces the persons in relation perspective, derived from Macmurray's work. It outlines the historical and cultural context leading to the emergence of modernism, and the response of personalism. It summarises John Macmurray's life and philosophy, focussing on his account of knowledge, its relation to the senses and the emotions, and his view of persons, society and religion. The paper goes on to develop a hypothesis about the rise of counselling and psychotherapy in Britain, linking it to the decline of religion, the conflict between individualism and collectivism, and the re-emergence of the persons in relation perspective. It concludes by posing challenges for the person-centred and psychodynamic orientations, and for counselling and psychotherapy as a whole.

INTRODUCTION

This paper has a personal significance for several reasons. First of all, I come from a northern Irish Presbyterian family, although I was born and grew up in Scotland. My father was a minister of the Church of Scotland who died in January 2003. He is very important to me, but the relationship is complicated because, as a child, I was in awe of him, and because from my early teens I knew that I did not believe in God. It was not until I came across the work of John Macmurray in 1989 that I began to entertain the idea that belief in God might not be the core of religion. This discovery has been slowly exploding in my soul, like a benign bomb, ever since. You can perhaps imagine my emotions when, sifting through his possessions with my brothers and sister, I came across two of Macmurray's books from the 1930s, with red underlines and the occasional marginal note in my father's handwriting. It was clear he had been deeply touched by Macmurray, as I have been 60 years later. In one of our last conversations – we were talking about the institutional church and its doctrines – he said to me, 'Of course, I don't believe in a lot of that stuff now. But I believe in Jesus'.

The second reason for its personal significance is that, ever since I took up the post of Head of the Centre for Counselling Studies at Moray House Institute (now the School of Education of the University of Edinburgh), I have been committed to the idea and practice of dialogue between the person-centred approach and psychodynamic perspectives in counselling and psychotherapy. We were the first postgraduate centre to adopt this orientation to counselling training. I have been challenged by the question of how best to express the common ground between them, coming as they do from such apparently different sources. In the present paper, and those to follow, I see myself as helping to excavate that common ground.

The third reason is frankly political, as well as religious. The global failure of communism in the 20th century lies not in the poverty of its original vision, but in its failure to put the personal at its heart. Instead, it put its faith in technology, in large-scale social structure and in an impersonal, coercive and frequently murderous collectivism, treating human beings and their relationships as disposable objects to be bulldozed aside. Personalists like John Macmurray entered into sustained dialogue with communism in the 1930s, but they were not heeded. We can still hear the voice of John Macmurray today, and we can learn and apply his lessons in the 21st century.

This paper was first presented at the joint *International Association for Counselling and Psychotherapy/European Association for Counselling* conference at Geneva in April 2003, on the theme of the counsellor and social responsibility. It begins with a question, an old-fashioned theological play on words: what is the ground of all our being as counsellors? I suggest that many of us do have such an orientation, which is indeed the ground of our being counsellors, but we are either unaware of it in the sense that we have never said it to ourselves out loud, or else we are diffident in talking about it, especially when speaking to those with political, economic or institutional power. We tend to talk their language, and tack towards their objectives, so that we can persuade them to make use of our services.

HISTORICAL AND CULTURAL CONTEXT

In what follows, I identify some of the key features of the persons-in-relation perspective. This entails outlining the thinking of John Macmurray, whose work provides the basis for it.

To do this I need to start with a very short history of the 19th and 20th centuries, mainly in Europe. The 19th century was characterised by rapid urbanisation, industrialisation and the flourishing of capitalism; the emergence of modern nation states in Germany and Italy; the weakening of the Austro-Hungarian empire; and the growth of British, French, and later German imperialisms. The cultural backcloth was romanticism, which began in radical iconoclasm and ended in regressive sentimentality. Grudging but significant advances were made in the direction of the representative version of democracy. The Christian religion got involved in a battle with positivist science about the creation of the world and the evolution of species, a battle it was bound to lose. In philosophy, Friedrich Nietzsche excoriated Christianity for hypocritical sentimentality, announced the death of God, and hailed the emergence of the superman. In personal life, the dominance of men over women and reason over the emotions and the senses had reached such a pitch by the 1890s that Sigmund Freud was driven to adapt such concepts as hysteria, repression and the unconscious in order to help make sense of some of the experiences of middle-class women in Vienna. Around the same time, Robert Louis Stevenson was writing *Dr Jekyll and Mr Hyde*, offering a way of explaining related phenomena in the male psyche, an analysis pointing in the direction of the concept of dissociation then being developed by Pierre Janet, and later adapted by Ronald Fairbairn. The end of the century saw the deepening immiseration of the urban proletariat, the spread of trade unionism among semi-skilled and unskilled workers, and the growth of organised social democratic, labour and communist movements.

This boiler-room of tensions exploded in various ways: revolutionary uprisings in Russia, Germany, and Austria, the suffragette movement, and above all the First World War. The 20th century proceeded as a three-way struggle between fascism, communism and representative democracy, accompanied by the emergence of modernism as a cultural theory, the creation and growth of the welfare state, and the decline of religion. After the Second World War a golden age of relative social security opened the way to the decline of deference, accompanied by the take-off of science and technology, and the hybrid radicalism of the 1960s and 70s, with its disparate strands of laid-back libertarianism, militant trade-unionism, marxism, student revolt, feminism, and gay liberation. The next phase saw the forward march of labour halted (to use E. J. Hobsbawm's phrase), and the rise of free-market economics and laissez-faire individualism. Radical intellectuals hailed the failure of the grand narratives and the emergence of post-modernism. That is the story line we have got used to hearing.

PERSONALISM

I want to add another story, a more creative and affirmative story, which starts with a significantly different response to the horrors of the First World War. The intellectuals of the 1920s were united in their view that the society and culture they had inherited was discredited. Ezra Pound summed it up in a terse phrase: 'a botched civilisation'. Pound, like many of his contemporaries, turned to fascism. Others turned to communism, others to a more moderate but still statist kind of social democracy. These are the stories that get told over and over again. What gets lost sight of is a story, which is of special interest to us as counsellors and psychotherapists, the story of personalism. I will argue that the narrative of personalism, far from having failed, has re-emerged, certainly in the UK, in the form of the popular turn to counselling and psychotherapy in response to the Thatcherite individualism of the 1980s and 1990s.

What is personalism? Briefly, it is a response to the distortions and hypocrisy of society and religion in the 19th century, which does not discard religion but seeks both to rediscover and reinvent its core meaning and revitalise its practice. The key ideas are that human beings are persons, that the heart of their being lies in their relations with other persons, and that the self-realisation of persons-in-community is an end-in-itself which should not be subordinated to other ends. Personalism is a radical social perspective, which shares the ends of human liberation and social justice with communism and social democracy, but holds that these ends cannot be achieved by subordinating the personal to the structural or by worshipping the state. To conclude this outline it is important to emphasise that these are normative, not descriptive statements. Personalism is grounded in positive values. It is not about going along with social trends in a rudderless fashion: it offers an orientation for living our lives. Personalism has its roots in the life of Christ and in aspects of the Jewish tradition, and takes a very specific, relational view of God, as we shall see.

I first came across personalism in the early 1970s in the work of the Brazilian adult educator Paulo Freire. I had been drawn to Freire because of concerns about people being treated as objects, as means to future ends, even within struggles for human liberation. Freire's work is a synthesis of many elements. The core of it is his commitment to the idea that oppressed people can engage with the world as subjects who know and act, not objects which are known and acted upon. He developed an approach to popular education, which centres around the practice of dialogue as a way of engaging with oppressive social reality. The personalist influences on Freire were Martin Buber and Emmanuel Mounier. There is no reference in his work to that of John Macmurray, and it wasn't until I read a remarkable essay by Ronnie Turnbull, entitled Scottish Thought in the 20th Century, in 1989, that I came to realise his importance. It is worth pointing out that Martin Buber knew and admired John Macmurray, seeing no significant difference between their ideas.

Throughout the following sections, I make extensive reference to John Macmurray's own work. His key books in order of first publication are:
– *Freedom in the Modern World* (1932)
– *Reason and Emotion* (1935)
– *The Clue to History* (1938)
– *The Self as Agent* (1957)
– *Persons in Relation* (1961)
With the exception of *The Clue to History*, these have all been reissued recently. I have also drawn widely from John Costello's excellent biography of him, published by Floris Books in 2002. John Costello is a faculty member of the University of Toronto, where he is director of the Jesuit Centre for Faith and Justice.

JOHN MACMURRAY'S LIFE

Macmurray was born in 1891 and died in 1976. He grew up in a Presbyterian family in Scotland. Presbyterianism is not a quietist faith which poses individual against society. On the contrary, it combines communal and private prayer with family and congregational worship, stressing the social responsibility of the person to embody the values of their faith in community, work and the wider world. John Macmurray's youthful personal journal shows how fully he internalised its values of fellowship and altruism. He studied philosophy and toyed with pacifism as the First World War approached, opting first to join the Royal Army Medical Corps and later becoming an officer in a fighting regiment. Immediately on his arrival in the trench where his platoon was stationed, a shell exploded killing two of the men he had just been talking to. Towards the end of the war he was seriously wounded and invalided out. Before that happened, on a visit home, he preached in a Presbyterian church in north London, urging the congregation not to adopt a spirit of vengeance towards the Germans, and pleading for reconciliation. This message was received with hostility. No-one would speak to him after the service. Reflection on these and other experiences radically reshaped Macmurray's view of religion. He was never tempted to abandon it, but from then on he distinguished between personal Christianity and the spurious Christianity of religious organisations, which he called the national religions of Europe. He never subsequently joined an institutional church, until he retired in 1959, when he relented and joined the Quakers, perhaps the least institutional form of Christianity.

John Macmurray had a successful academic career at the Universities of Oxford, Witwatersrand, London, and Edinburgh. He lived a life of commitment, broadcasting, opposing fascism, in dialogue with communism and the Soviet Union, and engaged in the struggle for world friendship and justice through the Christian Left. He affirmed *friendship* as the core value, analysing the causes of the First World War not primarily in terms of imperial rivalries, but in terms of distortions in values and actions. He highlighted pervasive hypocrisy, sentimentality, the substitution of gross materialism for spiritual yearnings, the myth of progress, and the deliberate cultivation of hatred of other nations: as his biographer John Costello puts it,

> The demonisation of the 'other' in order to hide inner contradictions and to enhance a self-image of moral rightness. (Costello, 2002)

Against this, he affirmed an apparently simple alternative: cultivation of the personal life.

HIS PHILOSOPHICAL POSITION: THE STANDPOINT OF ACTION

He starts from a rejection of Descartes' *I think, therefore I am*. Macmurray argues that it is a standpoint which isolates the self from others, splits mind from body and the spiritual from the material, and separates thinking from sense experience, feeling and action. Against the egocentric assumption that the self is an isolated individual, he puts forward the view that the self is a person, and that personal existence is *constituted* by our relations with other persons. He substitutes the 'You and I' for the solitary 'I' (Macmurray, 1995c, pp. 11–12).

Against Descartes' disembodied subject, who observes and thinks in isolation, he proposes the primacy of the self as agent, an agent confronted with other selves, each of whom reflects upon his or her activity. Action is primary. Thinking is vital but secondary: a subordinate activity which serves action. Reason, or rationality, which is much wider than thinking, begins in sense perception and crucially involves the emotions, which are the sources of our motives and our evaluations. In a memorable phrase, he defines reason as

> the capacity to act consciously in terms of the nature of what is not ourselves, [whether that is an inanimate object, an organism or another person]. (Macmurray, 1995b, p. 21)

In adopting this standpoint, Macmurray sought to overcome dualism, egocentricity and objectification of the other. He is not denying that persons are subjects, nor that they are and can be known as objects:

> A personal being is at once subject and object both; but he is both because he is primarily agent. As subject he is 'I', as object he is 'You', since the 'You' is always the 'Other'. (Macmurray, 1995a, p. 27)

> I can isolate myself from you in intention, so that my relation to you becomes impersonal. In this event, I treat you as an object, refusing the personal relationship.' (Macmurray, 1995a, p. 28)

KNOWLEDGE, THE SENSES AND THE EMOTIONS

Macmurray argues that the history of philosophy discloses three forms of knowledge:
- knowledge of the inanimate material world, which he links with mathematics, physics, the use of mathematical and mechanical metaphors, and formal logic;
- knowledge of the organic world, expressed, for example, in biology, linked with the use of evolutionary and organic metaphors, and dialectical logic;
- knowledge of the world of the personal whose form he set himself the lifelong task of articulating. He argues that the highest and most comprehensive form of knowledge is the mutual knowledge of two persons.

Personal knowledge, he argues, subsumes or includes the material and organic forms of knowledge. It does not supplant them, but it does put them literally in their place. They are vital dimensions of the personal, but personal life cannot be reduced to them. Personal knowledge is radically different from impersonal *knowledge about* something or someone. He makes a sharp distinction between *knowledge of* and *knowledge about*. Intellectual knowledge, which relies on concepts, gives us knowledge about things, not of them (Macmurray, 1995b, p. 43).

To understand more fully what Macmurray means by personal knowledge, and *knowledge of*, we need to return to his view of the relationship between knowledge and action.

> To act and to know that I am acting are two aspects of one experience ... if I did not know that I was acting I should not be acting ... I must know to some extent what I am doing if I am doing it. There cannot be action without knowledge. Yet action is logically prior to knowledge, for there can be no knowledge without an actual activity which supports it ... (Macmurray, 1995c, pp. 102–103)

This leads him to consideration of the part played by the activity of sense perception in knowing:

> [it is] through sense perception [that] I am aware of the Other ... the Other may be another thing, another organism or another person. (Macmurray, 1995c, p. 109)

He takes touch, rather than sight, as the paradigmatic sense perception:

> Tactual perception, as the experience of resistance, is the direct and immediate apprehension of the Other-than-myself. The Other is that which resists my will. (Macmurray, 1995c, p. 109)

Knowledge of is more than intellectual knowing: it begins with the senses which he calls the gateways of our awareness (Macmurray, 1995b, p. 39). To be fully alive we need to increase our capacity to be aware of the world through the senses, cultivating it for its own sake. As well as the senses, we need to cultivate our emotional life: our emotional life is us. He talks about emotional reason. All our motives, he argues, are emotional:

> Emotion stands directly behind activity determining its substance and direction. (Macmurray, 1995b)

though he acknowledges, with a nod in the direction of Freud, that quite often the emotions which motivate us are hidden from our conscious awareness. The cultivation of our emotional life is the cultivation of our direct sensitiveness to the reality of the world about us. Its aim is to develop

> the capacity to love objectively, ... the capacity which makes us persons. (Macmurray, 1955b, p. 32)

Not only do our emotions provide the motives for our actions, we depend on them also for our determinations of value.

As the picture builds up, we can see the inclusive view of knowledge that Macmurray is developing. We know the world through our senses (which, we need to remember, are directed both inwards and outwards), through our feelings, which are a deeply orientational form of knowing, and finally through the intellect. Intellectual knowledge is vital, but it is partial. It contributes *knowledge about* from the standpoint of the observing thinker, but it is incapable of generating the *knowledge of* that can only be achieved by persons as agents through cultivation of their senses and their emotions, and through their encounters with other persons. All thinking, concludes Macmurray, is for the sake of action, and all action is for the sake of friendship.

It should be noted at this point that far from being hostile to empirical science, Macmurray was an enthusiastic and informed supporter of it. He was keen to promote dialogue between the sciences, the arts and religion, which he saw not as antagonistic, but as involving different and mutually necessary forms of knowledge. He saw scientific knowledge as an abstraction from the full field of personal knowledge, and described it as involving knowledge of fact only.

REINVENTING RELIGION

Macmurray's reflections on his experience of the First World War, together with his passionate sincerity in personal relations and his commitment to freedom and social justice, led him to a radical reinterpretation of the meaning of religion.

According to John Costello, his Canadian biographer, his reading of Marx and Trotsky led him not to abandon but to reinvent his Christianity in a new, non-idealist form. He concluded that the institutional churches had abandoned any concern for the material dimension of life, substituting pie in the sky when you die: they had become purely spiritual. Macmurray observed that

> modern Communism might well be that half of Christianity ... dropped by the church ... coming back to reassert itself against the part that had been retained. (Costello, 2002, p. 199)

But this was not the statement of a man fighting a rearguard action to defend the indefensible in Christian tradition, dogma and doctrine: on the contrary, that is what he jettisoned. In its place, he puts what he calls the spirit of Christ, the personal, and the core value of friendship-in-community. By the personal, he is referring not to you and me in a cupboard, or in the nuclear family, or even in a nation, but to you and me in the world. In effect, Macmurray is re-translating the rallying cry of the French revolution as freedom, equality and friendship-in-community.

It is clear that Macmurray's conception of the personal is communal and political as well as religious. Religion is '...the personal life of humanity: it is bound up with the experience that makes us persons' (Macmurray, 1995c, p. xi). He writes:

> any community of persons, as distinct from a mere society, is a group of individuals united in a common life ... its members are in communion with one another; they constitute a fellowship ... the self-realisation of persons in relation. (Macmurray, 1995a, pp. 157–158)

He is not talking of a bounded, particularistic, localised community but of a universal community of persons in which each cares for all the others ... (Macmurray, 1995a, p. 159)

religion is the pressure to live in terms of the reality of persons who are not ourselves ... the urge to enter into full mutual relationship with other persons ... It is the force which creates friendship, society, community, cooperation in living. (Macmurray, 1995b, p. 62)

friendship is the fundamental religious fact in human life. (Macmurray, 1995b, p. 63)

religion [is] the slow growth of emotional reason in us. (Macmurray, 1995b, p. 65)

Communion is the keyword of religion. (Macmurray, 1995b, p. 65)

THE GOOD OTHER

Macmurray's mother was a powerful influence in his life, one to whom he remained deeply attached but from whose emotionally constricting and fundamentalist qualities he struggled to separate himself. John Costello gives an amusing account of Macmurray's attempts to answer his mother's demanding question: 'John, where is God in all this?' It is my view, though Macmurray might not have agreed, that the idea of God as an objective existent has become superfluous in Macmurray's vision of religion. Yet in each of his books, he finds a place for God. Here is one example of this process as it occurs in *Persons in Relation*. He is giving an account of the meaning of communion, which he sees as a celebration of fellowship, involving a communal representation or reflection of the community to itself. Consistent with the centrality of the personal, what has to be represented is the relation to a personal other. Macmurray continues:

how can a universal mutuality of intentional and active relationship be represented symbolically? Only through the idea of a personal Other who stands in the same mutual relation to every member of the community ... the universal Other must be represented as a universal Agent ... the idea of a universal personal Other is the idea of God. (Macmurray, 1995a, p. 164)

As the last step in this wholly intelligible but increasingly attenuated sequence of thinking, Macmurray finds a place for God as the universal personal other. In my view, this is convincing as an account of how our ancestors came to infer or invent the existence of God from their profound need for a universalised good other. As a proof of the existence of God, it is unconvincing. To put the matter positively, John Macmurray has by his passionate pursuit of the logic of the personal, discovered that 'God' symbolises and represents nothing more and nothing less than our universal need for and love of the good other.

SOCIETY AND THE DECLINE OF RELIGION

How, then, does Macmurray view society? This, I believe, is where John Costello is right to argue that he is a philosophical voice for the 21st century. Macmurray developed his key ideas in the 1920s and 30s, the period of the rise of fascism and communism, although it was not until the late 1950s and early 60s that he gave them their fullest formulation in his two series of *Gifford Lectures*, jointly entitled *The Form of the Personal*, and published by Faber and Faber as *The Self as Agent* (1957) and *Persons in Relation* (1961). His reflections on the societies he knew are just as relevant to the societies of the 21st century. He believed that the failure of contemporary societies could be explained by their disregard of the personal in favour of material and organic forms of knowledge, structure and action. He argued that the cultural crisis of the present is a crisis of the personal. To explain what he means, he refers to two aspects of the contemporary situation: the tendency towards an apotheosis of the state; and the decline of religion. As far as the apotheosis of the state is concerned, he sees it as involving the subordination of the personal aspect of human life to its functional aspects. John Costello is surely right to argue that Macmurray's assessment is relevant not only to the communist, fascist and democratic societies of the west in his day, but equally, and perhaps more strongly, to the current tensions between liberal democratic, social democratic, and traditional societies in the first decade of the 21st century.

On the impact on society of the decline of religion, his views are best represented by an extended direct quotation from the first chapter of *The Self as Agent:*

> The decline of religious influence and of religious practice in our civilisation … betrays, and in turn intensifies, a growing insensitiveness to the personal aspects of life, and a growing indifference to personal values. Christianity, in particular, is the exponent and guardian of the personal, and the function of organised Christianity in our history has been to foster and maintain the personal life and to bear continuous witness … to the ultimacy of personal values. If this influence is removed or ceases to be effective, the awareness of personal issues will tend to be lost, in the pressure of functional preoccupations, by all except those who are by nature specially sensitive to them. The sense of personal dignity as well as personal unworthiness will atrophy, with the decline in habits of self-examination … Success will tend to become the criterion of rightness, and there will spread through society a temper which is extraverted, pragmatic and merely objective, for which all problems are soluble by better organisation. In such conditions the religious impulses of men will attach themselves to the persons who wield political power, and will invest them with a personal authority over the life of the community and its members. The state is then compelled to perform the functions of a church (for which by its nature it is radically unfitted) and its efforts to do so will produce … a crisis of the personal … If we remember that history has brought us to a point where we must think of human society as a whole, and not limit our outlook to the confines of our own nation, then there

must be few who will fail to recognise ... that we are involved in such a crisis. (Macmurray, 1995c, pp. 30–31)

COUNSELLING, PSYCHOTHERAPY AND THE PERSONS IN RELATION PERSPECTIVE

But what has all this got to do with counselling and psychotherapy? Here I will have to confine myself to a short outline of a hypothesis concerning recent developments in British society exclusively. Church membership and religious practice, conventionally understood, have declined drastically across the United Kingdom throughout the 20th century. The exact pattern has varied significantly in the different nations of the union, but the broad trend is the same. The components of religious organisation and practice also vary, but the common elements are the central role of the minister, vicar or priest; the church service involving communal prayer and singing, the reading of the bible and preaching of the sermon combining exposition of biblical texts with their application to everyday living in society. To this must be added the sacraments of baptism, marriage and communion, personal and family prayer, and ministry through pastoral visitation, confession, forgiveness, and atonement.

As religious practice has declined, two mutually opposed trends which are in tension with one another have flourished, often in the same person. The first is the complex trend towards individualisation, and I would include in this complex Thatcherite individualism linked with self-reliance, enterprise, and free-market economics, along with more obviously psycho-social features such as individuation, self-actualisation, person-centredness, and the recent emphasis on autonomy and personal space. The second is the trend towards collectivism which again should be considered as a complex, including trade union, socialist, communist, ecological, feminist and gay movements, and various forms of single issue protest such as the anti-poll tax movement, and the recent activities of the Stop the War coalition.

For the present purpose what is significant about these trends is the tension between them, often expressed in the form of highly individualistic personal styles, preferences and behaviours, in combination with often strident collectivist behaviours and affiliations. This can be understood as an attempt to resolve a deep-seated conflict between the desire for personal autonomy and the need for relatedness, social security, and justice.

Traditionally, religions had achieved a resolution of this conflict based on the primacy of the community of believers gathered around their god, their doctrine and their practice of care which acknowledged the dimension of individual conscience through self-examination, prayer, confession, repentance, faith, and good works. In this sense, the personal has always been a recognisable dimension of religious practice. But this traditional solution is no longer available to post-modern man and woman, because of its perceived authoritarianism, its *imposition* of a set of revealed beliefs, values and practices for living. This helps to explain the enormous appeal of the Rogerian conception of an internal locus (and process) of

13

evaluation, which appears to free the individual from imposed, or introjected, values. This trend is reflected also through the growing preference for spirituality as (explicitly) opposed to religion.

What is particularly fascinating in the British context is to note that political expressions of collectivism peaked in the later 1970s and early 1980s, just at the time when individualism, free enterprise, and the rolling back of the state took hold and began to flourish from 1979 onwards. As this dubious battle (in Steinbeck's phrase) swayed back and forth, the 70s and early 80s saw the steady growth of counselling and psychotherapy which took off in the mid to late 1980s, with spectacular increases in the demand not only for counselling, but also for counselling and counselling skills training. The trend continued upwards throughout the 1990s, dropping slightly, and then levelling off with the return of a Labour government in 1997.

Some left-wing commentators have argued that the growth of counselling and psychotherapy represents the privatisation and individualisation of care. There is an element of truth in that case, but it is a typically structuralist reading of a social trend which has much deeper personal meanings. Our research on Voluntary Sector Counselling in Scotland, (Bondi et al, 2003), which focussed on the personal experiences and reflections of about 100 voluntary sector counsellors, trainees, and counselling agency managers, has confirmed what we knew anecdotally from the outset. A significant number of counsellors and psychotherapists come from activist left-wing (socialist, communist, feminist, and gay) backgrounds, from activist religious backgrounds (Protestant, Catholic, Judaic, Muslim, Buddhist), and often from backgrounds of committed activism involving both (for example, membership of the Iona Community, whose founder, George MacLeod, was an admirer of John Macmurray). No claims about generalisability are being made here. But there is enough evidence to encourage us to offer another possible interpretation of the growth of the demand for counselling, counselling training, and the counselling approach. This interpretation connects the growth of counselling directly with the persons-in-relation perspective as articulated by Macmurray.

Counselling and psychotherapy, on the part both of client and therapist, can be seen as a popular response to the ravages of predatory individualism, materialism, and nihilism, representing *both* a reaching out for help, a search for understanding of self, other, and society and a need to be personally known, *and* the embodiment of a wish to care for and know the other in an immediate, direct, personal way. It can be understood as the altruistic giving of oneself to the other, the offer to know the other through a mutual encounter, involving a deep respect for the other person's freedom and personal meanings, on the basis of equality of regard. The therapeutic relationship can be seen as a specific form of friendship-in-community. The parallel with Macmurray's ideas is certainly striking. The same case can be elaborated with reference to the significance of counselling and psychotherapy courses as learning groups or learning communities. These can be understood as the intentional creation of opportunities for personal relating which facilitate the growth of friendship-in-community. In this setting, personal *knowledge of* self,

14

other, and society is informed by *knowledge about* therapeutic theory, values and practices, with the aim of cultivating the capacity to help others as you yourself have been helped.

Just as religious doctrine – and arguably also God – has been de-centred in Macmurray's re-interpretation of religion, so too in the practice of counselling and psychotherapy training, while we see some continuation of fundamentalist attitudes in the core models or orientations of certain training courses, there is a growing trend in the direction of plurality within orientations, and dialogue between orientations, amounting to a willingness to learn, understand, and speak each other's language and seek common ground. The truths revealed by such gurus as Sigmund Freud and Carl Rogers have been brought down from the mountain to the community learning centre for critical consideration. We are coming to appreciate them not as gods but as fallible, good-enough human beings, who struggled to understand, to accompany and to help.

CHALLENGE FOR THE PERSON-CENTRED APPROACH

In conclusion, the persons in relation perspective which I am arguing is emerging in counselling and psychotherapy, contains some very hard challenges for us. Because time is short, I will confine myself to suggesting just two of these. One is a challenge for the person-centred approach, and the other for psychodynamic perspectives. I select these two because of their pivotal importance in the therapeutic culture of today. I have no doubt, incidentally, that John Macmurray would have valued both of these perspectives and engaged in constructive dialogue with them, but his position in relation to each would not have been uncritical.

The person-centred approach, as its name implies, centres itself on the person of the client and the person of the therapist. It affirms the significance of the personal feelings and meanings of both. It holds that the task of the therapist in the psychotherapeutic relationship is to accompany the client as s/he explores these feelings and meanings in a process that is deeply respectful of the client's autonomy as a person. If there is psychological contact between the two, and if the therapist's empathic acceptance is consistently communicated and experienced by the client, and felt to be real, the client will come to trust her own internal locus and process of evaluation, gradually becoming able to discard introjections usually from early caregivers.

From a persons-in-relation point of view this is unclear, not so much in its formulation as in its effect. It could be (and sometimes is) understood as encouraging a self-centred and hedonistic orientation: if it feels alright to me inside, then it *is* alright. Macmurray would see this as a distortion of priorities. For him, what is vital is not the person him-or-herself, but the person in personal relation with the other. It is our relations that are actually *constitutive* of our personal existence. What we take in from and give out to others cannot be reduced to the status of introjections, but includes a host of internalisations which have contributed to making us what we are now.

Macmurray's perspective argues for the giving of the self to the other in a mutual relation of knowing. This is altruism, but not to be confused (although it is often confused) with abnegation or disregard of the self. Macmurray would, I believe, have endorsed Gerard Manley Hopkins' celebration of the self:

> Each mortal thing does one thing and the same:
> Deals out that being indoors each one dwells;
> Selves – goes itself; *myself* it speaks and spells,
> Crying *What I do is me: for that I came.*
> (in Gardner, 1953, p. 51)

What both Hopkins and Macmurray mean by this is a full giving of the self to the world, to the other. It is not an egocentric being-for-self, but being-of-self-with-and-for-the-other.[1] This challenge also goes to the heart of the relationship between the person-centred approach and contemporary western society. Is the person-centred approach on the side of contemporary self-centredness and hedonism, or opposed to it? There is an ambiguity at the heart of the person-centred approach around this vital issue which needs to be addressed.

Having said that, Macmurray would profoundly value the person-centred approach, because of its emphasis on the embodiment in practice of respect for the person of the client. The emphasis on tracking and sensing the personal feelings and meanings of the client, of not imposing an understanding from another frame of reference, and of a congruent meeting of the person of the counsellor and the person of the client at relational depth, is in tune with his perspective. (In formulating the wording of this paragraph, I have drawn on the work of Dave Mearns and Brian Thorne, both of whom offer a more relational view of the person-centred approach).

CHALLENGE FOR PSYCHODYNAMIC PERSPECTIVES

Macmurray would be equally challenging in relation to psychodynamic perspectives. He would take issue first of all with its name: psychodynamics is a metaphor drawn from physics, and implies a completely impersonal view of the psyche as a field of conflicting forces. Macmurray would acknowledge that a person may indeed have such conflicts within them, but would reject the view that, as a person, they can be reduced to them. He would regard the 'treating' of a 'patient' conceived of as suffering from repressed drives and psychic representatives of drives, as involving the objectification of a person. While he would acknowledge that the object relations perspective is a qualitative advance on a theory based on impersonal drives, he would challenge the predominant view of the other as object implied in the name of this perspective. To Macmurray, the self is first of all an agent, in a subordinate sense a subject, and only when treated as a mere means to an end, an object. For object relations, he would insist on substituting personal relations, if the therapist/client relationship is to be a genuinely personal one.

His challenge to the psychodynamic perspective would not confine itself to the theoretical level. He would argue that ambivalence within psychodynamic perspectives as to whether the client is to be regarded as a person or as an object, has led, at its worst, to a partial depersonalising of the therapeutic relationship, in which the full self of the therapist as person is withheld from the client. For a mutual encounter in which the person of the therapist meets the person of the client, some psychodynamic practitioners have historically substituted a blank screen in which the client is denied a direct contact with the real responses, the real humanity of the therapist. He would call for a fundamental revision of psychodynamic theory and practice in this central respect. Such a revision has to some extent been undertaken, most prominently by Harry Guntrip, who explicitly acknowledges his debt to John Macmurray. That revision has been influential, but its impact is by no means pervasive.

Yet once again, Macmurray would deeply value psychodynamic perspectives, above all for their illuminating insights into the ways in which human beings are constituted by both their external and internal relations with other persons. Indeed, we know from John Costello that he drew heavily on Ian Suttie's *The Origins of Love and Hate* in developing his understanding of the relations of persons. I personally take the view that he was also influenced by the ideas of his contemporary, Ronald Fairbairn, although his biographer, John Costello, states he has not managed to find confirmation of this.

Another way of interpreting these two challenges is to suggest that Macmurray's ideas can be used to elucidate understandings that are already implicit in person-centred and psychodynamic practice. The challenges then resolve themselves into invitations to re-conceptualise that practice in the light of the persons-in-relation perspective.

CONCLUSION

Macmurray's final challenge to us as counsellors and psychotherapists considered as a whole body has to do with how we see therapy in society. We still tend to see the personal as private: we equate personal relations with relations within the family, with partners or with personal friends. The personal, on this perspective, is a private, encapsulated domain. And that is how many counsellors and psychotherapists see the concerns of their practice: as a private matter concerned with individuals abstracted or excerpted from the social matrix. We even refer to it as 'private practice'. But for John Macmurray, the personal extends in every direction. It is public, social, economic, political, ecological, and religious: it is universal. If, to revert to a useful materialist metaphor, we see persons as nodes in a multiplicity of networks, from the Macmurray perspective many of the nodes are persons and many of the lines of the networks are personal relations. (He does acknowledge that, while direct relations are personal, indirect relations are impersonal.) His is a normative, evaluative, and not a neutrally descriptive theory. The personal is primary. It is ethically of first and last importance. If we were to adopt the persons-in-relation perspective as a philosophy for counselling and psychotherapy in society, it would commit us to a position that gives therapy a particular kind of ethical basis, one that asserts the primacy of persons in relation in all social and global issues. Therapeutic work has a subordinate technical dimension which is important, but it is not grounded in technical rationality, nor is it primarily a method of problem solving. Its *tekhne* is a means constitutive of its ends, and its ends are self-and-other knowledge, knowledge of the good, and the reaffirmation of the universality of the personal relation of friendship-in-community.

NOTES

[1] Evidence for this interpretation of Macmurray's view of the self can be found in his earliest book, *Freedom in the Modern World*, first published in 1932, especially in the chapter on self-realisation.

REFERENCES/BIBLIOGRAPHY

Bondi, L., Fewell, J., Kirkwood, C., & Arnason, A. (2003). *Voluntary sector counselling in Scotland: An overview*. Edinburgh: The Counselling and Society Research Team.

Buber, M. (1959). *I and Thou* (2nd ed.). Edinburgh: T & T Clark.

Costello, J. E. (2002). *John Macmurray: A biography*. Edinburgh: Floris Books.

Fairbairn, W. R. D. (1986) (first published 1952). *Psychoanalytic studies of the personality*. London: Routledge and Kegan Paul.

Freire, P. (1972). *Pedagogy of the oppressed*. Harmondsworth: Penguin.

Gardner, W. H. (Ed.) (1953). *Gerard Manley Hopkins: A selection of his poems and prose*. Harmondsworth: Penguin.

Guntrip, H. (1971). *Psychoanalytic theory, therapy and the self*. London: Karnac.

Kirkwood, C. (2003). Reflections on dialogue between person-centred and psychodynamic perspectives in counselling training. *Newsletter of the European Association for Counselling*.

Kirkwood, G. & Kirkwood, C. (2011). *Living adult education: Freire in Scotland* (2nd ed.). Rotterdam/Boston/Taipei: Sense Publishers.

Macmurray, J. (1938). *The clue to history*. London: Student Christian Movement Press.

Macmurray, J. (1992) (first published 1932). *Freedom in the modern world*. London: Humanities Press.

Macmurray, J. (1995a) (first published 1961). *Persons in relation*. London: Faber and Faber.

Macmurray, J. (1995b) (first published 1935). *Reason and emotion*. London: Faber and Faber.

Macmurray, J. (1995c) (first published 1957). *The self as agent*. London: Faber and Faber.

Mearns, D. & Thorne, B. (1999). *Person-centred counselling in action* (2nd ed.). London: Sage.

Suttie, I. D. (1988) (first published 1935). *The origins of love and hate*. London: Free Association Books.

Turnbull, R. (1989). Scottish thought in the twentieth century. In C. Beveridge & R. Turnbull (Eds.), *The eclipse of Scottish culture*. Edinburgh: Polygon.

CHAPTER 2

THE PERSONS IN RELATION PERSPECTIVE

Sources and Synthesis

Key words and themes: innate need for companionship, tenderness, interest-rapport, play, love and its vicissitudes, development of a social disposition, the taboo on tenderness, psychotherapy as reconciliation, internalisation, inner world, ideal object and central ego, rejecting object and anti-libidinal ego (internal saboteur), exciting object and libidinal ego, dissociation, passive tolerance of contradictions, true freedom.

INTRODUCTION

This second paper moves towards a synthesis of the contributions of three great 20th century Scots: the philosopher John Macmurray (1891–1976), the psychiatrist and relational psychotherapist Ian Suttie (1889–1935), and the psychoanalyst Ronald Fairbairn (1889–1965). Here I discuss the contributions of Suttie, indicate briefly the significance of Fairbairn's contributions, and identify some key themes of the emerging synthesis. Reflecting on progress so far as if it were a football match, I would say that at this point we're about two thirds of the way through the first half.

Ian Suttie created an interpersonal and socio-cultural psychology in the 1920s and 30s, one which has been unjustly neglected yet is widely influential. A longer version of this second paper was first published in *The Legacy of Fairbairn and Sutherland: psychoanalytic approaches* (Routledge, 2005), edited by Jill and David Scharff. The section of it omitted here is the summary of the ideas of John Macmurray, which are fully covered in the previous chapter. The third paper, which follows this one, is concerned with Ronald Fairbairn's revolutionary account of the interpersonal nature of the basic inner situation, and takes further forward the task of articulating the synthesis.

Macmurray, Suttie, and Fairbairn all served in and were affected by World War I. They all drew deeply (and in different ways) on Scottish Christian traditions. They benefited from the Scottish educational tradition of training in philosophy, which enabled them to challenge Freud's thinking with confidence and authority, without devaluing his contributions. Lest we might imagine that Ian Suttie is the odd man out, the one who has gate-crashed the party, we must note that it was on Suttie's book, *The Origins of Love and Hate* (Suttie, 1935) that John Macmurray based some of his own thinking about persons in relation. Although Fairbairn makes no reference to Suttie in his published work, we know from his biographer, John D. (Jock) Sutherland, and from Fairbairn's friend and analysand, Harry

Guntrip, that he was influenced by Suttie's writing. Harry Guntrip records that Fairbairn said to him: 'Suttie really had something important to say' (Guntrip, 1971, p. 24). We learn from Fairbairn's daughter, Ellinor Fairbairn Birtles, that he and Macmurray knew each other and may have collaborated, and we know that Harry Guntrip was deeply influenced by both of them and attempted to integrate their ideas in his own synthesis.

The last 20 years have seen renewed recognition of the contributions of Macmurray, Suttie and Fairbairn. Their works have been republished. There have been critical reassessments of Fairbairn and Macmurray, and ground-breaking biographies of Ronald Fairbairn by Jock Sutherland, and of John Macmurray by John Costello. Their perspectives are now influencing thinking and practice worldwide. John Bowlby described Ian Suttie's book as:

> a robust and lucid statement of a paradigm that now leads the way,

adding:

> his ideas never died: they have smouldered on, at length to burst into flame … *The Origins of Love and Hate* stands out as a milestone. (Suttie, 1988, pp. xv, xvii)

THE CONTRIBUTION OF IAN SUTTIE

I am deeply indebted to Dorothy Heard for her painstaking excavations and lucid account of Ian Suttie's life and ideas (Heard, 1988). Ian Dishart Suttie was born in Glasgow in 1889, the third child of a family doctor. He graduated in medicine in 1914 and worked as a psychiatrist in Govan before joining the Royal Army Medical Corps. He saw service in France and in what is now Iraq. After working at Gartnavel Hospital in Glasgow, and hospitals in Perth and Fife, he became a psychotherapist at the Tavistock Clinic in London in 1928, continuing to work there until his untimely death in 1935. His wife Jane was also a psychotherapist there. They shared an interest in the ideas of the Hungarian analyst Sandor Ferenczi whose work Jane translated. Ian Suttie was by all accounts a vigorous, kind, brilliant, and intellectually combative man who was deeply missed by his colleagues. In his obituary, J. R. Rees, Medical Director of the Tavistock Clinic, describes his boyish gusto, and his passionate advocacy of ideas. Dorothy Heard quotes Jock Sutherland as saying that

> Ian Suttie could be assertive and confrontational in a way that was not always in his own best interests. (Heard, 1988)

I will offer a summary of Suttie's ideas, followed by close-ups of a selection of his core themes. Essentially, Suttie was engaged in an impassioned – and (sadly) one-sided argument with Freud, challenging Freud's instinct theory and replacing it with one based on the innate need for companionship and love. Suttie's only book, *The Origins of Love and Hate*, was written in a great hurry. His themes criss-cross, but the author's insight and passion carry the reader along. I have spent several months reading it closely, and have named the key themes in his own words as far as possible, organising them in a sequence in which the one leads easily into the next.

Suttie's key themes:
- the innate need for companionship: love, tenderness, interest-rapport, and fellowship
- psychic weaning and the development of a social disposition
- play and the development of cultural interests
- self and not-self
- consciousness and social mind
- the emotions, expression, and communication
- the taboo on tenderness
- culture and society
- society and the jealousies
- women, children, and men
- the critique of Freud
- science and the scientific attitude
- religion as social psychotherapy
- psychopathy as disturbance of the social disposition
- psychotherapy as reconciliation

In reading this sequence, you may have noticed certain significant features. First, there is an emphasis on interpersonal and socio-cultural dimensions throughout. Second, these are seen as closely related to each other: they are not in separate compartments. Third, there is an attempt to develop an overview, the sense of a vision of the whole of society, culture, disturbance and psychotherapy. The jigsaw pieces fit together, and the picture that emerges is integrated and comprehensive.

The innate need for companionship

Here, I offer a selective summary, starting with the ground-base of Suttie's perspective, the innate need for companionship, embodied in love, tenderness, interest-rapport and fellowship. In positing this innate need for companionship, Suttie is rejecting Freud's conception of the infant as a bundle of instincts generating tensions which require discharge, a process in which other persons, if they are needed at all, are needed only as a means to an end. What goes on between people, for Suttie, is more than the satisfaction of appetites. Suttie sees the baby as seeking relationships from the start of life, bringing with it the power and will to love, a love which has a special quality of tenderness, embodied in the devoted, loving ministrations of the mother, and the reciprocal emotion of tenderness in the infant. This loving tenderness requires for its satisfaction the awakening of an adequate response of appreciation on the part of the other. Enjoyment, appreciation, and company are sought on both sides: this is the interpersonal context in which bodily needs arise and are met. The vital point here is that love is social, not merely sexual, in its biological function. Suttie holds that there is an

21

organic basis to non-sexual love: it creates feelings of satisfaction in the respiratory, circulatory and digestive systems.

This love-need is directed towards the nurturing other, usually, but not necessarily the mother. The interactions involved are communicative as well as nurturing. The relationship involves mutual giving and getting, and generates a reciprocal sense of security. When this love is thwarted, the first result is anxiety. And when the thwarting persists, it can generate the frustration-reaction of aggression.

The development of interest-rapport

The early love relationship, before weaning, is fundamental to everything that comes after. It influences the baby's view of other people, which Suttie calls the social disposition. At this early stage, self and other are not discriminated. The baby loves its own body, its immediate concerns, the mother's loving attentions and the mother herself. Suttie argues that 'the bodily self ... is the first plaything shared with her' (Suttie, 1935, p. 37). In the course of these interactions, interest-rapport develops. As the not-self is gradually discriminated, play and fellowship grow. If things go well, the extension of interest from self-and-mother to other persons and physical objects broadens to include, potentially, the whole socio-cultural field. The implication of this account is that love generates interest-rapport, which gradually extends beyond the original love relationship. Love doesn't necessarily cease with the growth of interest-rapport, but the latter can become highly differentiated from the love in which it originated. New interest-rapport relationships with playfellows can now be established without the preliminary establishment of love.

As this picture unfolds, the nature of Suttie's achievement comes into focus. With his concept of the growth and spread of interest-rapport, he replaces Freud's concept of aim-inhibited sublimation of the sexual instinct as the explanation for the development of culture, prepares the ground for the work of Fairbairn, Winnicott, and Bowlby, and opens a door for interpersonal, and socio-cultural perspectives in psychology and psychotherapy.

Just in case the reader is tempted to conclude that Suttie idealises love, it is important to emphasise that the account, up to now, is based on relationships going well enough before weaning. They do not always go well enough, as we know: Suttie understands that love is an equivocal as well as a positive factor in human society. This becomes clear in his account of the process of psychic weaning, and the development of a social disposition, to which we now turn.

The development of a social disposition

The golden age of infant-mother absorption and responsiveness, in which love is unconditional, is brought to an end by weaning, the birth of another baby, cleanliness training, and the need for the working mother to leave her babies. The infant now develops an ambivalent experience of mother, a mixture of love-longing, anxiety, and anger, in which love is increasingly experienced as conditional. The child now adopts a life-role, a stance towards others and the world which seems to it preferable both to itself and others: this is what Suttie means by the development of a social disposition.

If the frustration of the love-need is very great, frustrated love converts into anxiety, guilt and finally into hatred. But to hate a loved person, at this early stage, is felt to be intolerable. The child therefore adopts one or more of the following interpersonal strategies:

– keep mother loveable now
– abandon mother as she is now, and replace her with mother as she once was
– seek a good substitute for bad mother (e.g. father)
– engage in love protest: anger, aggression, coercion
– become what is wanted.

These strategies produce certain intrapersonal and interpersonal results. The first can lead to feelings of inferiority or to melancholia. The second can lead to regression, fantasy satisfaction, or turning away from reality. The third can lead to paranoia, feelings of persecution by the bad other. The fourth can lead to the self-important exacting of services from others. And the fifth can lead to a denial of what one really is, and the substitution of a false self. In all of this, Suttie again anticipates Fairbairn and Winnicott.

It is worth emphasising that Suttie's account of development turns entirely on the actual, ongoing interpersonal situation between the child, the mother or primary caregiver, other loved persons and the whole physical and socio-cultural environment.

The emotions as transformations of love

Like Antonio Damasio, Suttie ascribes a crucial role to the emotions, arguing that they are nearly always socially related. In other words, the expression of emotion is a means of communication with others, and is designed to elicit a response. Its function is to keep individuals in rapport with each other: it is essentially social, communicating meaning and maintaining nurturing, playful and cooperative association. The means of emotional communication include the voice, crying, laughter, and all kinds of body language. These elements are apprehended together, not separately.

Suttie sees the emotion of love as primal and pivotal: all the other emotions are interconvertible forms of the urge to love. These transformations of love occur under the stimulus of changing relationships with the loved person, and include the following:

– love denied turns into hatred
– love threatened turns into anxiety
– love supplanted turns into jealousy
– love rejected turns into despair
– loss of the loved person turns love into grief
– sympathy for the loved person turns love into pity

23

– love thwarted turns into the quest for power, the quest for admiration, or the quest for possession, resulting in unstable, unbalanced and unilateral relationships.

The taboo on tenderness

The unity of the interpersonal and the socio-cultural in Suttie's thinking is demonstrated most clearly in his concept of the taboo on tenderness. For Suttie, tenderness is a primal reality, one modality of love. It is embodied in the activities and feelings involved in the non-sexual fondling relationship between baby and mother, and in the need for companionship with her. The repression of tenderness in our culture begins in the process he calls psychic weaning, in which the tender attentions previously enjoyed by the baby are withdrawn. This is experienced by the child as a withdrawal of the mother's love, and also as meaning that the child's love is not welcome to the mother. This thwarting of the child's tender feelings, grief over the loss of the mother, and anxiety caused by the change in her attitude, together strike at the root of the child's sense of security and justice. The child is now faced with a number of options: it can develop companionship with others; fight for its rights; regress; find substitutes; or submit and avoid privation by repression. The last of these options, repression of longings, is the major source of the taboo on tenderness.

But the process of repressing tenderness does not occur in the individual child-mother relationship alone. It has its cultural origin in the stoicism which has pervaded British culture, and British Christianity, for a very long time. Both parents, and the child's older siblings, will already be intolerant of tenderness, to a greater or lesser extent, reflecting the degree of stoicism in their own upbringing. The process is reinforced beyond the family, particularly among men and boys. The taboo on tenderness is expressed by upper-class parents who send their sons (and daughters) away from home to attend private single-sex boarding schools, and by the gang of boys who idealise manliness and repudiate any sign of babyishness and girlishness. Suttie characterises their state of mind as involving a reaction against the sentiments related to mother and the nursery, and describes these boys as 'a band of brothers united by a common bereavement'.

These attitudes and practices are transmitted from generation to generation. They appear to affect men more than women: in Suttie's view, this is because of women's nurturing role. Although the taboo on tenderness (which he distinguishes from the taboo on sex) has weakened somewhat, it has by no means disappeared. The concept of the taboo on tenderness is, in my view, a powerful tool for understanding societies and cultures throughout the world deriving historically from English and Scottish roots.

Society and the jealousies

The close interplay of the interpersonal and the socio-cultural is highlighted again in Suttie's discussion of society and the jealousies. The starting point lies in his debate with Freud. Suttie poses the question: is society a spontaneous expression of human nature, or an artefact of force? For Freud – on Suttie's account – society is maintained by the dominance of the male leader over his followers. Social behaviour is the outcome of repression by fear, and the fear involved is the fear of castration. Freud focuses on two jealousies of prime importance in the development of society: men's jealousy of male rivals, and women's penis envy of male partners, and men in general.

For Suttie, on the other hand, love is the mainspring of social life. The jealousies disrupt love and frustrate the need for it. The basic unit of society is the band of brothers and sisters under the same mother. Mother is the first moraliser, encouraging and enforcing mutual tolerance by means of the fear of loss of love. Freud, Suttie argues, only understands the effect of the fear-of-castration factor, not the fear-of-loss-of-love factor, in prohibition and inhibition. For Suttie, a physically weaker prohibitor can make a more effective prohibition. Of the two determining factors – fear of punishment and fear of loss of love – fear of loss of love is the more powerful.

Table 1. Summary of Suttie's account of the jealousies

Jealousy	Characteristics	Suttie's comments
Oedipus complex	The boy wants to get rid of father and get mother for himself. (Suttie acknowledges that Freud later modified his account of the Oedipus complex to incorporate a range of other factors.)	This holds good for patriarchal, guilt-ridden cultures, and in certain family circumstances.
Penis envy	The girl feels incomplete and inferior, and wants her father's or brother's penis for herself.	As above: Suttie adds a further comment on both the Oedipus complex and penis envy: these are neither the earliest, nor the most important, nor the most universal of jealousies.
Cain jealousy	The jealousy felt by the eldest child, of either sex, for the next child of either sex. (Cain killed his younger brother Abel while they were out of sight of their mother.)	The most universal, the earliest, and the most powerful jealousy for individual development.

25

Zeus jealousy	The man/father's jealousy of the woman/mother's child-bearing, lactating, and nurturing capacities. (Zeus swallowed his pregnant wife Mitis in order to bear her child Pallas himself.)	The lack of maternal hopes, anticipations, and satisfactions may account for male political and economic dominance.
Laios jealousy	The man/father's jealousy of the new child produced by the woman/mother. (Laios was the father of Oedipus, whose mother was Jocasta. Laios abandoned Oedipus on a hillside at birth.)	Suttie comments that this is the aspect of the Oedipus story neglected by Freud, and adds: the advent of the child enriches the woman's love life, but to begin with impoverishes that of the man.

It is impossible to overstate the importance of Suttie's contribution here. At the very least, he supplements Freud's narrow view. At most, he reorients our understanding of society, and socialises psychology. Having said that, I am struck by certain omissions. No mention is made of the jealousy of any child, at any point in the birth sequence, for the talents, qualities or popularity of another. Children's jealousy of their parents is also omitted. And his list is confined to jealousies within one family grouping, leaving out jealousies between individual members of different families, between families, classes or nations, and jealousies relating to inherited or accumulated differences of wealth, power and social or cultural capital. He omits any mention of jealousies, rivalries, comparisons and attractions arising among adults. He fails to distinguish envy from jealousy, using jealousy as a catch-all category. And he fails to discuss adequately the role of fathers in families: it is as if, in his polemic with Freud, he has swung too far towards the opposite extreme.

Having said all this, the general direction of Suttie's analysis is clear and convincing. It opens the way towards a social psychology based on love and its vicissitudes. In terms of psychotherapeutic practice, it shifts the weight of emphasis away from instincts and their representatives, and to some extent also from internal objects and their relations, on to actual interpersonal relationships both past and present. And it challenges us, as theorists, practitioners and researchers, to create a new balance and integration of all of these factors in psychotherapy.

Psychopathy[1] as disturbance of the social disposition

In his discussion of psychopathy, Suttie distinguishes organic impairment or disease of the brain (which produces symptoms without meaning in terms of social relationships), from psychopathy considered as disturbance in the relationship between an individual and his or her fellows, due to privations, inhibitions and distortions in the person's social or love disposition. Such disturbance generates symptoms which do have meanings, always connected with the individual's social purpose or aim. He calls these symptoms disturbances of rapport, listing them as follows:

- loss of interest in people
- loss of interest in things
- self-depreciation
- over-estimation of self
- anxiety
- despair
- anger/aggression
- regressiveness/return to infantile dependency.

His account of psychopathy stresses the role of emotions. He is particularly insightful with regard to the individual's attempt to

> increase its consequence to other people ... insofar as it feels it has no-one upon whom it can safely depend. (Suttie, 1935, p. 200)

Suttie's analysis helps us to understand the process of forming what he calls idealisms, which involve the child in imitating and seeking to emulate envied, outstanding figures in the environment. In a happy phrase for a desperately unhappy development, he describes psychopathy as

> an archaic and ... inept attempt to improve love relationships. (Suttie, 1935, p. 201)

Correspondingly, he sees psychotherapy as an attempt to assist the patient or client on his love quest, and set this upon lines more likely to achieve the desired results.

Psychotherapy as reconciliation

We turn finally to his conception of psychotherapy. In considering this theme, it is helpful to bear in mind his studies in sociology and social anthropology, his interest in the links between psychotherapy and religion, and his view that human psychology is practically always dealing not with the individual alone but with his or her relations to others.

Psychotherapy is ultimately about reconciliation, and involves the restoration of love-interest-rapport between the self and the social environment. Its aim is to overcome the barriers to loving and feeling oneself loved. Suttie writes:

> The ideal attitude (of the therapist) is very like that of Christ ... serene without being aloof, sympathetic without being disturbed: exactly what the child desires in the parent. (Suttie, 1935, p. 217)

He uses the metaphors of therapist as sacrificial victim (onto whom all hates, anxieties and distrust can be projected), and therapist as mediator or catalyst, by means of whose genuine engagement the alienated psyche of the client can reintegrate into society, not as an adaptation to a pathological norm, but as a person who is now capable of expressing his hate and his love.

A vital feature of this perspective on therapy is his view of the therapist as a real, ordinary human being, a product of his or her culture, with his or her own prejudices and inhibitions, and defended to some degree against his or her own needs and difficulties by the taboo on tenderness. Suttie is aware, from his own experience, of the anti-therapeutic effect of taking refuge in passivity and objectivity. He attacks those whose accounts of technique idealise passivity, arguing that they represent their relationships with their clients or patients as inhuman, impersonal and purely technical. For Suttie, the role of the psychotherapist is to offer

> a true and full companionship of interest ... [the therapist] shows by his understanding and insight that he too has suffered ... so there is a fellowship of suffering established. (Suttie, 1935, pp. 211–212)

Suttie refers to the therapist as a man of sorrows. He favours activity and responsiveness on the part of the therapist, and opposes what he calls the fiction of immunity from emotion. Endorsing Ferenczi's argument that it is the physician's love that heals the patient or client, he goes on to clarify precisely what love means in the therapeutic relationship. It is

> a feeling-interest responsiveness, not a goal-inhibited sexuality. (Suttie, 1935, pp. 212–213)

There is no question of the therapist using the relationship to meet his own needs, or engaging in *inappropriate* self-disclosure. Therapeutic love is an altruistic, non-appetitive love, focussing on the needs and growth of the other. What Suttie is saying is that such a relationship, if it is to be effective, cannot involve self-withholding. The therapist has to be fully present, a real human being communicating genuine emotional responses. A one-sided relationship, as he puts it, cannot be curative.

It is my contention, first, that contemporary psychoanalysis, psychotherapy, and counselling have much to learn from Suttie; and second that his contribution anticipates much of what has come after, including the work of Fairbairn, Winnicott, Bowlby, Guntrip, Sutherland, developmental psychologists like Colwyn Trevarthen, our contemporary interest in attunement and attachment, and the more recent contributions of neuroscientists such as Antonio Damasio who stresses the importance of internal representations of self and other in human relationships, and the vital role of emotions (Damasio, 2000).

My third contention is concerned with our human orientation towards living in the 21st century. It is analogous to the case so eloquently argued by Alasdair MacIntyre in the opening chapter of his book *After Virtue,* to the effect that, in contemporary culture, the language of morality has been fragmented and nearly destroyed. In the context of modernism and particularly post-modernism, morality, where it exists at all, has been subordinated to situational, structural and technological considerations. The dominant philosophical orientation, if it can be dignified with that name, is a self-centred consumerist hedonism, which celebrates our liberation from the dead weight of the past. Crocodile tears are shed over the failure of the grand narratives of Christianity, Marxism, psychoanalysis and feminism. My contention is that this perspective incorporates a purely negative view of freedom. Against hedonism, I argue that being human involves the challenge of finding a way of life (see Turnbull, 1989). This is a challenge that is communal as well as personal, and normative rather than merely descriptive. It asks, 'How should I live?' and not, 'What is everybody else doing so that I can do the same as them?' To struggle for the restoration of such an orientation is not to impose a single religious perspective, but to excavate and piece together an orientation for personal living of what Ian Martin has called the common life in community (Martin, 1987). This is the ethical imperative which underlies the attempt to construct a synthesis of the work of Macmurray, Suttie and Fairbairn.

THE DISTINCTIVE CONTRIBUTION OF RONALD FAIRBAIRN

The contributions of Ronald Fairbairn are discussed in the next chapter. Here, I confine myself to answering briefly the question: what distinctive contributions do Fairbairn and his followers make to our understanding of the persons-in-relation perspective? From Macmurray, I have argued, we take the philosophical and religious orientation. From Suttie, we take the creative shift from instincts and their vicissitudes to an understanding of the relations of persons in society, pivoting around love and its vicissitudes. What is missing from the picture they paint, Fairbairn fills in.

In swinging away from Freud's early focus on instincts, Suttie rightly emphasises real external relationships and socio-cultural values and milieux. But he has relatively little to say about our inner worlds. How do these external relationships affect us inside? Are they once-and-for-all experiences which simply accumulate in our memories like jam sandwiches or plates of porridge, or do they have an impact on us inside in some special way? Suttie's view of psychopathy implies that they do. They help to shape our choice of social disposition. But what exactly is involved, internally, in developing a social disposition? Suttie does not tackle that question in any depth. Fairbairn does.

Fairbairn gives us, for the first time, a convincing account of our inner world conceived primarily in interpersonal terms. He pictures a conscious central ego or 'I' relating to an ideal object, and a pair of split-off repressed parts of the ego: first, a rejected, persecuted part relating to a rejecting or punishing part of the object; and second, a longing, needy part relating to an exciting or tantalising part of the object. Added to that, the rejected part of the ego, which he calls the internal saboteur, persistently attacks the libidinal pairing. In all of this, Fairbairn continues to use the terms 'object' and 'ego', which in my view are better thought of as aspects of significant other persons in relation to aspects of the self. This representation of the repressive, rejective, aggressive and libidinal dynamics of the inner situation, so painstakingly pieced together in Fairbairn's *Endopsychic Structure Considered in Terms of Object-Relationships,* also applies to his unique understanding of dreams, seen as 'shorts' (short films) of conflictual intra- and inter-personal situations, both conscious and unconscious, with which the self is

29

currently struggling. His view of endopsychic (intrapsychic, intrapersonal) structure also has implications for our understanding of the transference/counter-transference relationship, and connects with his recasting of the concept of dissociation, of which he sees repression as a special case (Fairbairn, 1986; Sandler, 1976; Scharff & Birtles, 1994).

The careful attention which Fairbairn lavishes on understanding our inner situation has generated new insights on the part of those who have followed him. I am thinking here for example of Guntrip's dialogue with Fairbairn, leading to Guntrip's image of the repressed, regressed and withdrawn core of the libidinal ego, holed up in the schizoid citadel, inaccessible to real human contact; of Sutherland's suggestion that the links between the various self-other pairs consist of emotions; and of the Scharffs' modifications and applications of Fairbairn's model to therapeutic work with couples, families and groups (Guntrip, 1977; Scharff, 1994; Scharff & Scharff, 1991).

I want to make one final point about Fairbairn's contribution. His own analytic and therapeutic concerns are directed primarily towards understanding the interpersonal nature of the inner world, although he was also aware of the significance of the wider society and culture for inner world configurations: see, for example, his paper *The Effects of a King's Death upon Patients Undergoing Analysis* (Fairbairn, 1986). Sutherland's (1989) psychobiography *Fairbairn's Journey into the Interior* portrays Fairbairn in his socio-cultural context. Sutherland traces Fairbairn's development of theory to Fairbairn's self analysis of his own difficulties in the context of his family and culture of origin. Fairbairn's personal suffering is the suffering not only of a very private, brilliant, good man: it is also the suffering of a son, husband, and father growing up and living out his life in the Scottish and British society of his day. More specifically, his psychic suit was made of Edinburgh cloth woven out of threads of intense Christian idealism and professional devotion, episcopalianism with an undertow of Calvinism, sharply contrasting gender roles, kindness and reserve, warmth and distance, science and service. It would be fascinating to know exactly what Ronald Fairbairn had in mind when he said to Harry Guntrip:

Suttie really had something important to say. (Guntrip, 1971, p. 24)

My hunch is that he was thinking not only of Suttie's emphasis on interpersonal relationships and the role of emotions, but also specifically of his concept of the taboo on tenderness, a taboo which applied across much of Scottish society at least from the death of Robert Burns, through the Victorian period and the first two thirds of the 20th century, a taboo with which Macmurray, Suttie and Fairbairn all struggled in their different ways.

TOWARDS A SYNTHESIS

In this final section I discuss my working toward a synthesis, and I identify some of its principal themes. My aim is to integrate intrapersonal, interpersonal, and socio-cultural factors in a unified account of the theory and practice of psychotherapy and counselling. The synthesis will be grounded in Macmurray's philosophical, ethical, and religious thinking, which I refer to as the persons in relation perspective (a term adapted from the title of one of his books). This entails clarifying the distinctions and overlaps of meaning between the terms 'personal relations', 'object relations,' and 'persons in relation'. Briefly, 'personal relations' is used to refer to the direct relationships between human beings, whether past or present, both descriptively (that is, whatever those relationships happen to be), and normatively (that is, when each person involved is genuinely trying to consider and treat the other as a person rather than as an object).

The term 'object relations', which I dislike and use reluctantly, is nevertheless meaningful for accounts of the inner worlds of persons conceived in terms of their internalised images or representations of self and other, and the dynamic relationships between and among these self-other representations, when these are unconscious and/or have become to some degree dissociated, stuck or fixed. The term 'persons in relation' refers to a broader view of human beings in society, in any and every context, seen as persons in community whose personhood is actually constituted by their relationships with other persons. Because this is a normative as well as a descriptive view, and because not all human relationships are direct, the ongoing clarification of the meanings of these three terms is essential. It leads also to a consideration of the relationships between the personal, the structural and the functional. In the course of this discussion I draw particularly on Michael Fielding's illuminating application of Macmurray's thinking to the education of children in schools (Fielding, 2004). In this connection, it should be noted that Macmurray does not deny the existence or necessity of the functional, but argues that 'the personal is *through* the functional' and that 'the functional is *for* the personal' (Fielding, 2004, passim).

I now turn to some of the implications of these considerations for the theory and practice of psychoanalytic psychotherapy, family therapy, counselling and groupwork. We should be concerned primarily and pervasively with personal relations in our work with clients, whether the focus of the moment is on external or internal situations or both, and whether what is at issue is conscious, unconscious or dissociated. As John Macmurray acknowleged, persons are indeed objects, but they are much more than objects. They are subjects who are receivers or undergoers of their experiences, and agents of their actions, who construe and reflect upon those experiences and actions, and who, in their unique experiencing, acting, construing, and reflecting, encounter other persons likewise engaged. In short, human beings are persons in personal relations with other persons. This is true not only of our external interpersonal relations, but also, in a more complex sense, of our inner worlds, constituted as they are by the internalisation of previously external interpersonal relations. I did not take in my father or mother, or my brothers and sister, as objects. They are not bits of fishbone stuck in my psyche: they are significant other persons, however exaggerated, distorted and fixed some of my earliest construing of them may have been. While they are alive, there is a complex interplay of internal and often somewhat fixed personal ('object') relations, and externally occurring, here-and-now personal relations.

When they die, I carry within me the inheritance of an ongoing – and potentially developing – interplay between myself, my values and my socio-cultural environment, and their personalities, lives and relationships, their values, and the socio-cultural contexts from which they came and in which they lived out their lives. This has huge implications for how we should relate to our clients. In this connection, it is heartening to be reminded by Graham Clarke that Ronald Fairbairn wished to call his unique development of object relations theory 'personal relations theory' and only refrained from doing so because of his loyalty to Freud (Clarke, 2003).

From the basic assumption that psychotherapeutic work is an intersubjective collaboration between two persons, based on equality of regard, I proceed to my second theme. Persons are constituted not only by interpersonal relations, but also by real socio-cultural contexts and values which have been internalised and become parts of the self. The challenge of acknowledging the unity, the simultaneity, of the biological, the intrapersonal, the interpersonal and the socio-cultural is not primarily theoretical. It is a matter of experience and practice. It confronts us when we encounter another person.

When I took in my parents, I did not put their personalities in one box and their significantly different socio-cultural backgrounds in another. Nor did I continue relating to them, as I grew up, in a socio-cultural vacuum: on the contrary our relationships were interlaced with direct experiences and representations of post-war austerity, the life-saving welfare state, the developing cold war, the take-off of technology, the eruption of libertarianism, the decline of religion, and so on. That our personalities, our relationships, and our disturbances incorporate the interplay of all these factors, and that all of them come into play in the therapeutic relationship, is surely now beyond dispute. This interplay has been clearly demonstrated in the work of feminist psychotherapists like Susie Orbach in her work with clients whose difficulties revolve around eating and body-image, which are partly socio-cultural, as well as interpersonal, in origin (see, for example, Orbach, 1993). It has been demonstrated by Harry Stack Sullivan in his account of the painful tensions established in his youthful soul by the different socio-cultural backgrounds and expectations of his father and mother (Mullahy, 1952). It has been demonstrated by Jock Sutherland in his account of Ronald Fairbairn's personal development, and in his study of John Buchan's 'sick heart' (Sutherland, 1989; Sutherland, 1988).

This leads to my third theme. In our psychoanalytic and psychodynamic cultures, we are sometimes too narrowly (in the cases of a few practitioners, exclusively) preoccupied with inner worlds. Without abandoning that focus at all, we need to re-examine our understandings of the relationship of clients' inner worlds to their actual experiences of present and past external relationships, their socio-cultural milieux, their value systems and their ways of life.

This leads to the fourth, and final theme of the synthesis, which involves questioning our sometimes excessive emphasis on unconscious processes and repression as the sole source and locus of psychological distress. This is not to deny the importance of unconscious processes, but to suggest that society and culture have changed drastically since the days of Freud and Fairbairn. It was possible, in the 1890s, 1940s and 1950s, to argue convincingly that civilisation was based on repression. In the contemporary period, an equally convincing case can be made that our civilisation is based on continuous, intentional overstimulation, and on dissociation. Among clients seeking help now, while repression is sometimes a significant factor, many ingrained conflicts and difficulties exist in the domain of conscious awareness and are – very ineffectively – coped with by dissociation and the passive tolerance of contradiction. These processes are exacerbated by the fact that most contemporary channels of communication beam out messages implying that people are consumers who should seek, and get, everything they want, whether or not they can afford it, and whether or not it is good for them. The notions of the personal, of personal responsibility, of real freedom in John Macmurray's sense of the term, of the cultivation of the capacity to ponder, to weigh up, to make positive directional choices, and sometimes to say no, have been almost obliterated. For us, as psychoanalytic psychotherapists and counsellors, there is a challenging ethical task: to reaffirm the importance and the value of the personal life, and the perspective that society consists primarily of persons in personal relations.

NOTES

1. Suttie's use of the term 'psychopathy' now seems old-fashioned, implying a distinction between mental disease (psychopathy) and the science of mental disease (psychopathology). In contemporary usage, the same term, psychopathology, is used in both senses. Many psychotherapists would now challenge the use of either term for disturbances of the social disposition, accepting Suttie's account but not this term.

REFERENCES/BIBLIOGRAPHY

Clarke, G. (2003). Personal relations theory: Suttie, Fairbairn, Macmurray and Sutherland. Paper delivered at the Legacy of Fairbairn and Sutherland Conference, IIORT and SIHR, Edinburgh.

Clarke, G. (2006). *Personal relations theory: Fairbairn, Macmurray and Suttie*. London and New York: Routledge.

Costello, J.E. (2002). *John Macmurray: A biography*. Edinburgh: Floris Books.

Damasio, A. (2000). *The feeling of what happens: Body, emotion and the making of consciousness*. London: Vintage.

Fairbairn, W. R. D. (1952). *Psychoanalytic studies of the personality*. London: Tavistock Publications/ Routledge and Kegan Paul.

Fielding, M. (2004). Philosophy and the end of educational organisation. Paper delivered at the Philosophy of Education Society of Great Britain Annual Conference, Oxford.

Guntrip, H. (1977). *Psychoanalytic theory, therapy and the self*. London: Karnac.

Heard, D. (1988) Introduction: Historical perspectives. In Heard, D. (Ed.), *The origins of love and hate*. London: Free Association Books.

Kirkwood, C. (2003). The persons in relation perspective: Towards a philosophy for counselling in society. *Counselling and Psychotherapy Research, 3*(3), 186–195.

MacIntyre, A. (1985). *After virtue: A study in moral theory*. London: Duckworth.

Macmurray, J. (1938). *The clue to history*. London: Student Christian Movement Press.

Macmurray, J. (1992) (first published 1932). *Freedom in the modern world*. London: Humanities Press.

Macmurray, J. (1995a) (first published 1961). *Persons in relation*. London: Faber and Faber.

Macmurray, J. (1995b) (first published 1935). *Reason and emotion.* London: Faber and Faber.

Macmurray, J. (1995c) (first published 1957). *The self as agent.* London: Faber and Faber.

Martin, I. (1987). Community education: Towards a theoretical analysis. In G. Allen, J. Bastiani, I. Martin, & K. Richards (Eds.), *Community education: An agenda for educational reform.* Milton Keynes: Open University Press.

Orbach, S. (1993). *Hunger strike: The anorectic's struggle as a metaphor for our age.* London: Penguin.

Mullahy, P. (Ed.). (1952). *The contributions of Harry Stack Sullivan: A symposium on interpersonal theory in psychiatry and social science.* New York: Hermitage House.

Sandler, J. (1976). Countertransference and role-responsiveness. *International Review of Psychoanalysis, 3*(43), 43–47.

Scharff, D., & Fairbairn Birtles, E. (1994). *From instinct to self: Selected papers of W. R. D. Fairbairn,* Vols 1 and 2. London: Jason Aronson.

Scharff, D., & Scharff, J. S. (1991). *Object relations couple therapy.* London: Jason Aronson.

Scharff, J. S. (1994). *The autonomous self: The work of J. D. Sutherland.* London: Jason Aronson.

Sutherland, J. D. (1988). John Buchan's 'sick heart': Some psychoanalytic reflections. *Edinburgh Review, 78–79,* 83–101.

Sutherland, J. D. (1989). *Fairbairn's journey into the interior.* London: Free Association Books.

Suttie, I. D. (1988) (first published 1935). *The origins of love and hate.* London: Free Association Books.

Turnbull, R. (1989). Scottish thought in the twentieth century. In C. Beveridge & R. Turnbull (Eds.), *The eclipse of Scottish culture.* Edinburgh: Polygon.

THE PERSONS IN RELATION PERSPECTIVE

Counselling and Psychotherapy in the Contemporary World

Key words and themes: religious and political inheritances, the good other, religions as imaginative nourishment, loss of the good other, negative view of the self, basic inner situation, ideal object and central ego, rejecting object and anti-libidinal ego (internal saboteur), libidinal object and libidinal ego, aggression arising from separation-anxiety, aggression turned against the needy self, praise of the good other, getting your self-rejection in first, ethical values in society, the primacy of the other.

INTRODUCTION

This third paper in the persons in relation series was first delivered as a keynote presentation in Athens in the spring of 2006, at an international conference in the Panteion University of Social and Political Sciences, organised by the University's Department of Psychology, the Greek Association for Counselling, and the European Association for Counselling.

The original version of this paper included discussion of the contributions of John Macmurray and Ian Suttie, which are now omitted. Here I concentrate on the work of Ronald Fairbairn, and social, religious, and political dimensions of the synthesis.

THE PERSONS IN RELATION PERSPECTIVE

The idea that life has to be lived forwards and can only be understood backwards has powerful resonance for me as I look back over my own trajectory and the enormous transformations of European society and culture since the end of the second world war. I became conscious of beginning to form a personal point of view in the early 1960s, one that has gone on developing ever since then. But it is only in the last 15 years or so that I have felt the need to articulate and elaborate that point of view as a perspective, one which tries to unite a way of living, practising and relating, with a way of thinking which integrates psychotherapeutic, religious, and political inheritances to engage with the present and contribute to shaping a possible future.

I call it the persons in relation perspective, a phrase borrowed from the title of a series of Gifford lectures given by the Scottish philosopher John Macmurray at the University of Glasgow in the 1950s.

The resources I have drawn on for this paper are Scottish, with international connections. I don't see that as an expression of national chauvinism, but of my groundedness in a distinctive inherited culture, a culture which prides itself on its openness to Europe, the Middle East, and the wider world. I hope that our dialogue today will involve encounters between the particularities of my culture and yours. A question which therefore arises is: what are the personalist or persons in relation resources accessible to colleagues in Greece, Serbia, Turkey, Russia, Palestine, Israel, France, Holland, Switzerland, Germany, Italy, England, and so on?

I aim to do three things: first to identify the (for me) Scottish sources of the perspective and suggest how they come together in a synthesis. Second, to link this perspective with some of our common religious and political inheritances. And third, to suggest some challenges for counselling and psychotherapy as they position themselves in contemporary European and Middle Eastern society and culture, and in the wider world.

First, the sources and the synthesis. The more experienced I get as a counsellor and psychoanalytic psychotherapist, the less satisfied I am with an exclusive focus on our clients' inner worlds. I am equally dissatisfied with an exclusive focus on their interpersonal worlds. And I am exasperated by social-scientific commentaries which seek to reduce all meaning to the impact of broad socio-cultural, economic and technological trends or so-called 'structural' factors.

What I am seeking, and what I think our clients need, is a way of seeing, a *theoria,* which succeeds in integrating genetic, somatic, intrapersonal, inter-personal, socio-cultural and ethical dimensions with reference to our experience as persons and our practice as counsellors and clients.

The value of religious ideas and practices

What ground is available that will enable us to see these factors as belonging together? My answer is that we can find solid ground, a secure base for our theory, in the view of human beings as *persons in relation* most eloquently articulated by John Macmurray and Martin Buber. Martin Buber has declared that there is no significant difference between his view, as articulated in his book *I and Thou*, and that of Macmurray. He describes himself as the poet of this perspective, and Macmurray as its philosopher. I take that comment at face value, and today I will confine my contribution to considering John Macmurray's work.

For Macmurray, as for Buber, the ultimate reality of the other lies in God. Not everyone will feel able to go all the way with them on this point. I acknowledge, for myself, that I do not believe in the literal existence of a God present within and transcending all time, space, matter, and energy. What I do find real is the imaginative impact of the idea of God, when it is conceived of as symbolising (among other things) the good other, and our experiences, communications and relationships with good others, past and present, in our lives. I have, relatively recently, come to the understanding that religious practices, traditions, stories, buildings, attitudes, and imagery are best understood as providing deeply needed communal and spiritual nourishment. (I am a slow developer, and I acknowledge that many of you may have got to that position a long time ago!) They are imaginative attempts to understand, portray, and sustain core aspects of the human situation, placing at its heart our profound need for, and love of the good other, a need simultaneously personal and communal.

For me, this understanding makes religious ideas and practices not less but more valuable, more accessible, more convincing. I can now see that it was the problem of having to believe that religious statements were literally true that prevented me from allowing them to have their full impact on me.

Loss of the good other

I have come to make the – equally startling – connection that this is what we are concerned with in our counselling and psychotherapeutic work. What is at issue, for each person, and specifically for each therapist and client, is the loss or disturbance of a sense of the good other, existing for us externally in the world and internally inside ourselves; the interplay between our inner and outer sense of the other in this respect; and the impact all of this has on our sense of the goodness, efficacy and reparability of our selves, both internally and externally in the world. What is at issue, also, is our sense of having either purpose or futility, worthwhileness or worthlessness, in our lives; and finally a sense of the potential goodness or otherwise of the world in which we live. One dimension which particularly preoccupies me is the capacity, or lack of the capacity, to be open to receive and take in good experiences with others and with the world and to be affected by them internally in a way that carries conviction. I am thinking here particularly of clients who have entrenched internally highly negative views of themselves. One member of a psychotherapy group with which I am currently (2006) working articulated this understanding recently with great clarity. She said; 'I hate myself, I hate my body, and I realise that the logical implication of this is that I hate the whole of creation'.

THE CONTRIBUTIONS OF RONALD FAIRBAIRN

I turn now to consider the contributions of the Scottish psychoanalyst, Ronald Fairbairn, author of *Psychoanalytic Studies of the Personality* (1952).

For the first time in the modern world, in a series of papers published in the 1930s, 40s, and 50s, Fairbairn developed a way of understanding the construction of our inner worlds conceived in interpersonal terms. Unlike Suttie, he never made a break with Freudian language, but his revision of Freud is just as far-reaching as Suttie's. I am convinced that Fairbairn's revision draws on Suttie's and Macmurray's work. Let me try to outline his key ideas:
- the baby's ego or 'I' is present and whole at birth
- the baby, from the start, seeks a relationship with its mother or caregiver, called by Fairbairn 'the original object'. The word 'object' here simply means significant other person
- insofar as the baby experiences satisfaction in this relationship, all goes well

37

– insofar as the baby experiences frustration or deprivation in this relationship (and every baby does, because no mother or caregiver can be perfectly attuned to the baby's needs all of the time), several things happen:
  – the baby experiences separation-anxiety
  – the baby gets frustrated, and becomes aggressive in response
  – as a defensive measure, the baby internalises mother, psychologically takes her in, and in this process of internalisation, the baby splits off and represses two distinct aspects of her: her exciting and rejecting aspects
  – simultaneously, the baby splits off and represses two aspects of itself or 'I'. Fairbairn calls these two aspects the libidinal ego and the anti-libidinal ego: we might call them the vulnerable, needy self, and the rejected and rejecting self

  – the two internalised aspects of mother exist in relationships with the two aspects of the baby's ego or 'I': it is two self-other relationships which are split off and repressed
  – so now, instead of a whole self relating to a whole mother, we have a new situation of four relationships in the baby's inner world. Fairbairn calls this the basic endopsychic (or inner) situation.

Let me show you this in the form of two diagrams:

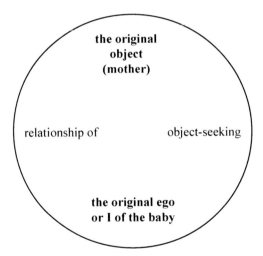

Figure 1. The original relationship situation.

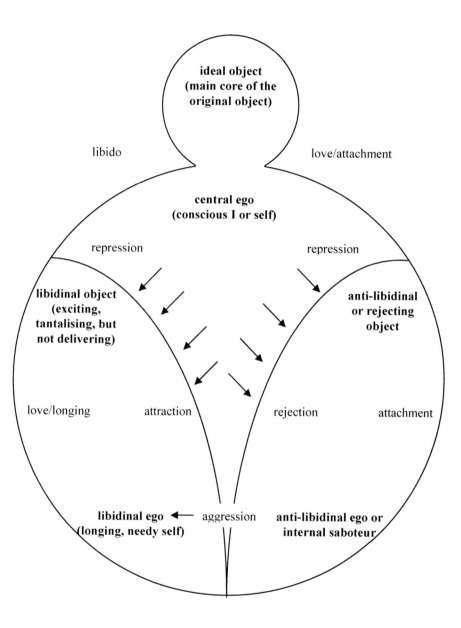

Figure 2. The new relationship situation (the basic endopsychic or inner situation).

Notes to follow Figure 2

1. The relationship between the central ego or I and the ideal object is both external (in the outer world) and internal (in the inner world).
2. The word 'libido' originally means sexual desire. Freud regarded it as a kind of love energy, to be contrasted with aggression. Fairbairn as always sticks to Freud's language and therefore holds to the libido/aggression distinction. For Fairbairn, we can take the meaning of libido to include desire, love-energy, and attachment.
3. The ego or I is that part of the personality you experience as being yourself. I think of it also as the core or executive part of the self, the part that believes it is running the show, so to speak.
4. The word object as previously indicated means significant other person. As you know, I prefer the terms other, or other person.

Four internal relationships

In this new inner situation there are actually four relationships existing simultaneously inside the self, one or more of which can be activated at any one time:

1. The conscious relationship between the central ego or I and the ideal object, a relationship of love/need/attachment.
2. The unconscious relationship between the rejecting, neglecting or punishing object, and the internal saboteur, a relationship of both attachment and aggression/rejection.
3. The unconscious relationship between the libidinal ego (the longing, needy, vulnerable self) and the libidinal object, which is one of allure, excitement, unsatisfied love-longing, and attachment.
4. Fairbairn adds a crucial fourth relationship, in which the anti-libidinal ego, the internal saboteur, itself already on the receiving end of aggression from the rejecting object, now turns on and attacks the needy, longing self, as if to say: don't be needy! don't be vulnerable! toughen up!

The second and fourth of these relationships represent Fairbairn's account of the phenomena of aggression turned against the self, one aspect of what Freud and Melanie Klein called the death instinct.

Fairbairn calls this whole picture *the basic inner situation*. It may seem quite far-fetched to those who have never suffered very much in their own lives, whose frustrations have been slight. And there is certainly no need to take it as a prescriptive picture of everyone's inner world, or indeed as the last word on the subject. But to those who have suffered neglect, torture, sustained bullying, rape, sexual or emotional abuse, scapegoating, double binds, or cruel depriving treatment of other kinds, and to those who work with them, it is painfully familiar.

Alternative conceptualisations

What Fairbairn did, 60 years ago, was to open up new ways of thinking about our inner worlds conceived, at least partly, in terms of emotion-laden relationships with significant others. And his ideas have inspired further ways of understanding what goes on inside each of us, new conceptualisations: for example, John Bowlby's concept of internal working models; the cognitive behaviourist concept of self-other schemas; the work of the person-centred therapist Dave Mearns who writes about working at relational depth and self-other configurations; Harry Stack Sullivan's me-you patterns; Antonio Damasio's account of ongoing neurological processes of making representations of the self, the object, and the impact of the object on the self; and so on.

This concludes the presentation of my three Scottish sources. I turn now briefly to consider the application of the persons in relation perspective to society, and the link with religion.

PRAISE OF THE GOOD OTHER

Let me begin by telling you what the connecting trigger was for me. It lay in a piece of information given to me by my own analyst, Alan Harrow. Alan told me that his analyst, Jock Sutherland, had once said to him: 'hymns are praise of the good object'. That throwaway remark was enough to enable me to make a link between the idea of having good-enough relationships with significant others in the external world, and the sense of having a good other or others inside you, in your inner world. As an example of these connections, I include here the English version of the text of an early Christian hymn:

Be thou my Vision, O Lord of my heart;
Naught be all else to me, save that thou art,
Thou my best thought, by day or by night,
Waking or sleeping, thy presence my light.

Be thou my Wisdom, thou my true Word;
I ever with thee, thou with me, Lord;
Thou my great Father, I thy true son;
Thou in me dwelling, and I with thee one.

Be thou my battle-shield, sword for the fight;
Be thou my dignity, thou my delight;
Thou my soul's shelter, thou my high tower:
Raise thou me heavenward, O Power of my power.

CHAPTER 2

Riches I heed not, nor man's empty praise, ☐
Thou mine Inheritance, now and always: ☐
Thou and thou only, first in my heart, ☐
High King of Heaven, my treasure thou art.

High King of Heaven, after victory won, ☐
May I reach heaven's joys, O bright heaven's Sun!
Heart of my own heart, whatever befall, ☐
Still be my Vision, O Ruler of all.

Translated from the ancient Irish (attributed to Dallan Forgaill, 8th Century) by
Mary Byrne, 1905, and versified by Eleanor Hull, 1912.
This version appears as hymn no. 87 in *The Church Hymnary: 3rd edition* (1973)
London, Oxford University Press.

Getting your self-rejection in first

From 2004–2009 I worked with girls and women suffering from severe eating
disorders, most frequently anorexia, occasionally bulimia. At first, I felt more than
a little at sea, until I realised that what was common to many of them was that they
had developed an intensely negative view of themselves internally. These
outcomes seem to happen as a result of the taking in of negative or negatively-
construed interpersonal experiences and harmful socio-cultural messages. These
self-other relationships, and these messages, get internalised as meaning-patterns,
as working models: they become negative internal states of mind-and-body, and
they influence the way these girls make sense of subsequent experiences. It
becomes more difficult for them to experience an external good other and thus to
develop and install inside themselves a secure sense of a good other. That in turn
affects their internal sense of their self. Sometimes it becomes so painful for them
to anticipate yet another attack, or another rejection, that they are driven towards
the solution of getting their own rejection of themselves in first. If you reject
yourself, if you say I'm crap, I'm shit, I'm rubbish, often enough in your internal
self-talk, or self-feeling, you may succeed in lessening the unbearable pain of
experiencing a real (external) rejection by another person yet again.

REAFFIRMING ETHICAL VALUES IN SOCIETY

I am arguing that a key part of our inheritance is our Judaeo-Christian inheritance,
and what Macmurray and Suttie single out as the core of it: the relationship of love
and its vicissitudes, the need for the good other, and a fundamental orientation
within ourselves towards the other: in short, what I am calling the persons in
relation perspective.

And it is clear to me that this is not just a private interpersonal and family
matter. The persons in relation perspective is a perspective for living in, and
shaping, family, community, society, the whole world. I would argue further that

some socialist, communist, anarchist, feminist, gay, liberal, and even conservative political movements have at their best also incorporated some elements of this same perspective. Sadly, they have not often been at their best. Too often, they have subordinated means to ends to disastrous effect, justifying their use of the most appalling actions, and uncritically worshipping the state, or the free market, or technology, as the principal means of achieving good ends.

You may wonder about the passion in my tone of voice. Why is he so concerned about reconnecting with out-of-date religious and political perspectives? Well, I do think that the decline and near-demise of an ethical perspective that is simultaneously personal and social in western society in the last 50 years is a very serious matter!

Let me remind you again of the epidemic of eating disorders in contemporary Europe and the USA. In the 1950s, organised religion could still argue a powerful case for a way of life grounded in ethical values. In the 60s and even the 70s in western Europe, it was still possible to argue a case based on a vision of the good society couched in socialist, communist or christian democratic terms, although the case was becoming less and less convincing, more ambivalent, more disappointing. In the 50s and 60s in central and eastern Europe you could still argue a case for socialism with a human face when confronted by Soviet tanks. Even in the 1980s, the case argued by the Polish workers in Solidarnosc was an ethical case. Not now. Nothing now seems able to stand in the way of the hedonist and consumerist messages of advanced capitalism, of affluence, of atomising individualism, of individual success, which dominate American, European and increasingly global society.[1]

Every day perfectionist young girls take in pernicious messages about being thin, about calorie counting, about perfect beauty, about not being successful enough or beautiful enough, about the packaged glossy rubbish that passes for food in the media. Older people like me and some of you here today can evaluate these messages and laugh at them, because we can refer back to older traditions. But many of you under 40 do not have such traditions to refer back to. Such people have nothing to defend themselves with. They are at the mercy of every conceivable kind of exploitative message. If there isn't a moral concern about this situation, there ought to be!

I am not arguing that the Christian, Judaic, Islamic, or other religious traditions are perfect. Manifestly they are not. They got homosexuality, lesbianism and the position of women in society badly wrong. But these are matters which can be challenged and changed. I am, however, arguing that religious traditions have got it right about hedonism, consumerism, and nihilism.

By allowing ourselves to get caught up in a fashionable libertarianism, and a fashionable anti-fundamentalism, we are in danger of throwing the baby out with the bathwater. We are in danger of losing sight of the vital contributions of the religious and political traditions of the world. They carried visions of a good way of life, they carried traditions of distinguishing right from wrong actions at personal and social levels, they carried forward discourses and practices of living by positive and – yes – normative values. They carried forward the history of the best efforts of human beings to create the good society and uphold personal responsibility within it. And they gave equal weight to thoughts, words and actions: they did not value words alone.

THE PRIMACY OF THE OTHER

Counselling and psychotherapy are not a set of techniques for glueing broken tin soldiers back together and returning them to function uncritically in society as it is. They arise out of an ethical attitude and are embodied in an ethical act, the altruistic act of caring for a personal other. The therapist is trying to be a good-enough other in interpersonal practice; trying to restore the client's sense of being deeply understood, reached at the heart, accompanied and loved for themselves. In doing this we assert the primacy of the other, our need for the other, and we challenge contemporary self-centredness and self-preoccupation.

In the first paper I wrote about the persons in relation perspective, I quoted a few lines from a poem by Gerard Manley Hopkins. Here they are again:

> Each mortal thing does one thing and the same:
> Deals out that being indoors each one dwells;
> Selves – goes itself; *myself* it speaks and spells;
> Crying *what I do is me: for that I came.*

Hopkins is referring to what we might call the *telos,* the purpose, of every organic thing, and above all of every living human being. This is in tune with all good religious teaching, and all good counselling and psychotherapeutic work. It is a call to be fully yourself in the world, and to give yourself fully to the world. It is the opposite of a call to be self-centred although it does involve knowing, valuing and – yes, even loving – yourself. It addresses the age-old human dilemma which comes alive again for every generation: should I be for myself, or should I be for others?

Love of the good other

In the Talmud, the answer given to this question takes the form of two more questions:

> If I am not for myself, who will be for me?
> If I am for myself only, what am I?

The Christian tradition answers:

> Love God, and love your neighbour as yourself.

Both the Christian and Jewish traditions endorse the following response in identical terms:

> Do to others as you would like them to do to you.

In all of these good questions and answers, the common factors are as follows:

- the existential and moral primacy of the other
- the primacy of our need for and love of the good other
- the call to each of us to reach, accompany and know the other, to enable them to rejoin the community and live as best they can
- the call to help others as we ourselves have been helped
- the call to know, care for and nurture ourselves.

These are the values that many counsellors and psychotherapists try to embody in our practice, and also the reasons why we do so.

NOTES

1   Since the financial crash of 2008, and the subsequent global recession, the messages of advanced capitalism, individualism and success are increasingly being challenged.

REFERENCES/BIBLIOGRAPHY

Bowlby, J. (1979). *The making and breaking of affectional bonds.* London: Tavistock.

Buber, M. (1959). *I and Thou*, 2nd edition. Edinburgh: T. and T. Clark.

Buxbaum, Y. (1994). *The life and teachings of Hillel.*

Damasio, A. (2000). *The feeling of what happens: Body, emotion and the making of consciousness.* London: Vintage.

Fairbairn, W. R. D. (1952). *Psychoanalytic studies of the personality.* London: Tavistock Publications/ Routledge and Kegan Paul.

Forgaill, D., Byrne, M., & Hull, E. (1973). Be thou my Vision, O Lord of my heart, hymn no. 87 in *The church hymnary*, 3rd edition. London: Oxford University Press.

Gardner, W. H. (1953). *Gerard Manley Hopkins: A selection of his poems and prose.* Harmondsworth: Penguin.

Macmurray, J. (1961). *Persons in Relation.* London: Faber and Faber.

Mearns, D. & Cooper, M. (2005). *Working at relational depth in counselling and psychotherapy.* London: Sage Publications.

Mullahy, P. (Ed.) (1952). *The contributions of Harry Stack Sullivan: A symposium on interpersonal theory in psychiatry and social science.* New York: Hermitage House.

Sutherland, J. D. (1989). *Fairbairn's journey into the interior.* London: Free Association Books.

Suttie, I. D. (1988) (first published 1935). *The origins of love and hate.* London: Free Association Books.

SECTION II

EXPLORING DIALOGUE

CHAPTER 4

SOME NOTES ON DIALOGUE

Key words and themes: dialogue, encounter, I, Thou, It, limitations of dialogue, the domain of the mess, convergence, difference, complications in dialogue, the impact of trauma and loss, trust, respect, meeting, connections, the unspoken, the need for a secure base, the dialogical nature of counselling and training relationships.

INTRODUCTION

First published by COSCA in *Counselling in Scotland* in 2002, these notes began life as a starter paper produced in my capacity as Senior Lecturer and Head of Counselling Studies at the University of Edinburgh. My colleagues and I were embarking on a rewrite of the postgraduate programme of counselling studies in preparation for its first academic review. Among other concerns, we planned to revisit the core orientation of the programme, which is a dialogue between the person-centred approach and psychodynamic perspectives. In this starter paper, I consider the meaning and some of the implications of dialogue.

Etymology of the word dialogue	words across or through
	(logos) (dia)
	from Greek dialogos, from dialegomai 'to converse'
Dictionary definitions	conversation
	conversation in written form as a form of composition
	discussion eg between representatives of two political groups
	a talk or conversation between two main characters, as in a play
Connotations	There is an association between dialogue and two people or groups, particularly because of the apparent contrast between dialogue and monologue (speaking solo). Paulo Freire makes extensive use of this in his early writings, posing dialogue against monologue, giving the first a positive and the second a negative flavour.
	In contemporary English usage, dialogue has developed, in terms of its connotations, clear differentiation from such terms as conversation, communication and exchange. In general, it has acquired a strong flavour of positive evaluation: that is, it is more than a neutrally descriptive word. It has acquired or accreted additional meanings around its core sense.

Some accretions:

Cognitive: questioning basic assumptions	From Socrates in Plato's *The Republic*, dialogue takes the meaning of sustained step-by-step exploration of a person's assumptions, their thinking, in holding a particular view on some matter. This occurs through a series of questions put to that person by Socrates. This can be summarised as the investigation of one person's basic assumptions or thinking in interpersonal dialogue between that person and another.
Relational: the encounter between persons	Martin Buber, in his book *I and Thou*, focuses on the interpersonal encounter between two persons. This he sees as qualitatively different from experiencing or perceiving the other person as an object: such perceptions belong to what he calls the realm of the It. And he goes on: 'But the realm of Thou has a different basis ... When Thou is spoken, the speaker has no thing: indeed he has nothing. But he takes his stand in relation.'
Collaborative action: knowing and acting on the world	Paulo Freire, in *Pedagogy of the Oppressed*, defines dialogue as the authentic or true word. A true word (as opposed to what he describes as idle chatter, verbalism, alienating blah) involves two dimensions: reflection and action. The implication is of a commitment to acting on the world in order to change it. However, there are key third and fourth elements in Freire's conception of dialogue. Firstly, it is not just two or a few people. To say a true word is the right of every person. Secondly, Freirean dialogue is directed towards communal action in the world: 'Dialogue is the encounter between men, mediated by the world, in order to name the world.'
	For Freire, there are limits to dialogue: dialogue is not possible in an oppressive relationship. It does not involve depositing or imposing one's ideas on another person. It is not an exchange of ideas, nor a hostile polemical argument. Freire argues that dialogue involves love, humility, faith in human beings, hope and critical thinking.

LIMITATIONS AND PROBLEMS

It is clear from the above list of accretions that the word dialogue is a value-laden concept. Very positive values are associated with it. Like other human positives, it is therefore available for idealisation.

What are some of the problems and limitations of dialogue?

The following contributions are taken from an outstanding paper given by Tracy Essoglou and Angel Shaw at a conference in honour of Paulo Freire's 70th birthday held in New York in 1991. In it, they argue that Freire's concept of dialogue fails to do justice to the experience of women, which is characterised by ambiguity, self-doubt, bitterness and self-censorship. They speak of the complexity of that which is unspoken and uncertain, in the following terms:

Women inhabit the domain of the mess, the inchoate, the epistemologically inadmissible.

Whole dimensions of subjectivity can be negated in dialogue.

In the absence of the validation of a multiplicity of languages, women are obliged to speak the master's language.

Language is a locus of power and servility.

The realm of the senses [and I would add, of the emotions, relationships and inner world – CK] is rendered suspect by the triumph of rationality.

There has to be an acknowledgement that women are in a constant state of defining themselves.

Quoted in Challenging Education, Creating Alliances: the Legacy of Paulo Freire in the New Scotland, Colin Kirkwood, *The Scottish Journal of Community Work and Development, 1998, Vol. 3.*

In my view, all of these comments are spot on. I would argue that they apply not only to women, but also to men. And they certainly apply to both students and teachers on counselling courses!

Another limitation is around people engaging, or saying they are engaging, in dialogue when they have other aims which may not be compatible with dialogue: for example, the use of dialogue as in effect the prosecution of war by another means. Take the Cold War between the West and the Soviet Bloc: there was even some rhetoric of convergence, but both sides were trying to win outright.

Some years ago, many of us felt great hope in relation to the progress of three significant dialogues: between the blacks and whites of South Africa, between Palestine and Israel, and the dialogue initiated by John Hume and others between the nationalist, republican and protestant traditions in Ireland ('it is people who are divided, not territory'). It is arguable that at least two of these dialogues have run into trouble because both sides have treated dialogue as another means of attaining their separate objectives (war by another means).

There is, particularly, but not exclusively among politicians, a tendency to use the word dialogue lightly, as a good-sounding word that can improve my image or associate me with positive values and help me achieve my own objectives. Whether this is a limitation of dialogue, or simple a limitation on the part of human beings, whom Alasdair MacIntyre would describe as lacking the virtues, is a moot point.

This consideration of limitations underlines the convergence dimension of dialogue as an objective, where convergence means a willingness on both sides to go beyond their present positions, to learn from, collaborate and find common ground with others. The late Janet Hassan, the child psychotherapist, referred to this aspect as expressing the objective of conjoining. The poet Bertolt Brecht, referring to the relationship between two people, described it as the third thing.

Dislocation and loss

A problem, rather than a limitation: this is the question of the extent to which dialogue is possible for people (many of us) who have experienced certain kinds of dislocation, disruption or suffering. Here I'm thinking a newish thought, not one I've yet formulated fully. I have in mind four or five sorts of situation, all involving different kinds of loss. First, there is the loss involved in moving from one place, home, landscape, people, language, and culture to another (dislocation). Second, there is the loss of a parent, caregiver, or sibling through death or separation/divorce. Third, there is the experience of abuse or betrayal of trust and the relationship complications that ensue. Fourth, there is the loss of capacities involved in becoming disabled through accident, illness, or genetic inheritance. And fifth, there is the loss involved in dramatic changes of economic circumstances through loss of job, home, income, and status. (These can and frequently do occur in combination.) All of them involve traumatic loss and change of both circumstances and relationships, and pose, willy-nilly, both the need, and the reluctance, to engage in new dialogues with new people in new conditions alongside mourning what has been lost. Some of us get stuck in the mourning (perhaps we all do, to some degree: the trauma is never entirely overcome), and we may not really or fully engage in the encounter/dialogue with the unwished-for new. We are to a greater or lesser degree alienated: a part of us is engaged elsewhere. This generates complications in dialogue.

DIALOGUE IN COUNSELLING TRAINING BETWEEN PC AND PD PERSPECTIVES

How does all of this apply in a counselling training programme that is trying to embody dialogue? The answer is: in many ways. Rather than start to list them, I want to draw this starter paper to a close by listing some gleanings and suggestions from experiences so far. These aren't in any special order.

There has to be trust and a sense of safety on the course. This seems to be a necessary (but not sufficient) condition for genuine dialogue. One key determinant in creating a sense of trust is the quality of the behaviour, relationships and fundamental attitudes of the tutors. There has to be a sense that the tutors are sincere, know their stuff well, share what they know to the best of their ability, but also share their not knowing, unsureness, and even their vulnerability. All this as well as having a capacity to enable or facilitate honest, searching explorations and reflections by the students.

For the inter-personal and inter-perspectival aspects of dialogue on a counselling course to be real, there has to be a genuine sense that the tutors like and respect each other and will go on listening and communicating with each other even when there are differences, misunderstandings, and the going gets rough. You cannot continue dialogue with someone you do not respect, and at the same time dialogue can't be just a fair weather phenomenon.

Convergence and difference

Dialogue can be about convergence or about difference. It is bound, often, to be about radically different starting points, stances, ways of knowing, and conclusions. But it is not, I think, a battle for victory by one side or another. Covert or overt contempt for the other point of view will put a blight on dialogue very quickly. Course members will sense it. My sense is that where difference is concerned, dialogue sets about patiently clarifying, exploring, deepening the exploration. That also applies where convergence is concerned: the convergence may only be apparent. Dialogue is not about making it all into one undifferentiated soup. Paulo Freire, at the conference already referred to, spoke about democracy as the courage to be different, to respect the difference and to try to learn from it. He went on:

I don't believe in unanimity. Democracy is the confrontation of difference and the necessity to overcome antagonisms ... it is possible for us to grow together in the differences, never trying to forget the differences: to get unity in diversity ... not to collapse us all into one.

I suspect that up until now we have given insufficient thought to what is not said, what is felt or thought and kept silent. Enabling/allowing more of it to be said involves a special kind of stance on the part of the tutor. Such a lot here turns on how the tutors behave, on their conception of how to be a tutor. They make a major contribution to creating the atmosphere of the course: the students contribute to that strongly as well, of course.

A powerful metaphor for an aspect of what we are trying to do is an image given to me by a friend when I was an undergraduate: he told me how much he enjoyed being at the edge of the sea, because three different elements meet there: the land, the sea, and the sky. The point is that they are different. And they actually do meet. Another linked metaphor is the meeting of languages. If you go and live in another country and immerse yourself in its language, lots of things can occur. One is that, paradoxically, as you become more aware of the language that is foreign to you, you become more sharply aware of your own language and culture. It's a sharpening of awareness due to contrast, but it's not – or need not be – an either/or relation. Looking at the Alps from a rooftop in the Veneto is not the same as looking towards the Highlands from a rooftop in Stirling, but it's a meaningful juxtaposition. There are differences, and there are connections.

The need for a good-enough foundation

Are there limits to the value of a dialogical orientation in counselling training? Probably. Our external examiner, Dr Gabrielle Syme, has highlighted one of them when she comments that the weaker students find the dialogue difficult, especially in the early stages. This is a most helpful observation. As soon as Gabrielle said it, I was aware (a) that it was true, and (b) of a certain defensive reaction on my own part. This touches on something quite important. It is fashionable, in our culture, to decry fundamentalism, and I understand why we do that. But much harder and more challenging is to understand the need for fundamentalism, which is, I suggest, at bottom, the need for a good-enough foundation. The etymology here is the Latin *fundus*, bottom in the sense of base, the hopefully solid ground on which a building is constructed. (In both Old French and Middle English, fundament means the buttocks, the solid base on which we sit!!) Contemporary relativism and nihilism have undermined many (particularly western and patriarchal) fundamentalisms, but have perhaps failed to address the need for something reliable that you can root yourself in. We, as counsellors and psychotherapists, particularly in the longer term work we do with clients who are deeply distressed in their early relationships, know about what can happen when that foundation is disturbed, destroyed or betrayed. And most of us have also experienced it ourselves to some degree. When we ask counselling students on our courses, as we do, to explore themselves as one of the four main strands of training, we are, in effect, asking them to explore what Carl Rogers calls their 'self-structure' and what Harry Stack Sullivan calls their 'self-system'. If they are to do this with confidence, what can they hold on to during this process? What will stay solid for them? What foundation can they rely on?

An image that recurs in my mind from childhood is one of two or three strong, mature beech trees growing in a cluster on a slope in a field. On the down-slope side their roots are partially exposed, and the observer can see how they have gripped some rocks embedded in the ground, and also gripped each other's roots. This is an image of a complex foundation.

A related if rather exaggerated image is the bible story about the wise man who built his house upon a rock and the foolish man who built his house upon sand.

Dialogical relations in training

Those of us who teach on a dialogical course usually have had our training in a person-centred or psychodynamic setting. Is there some sense in which these people are better grounded, more strongly rooted, or is it actually deceptive to say that any one perspective is pure and singular, sure and steadfast?

Is each of us not, in our own unique way, rooted around a particular sequence of relationships, experiences, learnings etc., which have some elements of wobble and plurality built in? Do we need to give more thought to what is the solid ground of our programme or is it clear enough? A meeting of two (or far more) different languages and cultures? A commitment to dialogue with and genuine relating to the other? Maybe it is clear.

I think I'm saying we need to be sure we have a grounded sense of what we're about. And we need to be able to create a learning environment in which the students experience that as a reliable, secure and consistent-enough experience. This places a lot of weight on the core tutors on the course, on their consistency, their knowledge, their capacity as teachers and as facilitators, their personal sincerity, and, above all, their relationships.

Maybe what I'm edging towards is that our core orientation is not solely that it's a dialogical course, but also that it's a persons-in-relations course. (The reference here is to the work of the Scottish philosopher, John Macmurray.)

A concluding thought: to me, the counselling relationship is inherently and essentially dialogical, a meeting of two people with different body-psyches, experiences, ideas, values, relationships, attitudes and languages. The counselling training relationship is also essentially dialogical, and it is not a contradiction of that fact that it is also a teaching/learning relationship. [1]

NOTES

[1] One of the formative experiences of my early twenties was observing a disputation organised by Father Anthony Ross, who was then Roman Catholic chaplain at the University of Edinburgh. The disputation was introduced as a medieval form of debate. One of the rules was that each side had to identify something central in the case put forward by the other side – something central, not marginal – that they could accept, and weave into their own argument. What struck me about this rule was that it was obviously designed to moderate the tendency to try to destroy the case advanced by the opposition comprehensively, by building in a requirement to achieve some common ground, some degree of convergence. It demonstrates a recognition of the centrality of difference in human affairs, and constitutes an attempt to engage with it in a way that is constructive. Coming as I did from a Northern Irish Protestant background, there was also a link for me with my encounters with Catholicism and with Catholics as persons. Considerations of this kind, generalised, underlie my sense of the existential necessity of dialogue in human relations and specifically in learning, in therapeutic work and in politics.

REFERENCES/BIBLIOGRAPHY

Buber, M. (1958). *I and thou*. Edinburgh: T & T Clark.

Freire, P. (1972). *Pedagogy of the oppressed*. Harmondsworth: Penguin.

Kirkwood, C. (1998). Challenging education, creating alliances: The legacy of Paulo Freire in the new Scotland. *The Scottish Journal of Community Work and Development, 3*.

MacIntyre, A. (1985). *After virtue*. London: Duckworth.

Macmurray, J. (1961). *Persons in relation*. London: Faber and Faber.

Lee, H. (translator) (1955). *Plato: The republic*. Harmondsworth: Penguin.

CHAPTER 5

DIALOGUE IN ITS LARGER CONTEXT

Only Connect!

Key words and themes: what goes on between, attunement, confluence, impact, presence, emitting and receiving, intersubjective knowing, means of knowing, subjects and objects, agents of knowing, accompanying, interweaving of means of knowing and objects of knowledge, unconscious communication, polyphonic score, relating, relatedness and unrelatedness, making meaning-full music.

This takes my earlier paper *Some notes on dialogue,* included here as Chapter 4, as read. *Dialogue in its larger context* was first published by COSCA in *Counselling in Scotland* in Spring/Summer 2004.

What I am interested in is what goes on between client and counsellor in the series of encounters that constitute the counselling relationship, and what that means to clients and counsellors as persons, in their lives.

I am interested in how people experience each other, and what they then make of that. Dialogue is important – words across, words crossing and re-crossing – but it is only a part of it, however crucial. It is part of something larger which is not primarily verbal.

I am also interested in observable behavioural dimensions, but it's more than that too. So it's not just words across (dialogue), and it's not just voluntary and involuntary movements and expressions (behaviour and body language), but something that is more comprehensive and includes all of these. I know this could sound like 'the mysterious' or 'the numinous' but I hold that everything is knowable, and can become clear. Unfortunately, in order to achieve clarity more quickly, our methods of knowing are often reductive to what can be easily observed, corroborated, measured and described. The trouble is that that approach tends to miss some of the key things that go on between counsellor and client.

So I don't want to devalue either behaviours and words or measurement and description. I want to locate and use these in relation to wider and deeper non-verbal processes.

This larger thing that goes on is difficult to name. Here are some of the words that get used: encounter, meeting, presence, attunement, resonance, barometrical registration, impact, reaction, response, representation. I'm allowing these words to come out and be written down. It's a whole thing. It fluctuates, flows changingly along like a river, except sometimes there are gaps, discontinuities (for example, passages of non-attunement) and these are also important.

The word confluence comes to mind. A confluence is the process of two rivers joining, their waters meeting, inter-impacting, mingling.

The fact that the menstrual cycles of women living together gradually 'harmonise', occur at the same time of the month, comes to mind.

The way a lot of women and some men often seem to intuit what another person is feeling/thinking/what's going on for them, comes to mind.

I want now – having circled around 'it' – to focus on what I think 'it' is. It is the total impact that one person has on another person when they are together in a room, only a part of which occurs through the use of words.

It is this something which occurs. It is this something to which we turn our attention. We try to attune (a) to what is occurring in ourselves and (b) to what we are receiving from the *presence* of the other. But these processes do not happen in separate rooms of the soul. It is the same person who is experiencing self and attending to other. The two processes relate to each other in various ways. Let me ponder this. In the Middle Ages there was this idea: all things that are, are lights: sunt lumina. All things go themselves (Gerard Manley Hopkins). They give out their light. In the counselling meeting, the client goes herself. So does the counsellor. Each emits/transmits, all the time, the totality of herself. The counsellor tries to be in receiver mode, receiving as much as she can of the client's transmission (which is her being, her emitting of herself). It impacts on and is received in the counsellor. Maybe there are three processes: first, I receive the transmission of the self of the client through all my receptors, the whole of my living conscious, preconscious and unconscious body; second, I continue my own process of being myself and attending to what is going on in me while the first process is occurring; third, the first process impacts on the second and makes it take certain directions. It 'selects' or plays certain notes in the second process, it colours the second process, impacting on its pace and rhythm, its content and quality. Some of this occurs outwith conscious awareness. And then there is a fourth process: how all this is perceived, sorted, named, linked up, reflected upon, analysed, and understood. It is only the fourth process that may vary from orientation to orientation. It is, in part, a process of naming and conceptualisation: what you think and say happened, and how you come to think about it.

This is the theme of experiencing and perceiving and naming and conceptualising: knowing. A cluster of issues here. A sequence (or is it a hologram? Or is it both?): occurrence, experience, perception, description, analysis. Let's try it out first as a sequence.

1. An event or events occur: objects or persons present themselves, in the presence of a person who is currently aware, and whose awareness is turned towards the presenting events.
2. The event(s) are experienced by the person, and focussed on: an emotional impact occurs.
3. The event(s) are perceived (apprehended, grasped) by the person.
4. The event(s) are named (described) by the person: verbal language enters the process.

5. The event(s) are explained and understood, contextualised and conceptualised and linked and analysed by the person.

This is a pretty normal sequence. The phases of course overlap, shade into each other. But not all events occurring in a person's awareness get to go through the whole sequence. Some stay at the stage of occurrence in awareness, some at the stage of experiencing with focus, some at the stage of apprehension, and so on. We might say that this is a sequence moving from non-verbal experiencing to verbal knowing, bearing in mind that while all knowing involves experiencing, not all experiencing results in knowing (unless we widen the meaning of knowing to make it identical with the meaning of experiencing, which is a possibility).

Having said that, I suspect that this so-called sequence is also a hologram: its phases are in some sense simultaneous, circling, swarming around and through each other.

As we move through the sequence, or move around in the hologram, the question 'What are the *means* of knowing?' becomes increasingly important. If we look at it as a sequence, for the sake of simplicity, we see that various means are required:

- sensing and directing attention
- undergoing and focussing on experiences
- grasping or apprehending focussed experiences
- attending to free associations, and pondering
- naming: using words and other representations
- analysing: using concepts and theories, making links, recognizing recurring patterns and emerging themes

But earlier in the sequence – indeed, from its very start – the person's basic assumptions are already in place and in play: space, time, three dimensionality, their assimilated theories, their schemas for organising their perceptions, and their orientation towards living. Some of these are universal, some vary from culture to culture, from epoch to epoch, from gender to gender, and from person to person.

The *object* of knowledge, right from our first awareness of it, requires *means of knowing* that are adapted to it. For an odour, the person needs a sense of smell, for a scene or colour, sight, for temperature and pressure, the capacity for skin and internal bodily sensations etc. To experience, focus and perceive a very tiny object, a microscope of appropriate design and size is required. For an object in motion at a distance, binoculars are needed. I am insisting on the obvious. And by the time you get to the later stages (if indeed they are stages), you are already into linking the object with other like objects – that's what naming is about. More so at the last stage: explanatory links, context, relations, abstraction, thematic investigation, synthesis.

I repeat: the object of knowledge needs appropriate means of knowing. The aim is to know the object in itself and in its relations, as it is, and not to mistake it for another object. What is the process, the object of knowledge, and the means of knowing when we consider the counsellor, the client, and their relationship? It is the counsellor – and the client – each as experiencing person, as subject, directing her awareness simultaneously towards her own experiencing self (her own living mind/body), and towards the self of the other, as a subject, and trying to register what is going on in and for the other and in and for herself. It is one person trying to know another person, *and* their own self, *and* the impact the second person is having on the first. I am spelling this out because it is not simply one person trying to know another person. There is also this focus on the two-way impact of the one on the other, that is, on a relationship. And further, I insist once again that we are concerned here with the knowing of two persons, not just one. There are two agents of knowing at work here, in an increasingly mutual relation of knowing. The object and the agent and the process of knowledge turn out to be plural! There are at least two experiencers and knowers at work. Plenty of scope for checking things out. Inter-subjectivity!

Another qualification: the counsellor and the client, each, is both subject and object. For herself, she is more experiencing subject, but the more she cultivates her capacity to attend to her own experiencing, the more capable she becomes of simultaneous awareness of herself as object as well as subject. To the client, the counsellor is object and perceiving subject. To the counsellor, the client is both object and subject, the more a subject the more the counsellor learns to accompany the client, in her own rhythms and terms, the more the counsellor glimpses the client's subjectivity, gets aligned with it. The client, to herself, is subject and object, object in so far as she experiences herself as the object of the counsellor's attention. This could go on. You get the point. Each gradually learns to relax attentively into this kind of relating.

As we go along the path of the 'means of knowing' sequence above, what *specific* means of knowing are actually used in the counsellor/client relationship? Yes, I know I am repeating myself, but hang on in there.

- direct perception, through the senses, of both the other and the self
- bodily sensations internal to both counsellor and client
- attending to free associations: whatever comes to mind, sensations, feelings, thoughts, songs, hymns, bits of poetry, snatches of prose, attitudes, memories, desires, colours, shapes, fantasies, hopes, notions, concepts, theories, tangents, jokes, moods – every conceivable and inconceivable thing that can come up as a free association
- a conscious awareness staying with, playing over, pondering and keeping in mind much of the above as it occurs and especially if it recurs
- the actual words, phrases, statements, non-statements, presence, silence, posture of the client/ the counsellor as (a) things in themselves, to be attended to, (b) things stimulating both reactions and responses in both persons
- patterns in the psyche of the counsellor or the client, which she begins to notice and about which she starts to think
- connections between those of client and those of counsellor in either or both of their minds/souls/bodies.

Now: a 'scientific' person, according to a Newtonian or 19th century physics stereotype, would say that some of this is subjective and unreliable. However, (a) contemporary scientists are interested in dreams, chaos, consciousness – they are not mechanists, they don't lack imagination, and (b) to be 'scientific' is to attend to the actual evidence presenting itself, and to go on attending and looking for patterns and variations, gradually aiming to get closer and closer to the object of knowledge in its actual nature by checking one's perceptions and developing and testing hypotheses.

I am also struck by the fact that thinking about this sort of 'evidence' presenting through these 'means of knowing' is stirring up two kinds of reflection in me right now. The first is that it is very like the material of the arts: poetry, novels, plays, paintings, music – words, tunes, colours, shapes, actions, flights of thought or imagination. The second is that there is a massive overlap or interweaving between the object of knowledge and the means of knowing – and this is also true in the arts.

'La conscience et le monde s'endorment d'un meme coup': this is a (vaguely recollected) quotation from Paulo Freire, quoting, in turn, from Jean-Paul Sartre. I think it means that consciousness and the world, that of which one is conscious, go to sleep at the same moment. They are bound up with each other. If consciousness goes to sleep, the world, of which it is conscious, is no longer present to consciousness (except, of course, in dreams). Consciousness is always consciousness *of*, or *with*. Consciousness takes the form of (is an apprehension *of* and *with*) the object of which it is conscious. And the means of knowing an object are elaborations of consciousness itself. You could even risk saying that the means of knowing, in use, become pregnant with the objects of knowledge: the former come to contain representations of the latter.

In the counselling relationship, the consciousness of the counsellor (aware of client and self in the same space/time flow) is only a second means of knowing the consciousness of the client. The primary means of knowing the consciousness of the client is of course the consciousness of the client. The client is increasingly as time goes on aware of her own consciousness and that of the counsellor.

I do not want to get away from this difficult, apparently confusing nexus of relations in which the means of knowing and the object of knowledge are so interwoven. I want to see it more clearly.

I want to know more about what and how the counsellor experiences, perceives, describes, names, and how this connects or does not connect with what the client experiences, perceives, describes, names. I want to follow the subtle shifts, the hesitancies, the puzzlements, the mistakes, and what else comes to mind. I would like each to be able to report what occurs to them as close as possible to the time at which it occurs to them. I would like to link these, or to see if they are linked. I think they are often linked. What is the nature of the linkage? One famous expression of it is the notion that the unconscious of the client communicates directly with the unconscious of the counsellor, without going through the consciousness of either.

This links with the notion of the barometrical relationship (barometer and weather) which I got from Jo Burns. It links with Dave Mearns's concept of the unspoken relationship. I want to know how the total stream of consciousness (and preconsciousness) (and unconsciousness) of the counsellor relates to the total stream of consciousness (and preconsciousness) (and unconsciousness) of the client. That's what I mean by dialogue in its larger context. Formally, what I am after might look like a polyphonic score, constantly improvising, consisting of simultaneous parts, voices, tunes, instruments, interweaving strands:

- part 1: what the client says and does
- part 2: the client's stream of consciousness, simultaneously with part 1
- part 3: what the counsellor says and does
- part 4: the counsellor's stream of consciousness, simultaneously with part 3
- part 5: the connections the client is making, and sometimes communicating, as the whole polyphony goes along
- part 6: the connections the counsellor is making, and sometimes communicating, as the whole polyphony goes along.

I would like to learn better to listen to and hear this score, in its totality, playing as it goes along, so that I can get more of the harmonies, the dissonances, the connections, and the lack of connections, the counterpoint, the themes and their development.

What I am interested in is what relating, relatedness, and unrelatedness look, feel, and sound like as they are happening, as they are going along. Come to think of it, that is close to what I am trying to do in a counselling session, and as the relationship deepens, I think it is what the client is doing too.

Increasingly, we are learning to connect and notice non-connections. We are making a particular kind of meaning-full music together. And that was E. M. Forster's plea: 'only connect!'

SECTION III

APPLYING THE PERSONS IN RELATION PERSPECTIVE IN COUNSELLING AND PSYCHOTHERAPY

CHAPTER 6

THE ROLE OF PSYCHOTHERAPY IN THE IN-PATIENT TREATMENT OF A TEENAGE GIRL WITH ANOREXIA

A Dialogical Narrative

With Three Letters by Anna Other, and a Reflection by David Tait

Key words and themes: eating disorders, anorexia, multidisciplinarity, family work, group work, dialogical relational psychotherapy, socio-cultural context, traumatic events, attunement, sibling rivalry, aggression, perfectionism, dreams, free associations, dialogue, respect for persons, persons in relation, persons in community, self-other-culture-world system, core relational thematics.

This paper was first delivered at a meeting of The Scottish Association for Psychodynamic Counselling in Glasgow on 6 March 2010.

INTRODUCTION

I count myself lucky, in the very week in summer 2004 when I retired from the University of Edinburgh, to have spotted an advert for psychodynamic psychotherapists to work with people with severe eating disorders at the Huntercombe Hospital Edinburgh. I thought: I know very little about this, but it sounds really interesting. And it was. I spent five fascinating years at Huntercombe, leaving in the summer of 2009.

I don't want to spend a long time setting the scene. Many of you will know about the existence of the Huntercombe Hospital Edinburgh at Ecclesmachan, just north of Uphall in West Lothian. It's a fine Georgian building near the top of a long tree-and-rhododendron-lined drive between a golf course and the Oatridge Agricultural College. It has beds for up to 22 people: the youngest about 11, the oldest at that time 54, with one floor for the under 18s and one floor for the over 18s.

Multidisciplinarity

The under 16s have a school with two teachers. There are cooks, and a dining room for each age group. There is a dietician who has a pretty vital role to play, as you can imagine.

There is a hospital manager who runs the whole place, and a medical director who is in charge of the work of the multidisciplinary team. The medical director is also consultant psychiatrist for the work with the over 18s, while his colleague, also a consultant psychiatrist, specialises in child and adolescent work and manages the under 18 side.

Working with them are another three staff grade psychiatrists, a clinical psychologist, three psychotherapists, an art therapist, and a social worker. The biggest single team is the nurses and care assistants: around five of each, led by a nurse manager. (The hospital, at that time, had no family therapist: other staff undertook family work. A family therapist was subsequently appointed.)

Most of the staff are women, and most of them are young. In the case of the nurses and care assistants, most are under 30, and in the case of the rest of the staff, usually under 40.

Huntercombe is a well-resourced, well-run hospital with a caring and learning culture. It is a good place to work.

This will not be an academic presentation in its style, although I have read a lot of academic and professional papers on work with people with eating disorders. I want to give you just a taste of that background. I am going to concentrate almost entirely on anorexia nervosa, and on our engagement with one person.

Anorexia: A disorder of contradictions

Professor Bryan Lask, who is internationally renowned for his research into eating disorders, has written that anorexia has been variously conceptualised as an eating disorder, an anxiety disorder, a delusional disorder, a self-esteem disorder, a phobic disorder, an obsessive compulsive disorder, a body dysmorphic disorder, a neuro-developmental disorder, and also as a reaction to socio-cultural trends. It is a disorder of contradictions, for example: fat/thin, full/empty, starve/binge, hair loss/lanugo hair, food obsession/food avoidance, low self-esteem/perfectionism, control/loss of control, fragility/strength, etc. It is seen as a complex illness with psychological, sociological, physiological, and neurological components.

Almost all the patients in the hospital were female over the five years I worked there. I worked directly with around 60 women or girls, and perhaps three boys or young men.

They came to the hospital because they were seriously ill, and because treatment at home or on an out-patient basis had not been successful. In many cases, their lives were at risk. Over those five years three newly arriving or former patients died. That the number of deaths was so low is, I think, a great achievement on the part of the hospital.

Treatment was in the first place aimed at physiological stabilisation and then at gradual weight gain. Much but by no means all of the work revolved around meal planning, eating, monitoring of eating, and so on. Getting medication right also had an important part to play. Medication was prescribed for some patients with other psychiatric problems, for example depression, not for the eating disorder itself. Because I have no medical expertise I will say little about this except insofar as the patients talked to me about food and their bodies; how they saw and felt about their own bodies and other people's bodies; how they saw and felt about eating, and about other people's eating; how they avoided eating and got rid of food. And they spoke to me about how their medication was working, or wasn't working.

My work, and the work of my fellow therapists, was undertaken in three or four main contexts: one to one psychotherapy, group psychotherapy, family work, and the daily community meetings. But I don't want to give the impression that this work was carried out separately or at a distance from the rest of the life of the hospital. The psychotherapists were in daily contact with the psychiatrists, the nurses and care assistants, the psychologist, the social worker, the cooks, the dietician and the management team. That is one great advantage of everything being on such a small scale. Everything is to a greater or lesser extent integrated. Developments in one area inevitably and instantly impact on other areas.

Theoretical perspectives

That leads me on to another key factor: multidisciplinarity inevitably means a multiplicity of theoretical perspectives and ways of working. When I first went to Huntercombe, the medical director and his fellow consultant psychiatrist shared a psychodynamic/applied psychoanalytic perspective. They were influenced by Freud, Klein, Suttie, Winnicott, Fairbairn and Sutherland. So that was the dominant discourse in staff meetings and in the journal club, modified of course by their long experience of the realities of being in charge of NHS in- and out-patient services. The clinical psychologist at the time adopted a cognitive behavioural and cognitive analytic perspective. One of my fellow psychotherapists, the therapies manager, described her orientation as integrative, which she explained as adopting a flexible approach, making use of a variety of theories and techniques according to patient need.

Since the retirement of the first medical director, and the departure of the first child and adolescent consultant and the first clinical psychologist, a new situation in terms of theoretical perspectives obtained. The second medical director, although drawing on some psychoanalytic understandings, was more orientated towards cognitive behavioural therapy, dialectical behaviour therapy and mindfulness, and the second (child and adolescent) consultant was a group analyst with a strong orientation towards the therapeutic community perspective. And the new clinical psychologist had a range of interests: CBT, mindfulness and integrative psychotherapy.

A change also occurred in the economic and institutional context in which the hospital operated. An agreement had been reached with the NHS in Scotland that the hospital would work solely with referrals from NHS health boards, mainly in Scotland, but sometimes also from Ireland, and still occasionally from England.

At the same time, a much tougher and more restrictive position was now taken on length of patient stay. Where, in the first two years or so of the hospital's life, the length of stay was variable (for example, two patients stayed for two years) the assumed norm became a stay of three or four months, with any extension beyond that only in exceptional circumstances and by agreement with the consultant psychiatrist in charge of eating disorders work in the referring health board.

On the basis of these developments, which have included sustained dialogue with referring hospitals and health boards, the hospital has succeeded in expanding its work significantly, and has, I believe, made a valuable contribution to Scottish society.

Socio-cultural context

I nearly said: that is all that needs to be said by way of introduction. But it isn't. Those of you who know me well will not be surprised when I draw your attention to the vital importance of the socio-cultural context, of socio-cultural factors, values and trends in the growth of eating disorders. Two stories will do to illustrate this point. First, the role of television. Until 1997 there were no known cases of eating disorders in one of the main South Sea islands. That year, television programmes from throughout the world became available on the island. Within 18 months the first case of an eating disorder was reported. Second, the role of women's magazines like *Hello*. Almost all the patients, or certainly the girls and younger women, are very preoccupied with these magazines, with *Big Brother*, and with violent and soft porn films and DVDs. Their role models are women like Victoria Beckham and other WAGs (wives and girlfriends), and celebrities. As you know, these magazines are mainly visual. The subjects' faces and skin are airbrushed. Most shots are of women in bikinis or revealing outfits. What text there is, is invariably about who is leaving whom, and who is getting together with whom, who is fat and who is thin, who is pregnant, who is happy and who is distressed. It is worth noting that this interest is not confined to the patients. These magazines are available in the nurses' room, where almost all the staff have their lunch, and all the female staff read them and talk about them. Occasionally I used to flick through them too.

To sum up so far: we are talking not about psychotherapy on its own, but psychotherapy as one collaborating part of a multidisciplinary team where the typical concerns of psychotherapists with personal feelings and meanings, past and present relationships, traumatic events and experiences in the family, school and community are always interwoven with concerns about medication, about eating, about weight gain or weight loss, about BMI (body mass index), about targets, about getting home for a weekend, about dates for discharge, about exercise whether secret or permitted.

Working with women and girls

What is it like for a male psychotherapist to work with these girls and these women? The first thing that struck me was that they were prisoners: the front and back doors and the doors of the conservatory were normally locked. The rationale for this was to protect the patients from themselves, and potentially from others. A patient leaving the unit might self-harm (very common in eating disorders), or come to grief in severe weather. Any detached house in the countryside is prey to unwelcome visitors, and at Huntercombe that was not just a threat to property, but potentially to vulnerable young women.

The second thing was how skeletally thin they are. The third thing is that, without exception, they all think they are fat. To see them eating is a painful sight. They look down. They eat very slowly. They do not want to eat. They attempt to cut their portions into tiny fragments, and the nurses and care assistants firmly tell them that they can't do that. They get up to all sorts of tricks to avoid eating, lose food, vomit or induce diarrhoea. In all of these respects, one is seeing them as objects, from the point of view of an interested spectator. There is no point in pretending that they, and we, are not objects, since that is one dimension of our existence, that we can be seen and treated as objects.

But we are more than objects, we are subjects who know and act, we are persons in personal relations with other persons, with personal meanings, personal aspirations, personal fears, and personal stories. And that is what we as psychotherapists are concerned with: to treat persons with respect as persons. The corollary of that, I believe, is that we need to be genuinely persons ourselves, so that in our relationships with our clients, we are sincerely being persons in relation to persons.

DIALOGICAL RELATIONAL PSYCHOTHERAPY

Now I want to do two things. The first is to outline how I worked with these patients. The second is to read you a selection of my reflective notes on psychotherapy sessions with a 14-year-old girl with anorexia, whom I will call Anna.

I'll start with my approach to the work. At first I felt I understood nothing of what was going on, particularly in the over 18s psychotherapy group and in what was then called the anger management group. I paid a lot of attention with my eyes and my ears and my whole self. During that first year it seemed to me that the girls often whispered in a voice as low and soft as their lanugo hair. I frequently couldn't hear them. Yet miraculously my fellow group facilitator, one of the other psychotherapists, could, and she seemed to be instantly in rapport with them. I remember thinking of that picture on the cover of *Families and How to Survive Them,* of John Cleese and Robin Skynner looking in a window at a woman breastfeeding a baby: the male as baffled outsider.

Developing an approach

I realise, in retrospect, that I soon moved out of that position. I quickly grasped that if you thought you could do psychotherapy as a Freudian blank screen, self-withholding, looking into the distance and saying nothing or next to nothing, you would have had your chips and might as well leave. But simultaneously I remembered reading a book about the work of the great American psychiatrist Harry Stack Sullivan. Sullivan reports how he learned to work with deeply withdrawn patients. He would go into the room they were in, usually in bed with their eyes closed. And instead of asking questions and just listening, he would talk about anything that came into his head, changing topics as his own awareness and free associations and hunches flowed along, always keeping an eye on how the silent, closed, withdrawn patient was reacting, or not reacting. When the patient opened his eyes or made a movement or a comment, Sullivan knew he had connected. As women in the west of Scotland used to say, he had got a click. And then they were into some kind of dialogue.

In the one to one work, and, in a slightly different way, in the group work, I adapted Sullivan's approach, and I modified it further by my reading of Ian Sutties's great book *The Origins of Love and Hate,* and the writings of Susie Orbach, John Macmurray, Harry Guntrip, Ronald Fairbairn, and Jock Sutherland.

The task is to attune, to get on the patient's wavelength, and you do that by being your self, and by being very interested in and welcoming and encouraging of their self. Always attune. Always accompany, always try to get alongside the person. Always be yourself, don't be fake, pay constant attention to what is coming up in you, and welcome it and wonder about it, and sometimes share it while acknowledging it as yours. And sometimes ask: does that resonate with anything that's going on in you? It frequently does, and it is frequently helpful, not as an interpretation, but as a resonance, an attunement, sometimes a harmony, sometimes a counterpoint. A means of making a direct connection.

This approach is guided, of course, by a very simple moral framework. You are there, being yourself, not to indulge yourself, not at all to meet your own needs, but to attune, to get alongside, to enable, to facilitate, to draw out, to encourage, to value and validate, to welcome, to encourage that person in the facilitating environment that you are trying to create, to help them understand themselves and their relationships and bring their meanings and themes to light. My favourite quotation of all time is from Gerard Manley Hopkins:

> Each mortal thing does one thing and the same:
> Deals out that being indoors each one dwells;
> Selves – goes itself; *myself* it speaks and spells,
> Crying *What I do is me: for that I came.*

But selves, of course, are not selves in isolation, even although, as the poet Tom Leonard says in response to John Donne:

> No man – or woman
> is an island.

> Oceanography, however,
> is not a science to be despised.

Family and relationship maps

So the next thing I do, once we have got alongside each other, is to invite the patient or client to make a family and relationship map. This is *not* a genogram. It is a homemade map, a personally-made map. I bring along a large sheet of paper, with pens and markers, and we sit alongside each other at a table. And I invite the girl or the woman to put her own name and age in the middle. And, in the space around, to add the names and ages of her sisters and brothers in the order that they were born. And then her mother and father's names and ages. And then aunties and uncles. And grannies and grandpas. And then husbands and partners and boyfriends and children and so on. And all the time I am showing a genuine and lively interest in this person and her relationships. And gradually this map, this personal picture fills out. And we add little notes where explanation is needed. I explain that I have a terrible memory, and that this is going to be really useful to both of us. I say: you are explaining to me all about your relationships and what they mean to you. And I am explaining to you something that in a sense you already know: the importance of human relationships. In a real sense, I say, we are our relationships, both past and present. We are persons in relation.

It may take a whole session to make the map, or even two sessions. Then I ask if we can make a copy, a photocopy, and if I can keep one and she will keep the other. I ask her to bring her family and relationship map to every session, every time we meet.

Once that phase of our work seems to be completed, we can go off in a number of possible directions, and which we take is decided by our continuing inter-subjective dialogue. We may go off into the telling of a personal life story, or we may go into dreams and free associations – or both. I want, now, to say a word about each of these two directions.

First, personal story. Some patients are like Coleridge's ancient mariner. They have had some terrible experiences and they need to tell you about some or all of them and they need you to believe them and treat their revelations with all the seriousness they deserve.

Emerging themes

A major theme that emerges in some stories is occasional, or in a few cases, sustained bullying at school and/or in the home or local neighbourhood. For some girls this has been sustained through primary and secondary school and even – in one case – into adult life in a psychiatric hospital. I will never forget her story of being raped by two other patients in a hospital while the staff's attention was elsewhere, and then having something that looked like a letter pushed under her door by her tormentors: it contained a fragment of broken glass with a sharp edge, and she explained to me that they and she both knew that this was an invitation to cut herself, which she did.

Another theme is estrangement or persecutory relations between a female patient and one parent, often a father, with the mother turning a blind eye to abusive or violent behaviour.

Another is the torment of experiencing ongoing conflict between one's parents, often lasting for years, sometimes throughout one's childhood. This kind of experience is often more disturbing than actual separation or divorce.

71

Another is a whole range of variations on sibling rivalry, leading to bullying, violence or extreme competitiveness between the patient and another sibling, usually with the patient as victim.

Another is the kind of thing that often seems to go on among girls at school: intense rivalry around good looks, physical attractiveness, intelligence, high or low achievement in studies, or sports, or friendship, or all three, leading to ostracism, mockery or, again, to bullying.

Another area is specifically sexual abuse, and in my experience this is the one area about which girls will not speak to a male psychotherapist. Indeed, in most cases they will not speak to anyone at first, even to the most empathetic and kind female staff. But gradually, often very reluctantly, they choose a woman they feel they can confide in and it does emerge, and that can be most difficult to deal with when it involves sexual abuse by a father, a brother, or an uncle who is still in the family. The problem here often is that the girl will first disclose the abuse and then withdraw from the discourse, leaving the girl herself, her family, the team, the social worker, and the police in an uneasy, unresolved, tormenting, debatable land where progress can be very difficult.

Yet another area is that of non-sexual traumatic events, such as the sudden unexpected death of a sibling. These can mark a child and scar a family, sometimes for life. The initial impact – the emotional shock – of the trauma becomes frozen in time, ever present, a state of affairs which may continue for years. The task of the patient and their psychotherapist is to work together through telling and re-telling, sometimes dreaming and re-dreaming, aiming gradually to detoxify the initial impact by exploring and then re-evaluating its outworkings in terms of stuck feelings, attitudes, relational patterns and cognitions. This working through needs to be undertaken patiently, collaboratively, slowly, because there is a real danger of re-traumatisation. The best outcome (not always achieved) is that through the gradual processing-in-awareness discussed in chapter 5, the grip of the trauma in the present is loosened. As the emotional investment diminishes, the events themselves can recede into the past like the traces of other occasionally remembered occurrences, allowing the person to move forward in their development again.

Two or three deeper themes can be said to emerge from all of this. One is sibling rivalry, obviously. Another is quite astonishing levels of perfectionism. 99% is not enough because it is not 100%. 100% is not enough because the moment you have achieved it you feel you will never manage to do it again. The third is intense negative self-esteem. One writer whose work I admire, Peggy Claude-Pierre, mother of two anorexic girls and author of *The Secret Language of Eating Disorders* (Random House, Canada, 1997), conceptualises this as 'confirmed negativity condition'. Whatever you call it, and however you explain it, it is deeply embedded in just about all girls and women with anorexia and bulimia. Is it turning aggression against the self? Is it getting your self-rejection in first, before you are rejected by a significant other or others? Or what exactly?

Relationship to aggression

This theme can be linked to a wider theme: the girl or woman's relationship to her own aggression. When I was first asked to take a co-facilitating role in the anger management group, I was most reluctant to do so. The group was really organised around the problems and themes of one patient who was intensely angry both with herself and anyone who tried to get close to her. She was committed to remaining ill, and has succeeded in defeating every hospital to which she has been sent.

In my view, the deeper problem was not anger management, but a much broader question of women's and girls' relationship to aggression. The person whose writing I have found helpful in this connection is Karen Armstrong, author of *A History of God,* and *The Great Transformation.* She is a brilliant historian of the emergence of the great religions, and her case is that these emerged over a 1,500 year period, about two and a half to four thousand years ago, in response to recognitions in China, India, the Middle East and Greece of the need to do something about rampant aggression of all kinds in all the major societies of the day.[1] The problem is not so much management of anger as what to do with one's natural aggression. I have found myself using the term 'good aggression', and frequently challenging both young and older women in the renamed exploring anger group: what do you do with your aggression? What happens to it? Where does it go?

On one occasion, during just such an exploration, I told the group that I was remembering what I had read about people who had little dolls into which they stick pins to bring about harm to people who have harmed them. One of the group members, a young woman in her early 20s who wore her resentment like a lapel badge, said: oh, I've got one of those, I do that, and proceeded to tell us who it was directed against.

Some psychoanalytic psychotherapists lay a great deal of stress on the Oedipus conflict, claiming that it is universal, and sometimes – or so it seems to me – arguing that deep down every case is Oedipal. I believe that is an example of massive over-generalisation. Many of the girls and women I have worked with in the area of eating disorders have never got anywhere near the Oedipal phase of relating. In psychoanalytic language, I would conceptualise some of their difficulties in terms of what Margaret Mahler called the separation-individuation process, or putting the matter in terms of positions (here I'm thinking of Melanie Klein's paranoid schizoid and depressive positions) I would argue that many of them are in the position recently identified by Thomas Ogden as the autistic contiguous position.

Dreams and free associations

Before offering you some illustrations from the dialogue between myself and a young female patient, let me now say a word about the importance of dreams and free associations. Here you will be perhaps surprised to learn that to a very considerable extent I am a convinced Freudian. Freud used to write down the dreams of his patients and ask them for their free associations. That is exactly what I do, and I do it in the session when the patient announces that she has had a dream. On the first occasion they bring a dream, I explain the idea of free associations and non-censorship, giving down to earth examples. Then I invite her to tell me her dream and I write down every single word she uses. I read it over again aloud to her, and as I do, I divide it into sections. I then read section one over slowly and ask her to note her associations and tell me what they are. I emphasise that anything that comes to mind however tangential or apparently irrelevant, including clarifications, jokes, memories, feelings, thoughts and so on, counts as a free association. I write these down. Then we go on to the next section, and again I write down her associations. And so on. Then, once she has shared hers, I give her my associations. Then I invite her to say what she now makes of the dream as a whole, in terms of its meaning for her. I join in with her in that process, so that by then, we are involved in a dialogue about all the feelings and meanings involved in the dream.

Many patients have found this process helpful. I also sometimes use simple relaxation processes, and quite often, we go out for a walk, particularly when the patient seems to be stuck or unable to work.

I call my way of working dialogical relational psychotherapy, and I regard it as a personalist adaptation of psychoanalytic psychotherapy.

ANNA'S STORY

Now I'm going to present some material from my reflective notes of sessions with one particular patient, a young woman who came to the hospital about seven years ago, then aged 14. We will call her Anna. Information which might identify this patient has been disguised. Anna has given her permission for this material (hers and mine) to be used. She had a six month in-patient admission, leaving at the age of 15. The other key dramatis personae are her father, then aged 58, her mother, then 47, and her brother, then 19. I saw Anna twice a week for one to one psychotherapy for nearly six months.

I will then present, with minimum comment or interpretation, Anna's subsequent letters to me, and a third letter she wrote to Anorexia with a capital 'A'.

You need to know that she had been a very good football player and had had a trial for her national team. Her brother was also very good at football, but whereas Anna was ultra competitive, Jim was very laid back. Her father took a very informed and enthusiastic interest in football, discussing the team's and Anna's performance with the team manager after each game.

Much of the time, during the psychotherapy sessions, Anna stands up. I accept this, even though I know that the nursing staff disapprove.

The referral letter from Anna's consultant psychiatrist gave her weight as 40.9 kg, in her clothes, and her height as 5 feet 4 and a half inches. On first being weighed at Huntercombe Hospital, wearing t-shirt and pants, she was 36.1 kg. Immediately before her departure, she weighed 40 kg, again in t-shirt and pants, and measured 5 feet 4 inches. She had succeeded in her consistently stated objective of putting on no weight. She was discharged at the request of her referring health board where her treatment was continued in another institution.

One aim of this presentation is to show something of how I work in practice. It is not a model of easy success, but captures aspects of our relationship and work together as it moves along, in and out of attunement, in and out of understanding. It's a slow process in which you sometimes feel you're getting nowhere: you're never entirely sure if you've cottoned on to a significant theme or not. You hang on in there, sometimes with a sense of two steps forward, three steps back.

As time goes on, nevertheless, you begin to have a sense of having identified, together, a bunch of emerging, developing, interweaving themes. These are the themes of her self, her self-system, what I now prefer to call her self-other-culture-world system as it flows along: her core relational thematics.

One strand of that process is the emerging sense of her-and-me in dialogue, learning to communicate, learning to put her themes into words, learning to mentalise as Bateson and Fonagy call it, tolerating feelings and reflecting on experiences, trying out tentative thoughts and sharing them. Thirty years ago, Marie Cardinal called this process finding 'the words to say it' (Cardinal, Picador, 1984).

EXTRACTS FROM CK'S REFLECTIVE PROCESS NOTES

8 December
At our second meeting there was a more frenetic atmosphere. Anna explained to me that she'd just returned from the group walk, during which she'd had a terrible conflict inside her head. Part of her wanted to go very fast, to get her cardiovascular rate up, which she ought to do to keep her fitness, another part felt she should walk with the group at the group's pace. But when she did walk at the group's pace, she felt very guilty that she hadn't gone for it, meaning walked very fast. I had a strong sense of her being driven by internal forces that were on the verge of being out of her control.

Then she returned to her life story, to the point where she thinks 'it' began, at the age of 11. At school from age 8 onwards there was one girl in particular with whom she and others didn't get on, who bullied everyone including Anna's friends. Anna, who was already very competitive, stood up to her. The story became a familiar one of girls being highly competitive with each other, having best friends, being dropped and replaced from time to time. Jean was her best tennis friend when Anna was 8. Later Anna's mum asked for Anna to be separated from Jean.

Anna didn't want to be podgy and horrible like another girlfriend: she wanted to be thin. She didn't want to be laughed at like her friend.

The girls kept making a best five list, a list of girls who were all liked the best. Sometimes they asked the boys to make the list. Anna was on this list and she wanted to stay on it.

Above all, Anna wanted to be liked.

She feels very embarrassed about all this, doesn't want it to be known or joked about.

In the summer when she was 11, there was a summer sports camp. Here she felt tremendous pressure on her to lose weight. The day before the sports day, Anna was running manically (her word) and exhausted herself. That summer she lost a lot of weight. Likewise she exhausted herself with her male friend Sean with whom she played football at home.

I have no hunches or insights to offer yet! (CK)

14 December

A lot about training and fitness. How short a time it is between age 11, when it really took off, and age 14 (now).

The trials seem to have been particularly stressful: often she didn't want to go. Slow running, followed by sprints, followed by build-ups. Her preparation for them seems to have sometimes been enjoyable, but more often it sounds like something she felt she had to do, had to really drive herself to achieve higher and higher. Now she's very worried about having lost her fitness. I've noticed she's pacing the corridor upstairs, but my sense is that her more ferocious attempts to up her cardiovascular rate have lessened.

She uses the name of her country in a strange way, as if it's half a training institution, half a personification. It has special power. The way she says it seems odd to me. Very striking. As if it has a life of its own. She paints a picture of selectors in blazers. I have an image of her, already too thin, going to have a trial.

What I notice I haven't done yet is ask her to dwell on her relationships with Dad, Mum, and brother Jim. She always harks back to the trials. I said to her you know I've got a memory of a story about lapwings in a field: they flutter and swoop and dive over here, but what they're really trying to do is distract us from their nest which is over there. I said to her: I find myself wondering if that's what you're doing in your sessions here with me.

18 January

Dad sounds like a serious, hard-working and committed man, and – so I imagine – a very able one. He watches all Anna's games. He analyses and discusses the whole of each game afterwards with her coaches. He doesn't like players to be prima donnas. I introduced this term into our discussion, and Anna was astonished, because it's the word Dad uses. He thinks the teamwork and the build-up are important, the midfield play. It doesn't matter who scores the goals. So Anna tries to play well in this cooperative midfield build-up, but she wants to be seen to have made the moves, for example the long difficult pass. She wants to be noticed herself for having made these moves.

Once a fellow team member said to her as they trooped off the pitch, and Anna was crying: but Anna, you've scored four goals! Why are you unhappy? Anna didn't feel she'd had enough recognition (from her Dad, I suspect) for what she had done.

I told her a version of the Narcissus story, and talked about what it might mean if we thought about it interpersonally: that Narcissus felt he'd not had enough recognition for his own self, his own contribution, his beauty, his very existence, and he was straining to get the extra recognition he needed by looking at the reflection of himself in the water. She said that that was exactly how she felt herself, that was why she still felt unrecognised in the relationship with her father.

I'm beginning to see Anna in terms of Kohut's idea of narcissistic deficit. The person who may seem to some like a spoiled brat in fact may not have had enough attuned/accurate recognition of what she is and what she has achieved.

Later that day I added the following to my notes: I remembered that I had talked to Anna about the distinction and relationship between being valued for what you do, and being valued for what you are, and I gave her the quotation, from Yeats's poem For Anne Gregory, which had been coming into my mind:

That only God, my dear,
Could love you for yourself alone,
And not your yellow hair.

I feel that Anna has internalised, or been colonised by, all the values and practices of exercise/keep fit/healthy eating which she refers to as 'the nation' for short. The nation expects, nay demands, training to the highest level. In this sense the nation is a powerful introject, a superego telling her what to value and what to do. If she doesn't do it, she feels guilty, because she hasn't done what she ought to have done. But there's more to it than that. It also gives her the satisfaction, which she needs, of feeling superior, superior to everyone else, because she's fitter and better. And I think that links directly to what she describes as her father's sense of superiority to what is common, what swears, what is vulgar.

1 February

Anna returned from the group walk crying hysterically. I managed to calm her down with fatherly cooing, and went along with her to the room we use for psychotherapy. Difficult to remember what actually happened in this session. Much to do with a process of attunement between her and me, which calmed her down. I have this sense of her as a little baby, a little girl who isn't held in a way which enables her to feel calm inside. I asked her about Mum. She said Mum spent time studying at the university and doing part-time and (if I was understanding her right) not high-status work. I found myself wondering where Anna 'is' between her high status father and low status mother. She looked really tired as if she needed to sleep. I encouraged her to sit down and basically talked and soothed her into a calmer state. No scope for insight here, just holding.

2 February

Next day. Major session. Anna, moody child, tantrums, I'd kick and scream, I was attention-seeking, I'd get upset and scream and scream and scream, so my mum would come, age 5 or 6. I knew if I did it long enough she'd come. But then, when she came, and try and hug me, and I would want to, but I just remember pushing her away. I wanted her to come, and then I got embarrassed when she tried to hug me. I thought it was cool to not be hugged – that was probably when I was a bit older. When I was at school aged 7 I was friends with boys aged 10, and I cared what they thought, they thought it wasn't cool to be hugged. On hols with my family, when I saw a group of boys and girls, I felt embarrassed to be with my parents at all. When I was about 10 or 11, same year as I got anorexia, I went into town with boys and girls, I tried to make other people who were with their parents, random people in the street, feel as I felt, embarrassed that they were with their parents. We were having such a good time. I always wanted to be a tomboy. I was always hanging around with boys, and they were streetwise.

Mum doesn't really do anything. She goes to work and does the cleaning. She doesn't really have an interest as such, that's why I can't really describe her. Me and my Dad and my brother, every weekend we would go somewhere, we took turns at choosing where we would go. We used to play football, all three of us, and then we watch football. Age 6, 7. And we used to go swimming together. And I don't know, my Mum never came. I don't know what she was doing. We used to go go-karting – that used to be my decision, cos I loved it. And I used to brag to my brother that I could go faster than him.

I said: Mum seems to be out of it for some reason. Anna replied: yes, cos it was always me and my brother and my Dad going for walks, going to the woods with the dog. I (CK) asked: did you ever cuddle the dog? She replied: no, I didn't like the dog. I used to make myself sit there and stroke it sometimes, as if I loved it, but I didn't. Now when I feel really guilty about eating, I wish I could be cuddled – but not by my parents, by friends. I really like Dana (the hospital's social work assistant), I really like her, she looks out for me, we were going on a walk, I felt really upset, and I wanted to be hugged by Dana. But I don't want to be seen as a lesbian.

Anna remembers crying when her mother had to leave her at nursery. She didn't want to be left. Mum says she couldn't leave me anywhere.

I used to go to swimming lessons. I waited to the end and I asked the coach person: was my dive the best dive? At parties, I didn't like it, cos I didn't speak to the girls, cos I wasn't friends with them, and the boys didn't want to speak to me cos I was a girl. I was always on my own – felt I shouldn't be there – felt the same at my cousins' house.

At this point in Anna's treatment, in consultation with her consultant psychiatrist and the nurse manager, and Anna herself, we decided to invite her parents to visit the hospital for a joint meeting. My letter of invitation said: '... a meeting between yourselves, Anna and myself would I feel be very helpful, the aims being to support the one-to-one psychotherapy work and yourselves as parents, to make cooperative links between us and create a sense of a shared project. I would see this not as family therapy, but as joint family-and-hospital work.'

1 March
Anna is very stuck, and I'm stuck with her. Anna still stands up throughout the session. She feels guilty about eating. I said to her that I would never order her to sit down, because then it would be me who is in charge. Her only initiative at one point two thirds of the way through the session was to ask: do you think it's my competitiveness that causes my anorexia? I said: what do you think yourself?

I think she doesn't know how to be a girl or become a woman. She has identified to a great extent with boys and men.

8 March
Today I attempted to confront Anna with my view of the nature of her and our stuck-ness. I am crapping it in relation to her Mum and Dad's imminent visit, and seeming to have nothing to show for all our work. I decided it might be a good idea to invite Anna to summarise our work together and say to her Mum and Dad what she has learned from psychotherapy.

On the one hand, she says she wants to become a feminine woman: breasts, bottom, fullness, etc. And I believe her. On the other hand, she doesn't want to put on any weight, because (she says) if she does it will gradually take her to a place where she will become fat. I said to her that that was anorexic thinking, which works to prevent her putting on any weight at all, so she'll continue to be thin, continue to damage her body. I said I would give her a written guarantee, signed by me, that she wouldn't get fat, ever. I realised that was way over the top, and possibly untrue as a prediction, but I think she heard it and partly believed me.

15 March
Anna's own notes on what she has learned from psychotherapy:
− Crave attention from parents
− Always analyse from others' perspective and how they perceive me
− I fear being normal
− I fear being disliked if I put on weight
− Hugely competitive
− Focus too much on food rather than the underlying problems
− Don't want to get to a 'normal' weight because then it might be possible to get fat
− All the time I stand up so that's saying Anorexia is winning
− Colin makes me see that I am very underweight – dangerously
− I want to be accepted as and by boys (I think this means 'as a boy and by boys' – CK)
− I fear growing up
− I'm scared to let go of my anorexia because I feel comfortable.
Anna wrote these notes at my suggestion, but I was not involved in drafting them. They are verbatim.

30 March
[I was on holiday. The following extract is taken from a female colleague's notes after a session Anna had with her in my absence.] She is in a real quandary between hating how she looks (thin, anorexic) and fearing to get fat. I found I wanted to support her to be in the quandary rather than lurch from one side to another, and she did seem to understand this idea. PS: She made particular reference to her mother, not her father. I thought this was interesting as I have had the picture that it is her father who has been more dominant.

12 April
[CK has returned.] Last week and this week we have been focusing on her relationship with her mother, with whom she has a powerfully ambivalent relationship. On the one hand she feels very embarrassed by her mother, for example when she wore pink corduroys and chanted 'Toys are us! Toys are us!' in the car park. On such occasions she wants to have a young, slim, elegantly/ fashionably dressed mother. And on the other she likes her 'cushioned' mother, the mother who is motherly with breasts, tummy, softness. I am reminded of the fact that that sort of motherhood is attacked and denigrated in our culture, and in its place is the fashionable, young, slim, model figure.

13 April
Today Anna brought a dream. I asked, and she gave me permission, to write it down. We divided it into two sections, and I read these back to her, one at a time. After each, I invited her to tell me her free associations and the emotional impact on her of that part of the dream. After she had finished, I gave her my own associations and comments, and I invited her to tell me her thoughts and reactions in response to mine. Before we started, I took her through a simple relaxation procedure: talking slowly about being aware of her feet, ankles, calves, thighs, tummy, chest, neck, breathing, head and shoulders. I invited her to sit down, and she did so. After 25 minutes she asked permission to stand up and I agreed. She remained standing, as usual, for the rest of the session.

Here is the text of her dream, and our dialogue, as far as I was able to record and recall it later.

I went to the Astroturf. I went with my brother and my Dad, and I was trying to practice against my brother and I was really good and I was getting round him and things. And then the dream kind of changed. And I was in a car with my cousins and my Mum, and at school, but we weren't at school. People were walking by, and we were going up a hill that was really, really steep, and there were loads of cars behind us and in front of us, and coming down the hill you know that big ENVIROCLEAN van, more like a lorry really, and it was coming down towards us down the hill and I was really scared, so my Mum had to keep hill-starting cos she kept stalling, and I kept thinking we're going to fall down the hill backwards and eventually we got round the big ENVIROCLEAN van. And then the dream kind of ended.

(Note: the ENVIROCLEAN van is an example of what Freud would have called a 'day's residue'. According to Anna, it came up the drive regularly to the hospital to clean out the sewers. CK)

I said to Anna that I wanted her to relax and pay attention to whatever came up for her as I read through the first section of the dream. Here is what she said: Just thought that Colin will think: my Mum's not there. I just see a picture of the Astroturf. I like it. About the football, I have butterflies in my stomach just now. I just remember the feeling of when I used to play football and get really nervous before the game. Then when I played for the country during the game I was nervous. I don't think I was good enough to play for the country really. It was an anxious kind of nervousness. But I'm not anxious about it now, but I was then. I asked her: how did you feel in the dream about being with your brother and Dad? She replied: that's just how it was, that's just normal. In real life, I always tried to get round my brother, playing football, but I never did. It feels good to have got round him in the dream.

I then offered Anna my own thoughts about the first part of the dream and invited her to say what she thought of them. I said I thought that it was about her being very rivalrous with her brother, desperately needing and trying to get past him, to surpass him. It showed how important competitive football had been to her, and still was, as a way of surpassing her brother and maybe even becoming a boy like him. And taken together with her comments on the dream, it seemed to show how her driven approach to playing football somehow made her anxious, and it made me wonder if this symbolised her approach to her whole life. I said that I wondered if she had been trying too hard all her life, trying to do more than she could actually manage, be something more, or something different, from what she was.

I then read part two of the dream to her, for some reason leaving out the passing reference to school, which we returned to later. And again I asked her for what came to mind and what it felt like.

She said that at first it felt fine, okay being in the car. Then I was scared in the car. I thought we were going to die, going to roll down the hill backwards. It was very frightening. Then she reported that three days ago in real life the big ENVIROCLEAN van was coming towards her and Jean in the Huntercombe minibus, and Jean kept having to go backwards and we kept wiggling across the drive. Wiggling? I asked. Wiggling, she repeated. The van eventually got past. It felt quite funny when Jean was trying to reverse cos she couldn't reverse in a straight line. I asked if she had any thoughts or feelings about the van in the dream. She said she didn't, she just kept seeing it, visualising the dream. She said she was really scared when her Mum had to hill-start after repeatedly stalling. She also felt very sorry for her. Then she said: when we got round the van, we were safe.

I then read her the short school section of the dream and asked what came to mind. She said she was thinking of the end of the day, when people from school used to walk down the street, and she was in the car. For some reason she was just driving past the school. She added: we weren't really at school, it was just people in school uniforms. She reported a memory of her brother learning to drive the car, when she was in the back seat. He couldn't get started on the hill, and kept stalling. (At this point I found myself thinking of blocks to learning.)

Anna had nothing further to add about this part of the dream, or the dream as a whole. I said I was wondering, first, if the dream was about trying very hard and finding life very difficult and at times frightening. The steepness of the hill might symbolize life as involving a steep learning curve, and how hard it was to live in a high-achievement, perfectionist sort of way, with such high aims. She said she agreed with that. I said that I wondered if stalling, slipping backwards and reversing in an out-of-control sort of way might represent her really feeling stuck just now, not wanting to put on weight. And I added that both her mother and her brother were in the dream or associated memories, both learning to drive and stalling or in danger of slipping back, and that was reminding me of her mixed feelings about her mother and her rivalry and identification with her brother, who is so laid back. Then I asked her what the van might mean to her, adding that I wondered if it might have something to do with her feelings about sexual relationships. I asked if she knew anything about sex, and she replied that she didn't. She thought the van represented her anorexia.

19 April
She reported another dream, as follows: I can't remember a lot. I was playing football and I was against this girl from the national team, and then the game finished and I went over to say 'well played!' and she just ignored me and pretended she didn't know me and that I wasn't even speaking to her. And so I said to her: why are you ignoring me? And really stood up to her, which I didn't in real life, and so we started shouting at each other, and that's it really.

In response to my invitation to say what was coming to mind, she said: I wish I'd stuck up for myself when I was playing for my country, but I didn't think I was good enough to be there. I felt inferior to everybody else socially and in every other way, and this girl had been there, and I had spoken to her before, but when she got into the clique, she didn't speak to me. I just kept remembering my first trial for my country, and all these horrible people there, who made me feel really bad and not good enough.

Before our session today I had heard from one of the nurses that Anna had had several tantrums over the weekend when she had not got her own way. 'She threw a knife in the dining room and was lucky not to hit someone.' I had been aware of Anna's tantrums, some of which occurred when she was refused permission to go home for the weekend. I had an uneasy feeling that we were not addressing these tantrums, and still not making any impact on her steadfast refusal to eat more than would keep her at her current weight. I bumped into the head teacher of the school in the corridor, a kind, experienced and empathic man who got on well with Anna, and asked him if he thought her tantrums were spoilt self-indulgence, or coming from somewhere deep beneath the surface. He said he thought it was the latter.

During the later part of our session I told Anna I'd heard about her angry behaviour, and asked if she would like to talk to me about it. She said a new temporary chef had been on and had produced a meal of sausage and gravy which was pretty horrible. I had already heard, from another patient, about this meal and the chef's behaviour. I said to Anna that I was wondering if her angry feelings about the food and the chef might also be coming from somewhere deeper down. I asked if anything we had talked about in our recent sessions had stayed with her. She said she had been specially struck by my comments about her mixed feelings, especially hostile feelings towards her mum, and she had had that idea in her mind when she was with Mum and Dad at the weekend. Several times she had felt irritated and annoyed with Mum, but had managed not to spoil the day with them.

I commented that her angry actions might be related to the underdevelopment of her capacity for tolerating mixed feelings. I hoped she would gradually get more used to experiencing her angry, hostile feelings without actually hitting out. She said she felt she had managed to do that at the weekend, when they were out horse-riding and Mum had refused her request for a drink.

26 April

Another dream! There was a flood. Joan (another patient) and I were in the shops looking for clothes, and then I was Kate Moss and I bought £150 worth of clothes but had to do it before the tide came in. And then I was a shoe, and I was spying on people. And then I got washed away (while still a shoe). And suddenly I was me, and there was my mum, my aunt, my gran and my cousin Jim and we were walking on the beach because my gran wanted to show my mum where the rugby pitch used to be on the beach, and I had turned back because I had lots of bags with me, and my mum was really angry that I had turned back, but then my mum caught us up because I had lots of bags with me and I was slow. And then the tide came in and it went through the alphabet and if your name started with say the letter 'a' (which of course Anna's did), and you were nearest to the water, it would get you, but we finally got safe inside the pub. Then we were at the Pleasure Beach and I had said I would go on the Pepsi Max ride but when I got there I didn't want to because I was scared the bar that kept you in would open when I was on it. And I would fall out. And then my mum got really angry with me because she said it wasn't fair on my cousin Jim, because I had originally said I would go on it. And I didn't and we were both given £1 each. And I spent 15p on the game, that big hand thing that grabs sweets or teddy bears – and I put 5p into it and you're guaranteed a prize and I got 3 three packs of wine gums, a lolly and a gobstopper! And that's it.

Anna's free associations to elements of the dream:
- Kate Moss: just that Kate Moss is really pretty and I would like to look like her.
- Shoe: (Anna smiles.) I can just picture the shoe. I can picture the dream. Quite nervous cos I'm trying to hide from these people I'm spying on. Being the shoe is a disguise.
- Washed away: really worried cos I thought we were going to get swept away by the tide.
- Rugby pitch: The beach had eroded so the rugby pitch wasn't there anymore. Just the green grass and the posts. Our school's quite big on rugby. I've always been into football rather than rugby.

- Mum/tide: just think of the clothes bags. I love shopping. I'd love to fit into the clothes that I like. Feel I don't cos I'm too thin. Longing to be a bit fuller so I fit. But part of me likes being this weight … Mum carried on to look at the rugby pitch but cos she was much quicker – she had bags too – she didn't think I should've turned back, and she said that I should believe what she was saying … It came into my mind that I should eat everything I'm given. Cos I've just had an argument with her this morning. Cos I wanted to ask Jane the dietician could I get something off my meal plan, and Mum said I should eat everything, and ask for more, and that I should believe her that I wouldn't get fat.
- The tide: I'm really scared of it. Wasn't just the tide, it's the massive floods … don't know, just scared I'm gonna get washed away. I don't really think about it. When there are floods in the world, like the tsunami, I get scared.
- Alphabet: you could see the letters of the alphabet. If you were nearest the tide, with your name beginning with the letter the tide stopped on, then you'd get dragged in, and you'd die. Just remembered a bit of another dream I had, there was snow in it. Can vaguely remember it but can't explain it. Snow – in real life I don't like snow.
- The ride: we were going to go with my cousin at Easter but didn't end up going. I was talking about roller coasters with Dana and I'm more scared of falling out than the actual ride. If I fell out I'd die or really hurt myself.
- £1: got £1 yesterday and swapped it for 10ps, that's what I did in the dream.
- Mum/cousin Jim: I felt bad – I'd let him down, but I was too scared.
- Rugby: talking about rugby yesterday, me, Jeannie, and Rhona. Rhona loved to play rugby. I said touch rugby would be OK, not full rugby.

26 April

Another session later the same day. I wanted to give her some of my own comments about themes and possible meanings embedded in the dream, and hear what she thought. I regarded it as a really resonant dream. The themes I identified are as follows: the theme of control, and fear of loss of control leading to death, or to growing up; the theme of choosing a celebrity model to imitate, to model yourself on; the excitement of buying clothes which would fit her and look good on her if she put on weight; the theme of rugby not football in the dream because, I suggested, rugby involves tackling and getting close to boys, which she both wants and doesn't want; her compromise solution of touch rugby minimizes the physical contact; the theme of her ambivalent relationship with Mum. On the one hand Anna wants to become independent of Mum, on the other she wants to learn from her and accept her good advice. She is being followed by Mum, challenged by her, and running away from her. The core of her argument with Mum is about control, control over the intake of food. Anna wants to be in control, but to her control means eating less, eating only what she chooses. The solution I said was for Anna to develop a more sophisticated and flexible form of control, which would include her becoming able to accept some feedback from Mum and others without feeling she'd lost her self.

The theme of fear of loss of control leading to catastrophe is critical, expressed again in the important alphabet section of the dream. 'A' is for Anna, first letter, first person, numero uno, most important person. If she loses control she feels she'll be swept to her death.

The next bit of the dream is an attempt to wrestle with and modify this self-centred, control-centred narcissism. Mum tells her she should be concerned with what her cousin wants and not be totally self-preoccupied. Anna understands that and feels guilty, but her fear of catastrophe overrides this beginning of concern for the other, in favour of continuing self-preoccupation.

The final theme is a kind of joyful wish to regress, go back to being a little girl, who triumphs over all frustrations and tellings-off by getting wine gums, a lolly and a gobstopper! I said: sometimes, when we're 15, we just want to go back to being a kid again. And sometimes we want to try growing up and eating more and getting to know boys.

3 May

Anna, who looks much brighter and healthier than she did when she first came, but hasn't put on any weight, tells me about her terrible weekend at home with Mum and Dad. She had four whole days which sound like hell. She ate on her own, not waiting for her parents' food to be ready. She ate what she wanted, not what was carefully and thoughtfully prepared. Behaved rigidly. Threw away all the good work of the last few weeks. Oh, hell! I can feel my own frustration. No wonder her mother ended up shouting at her. Shepherd's pie. Lamb roast. Spaghetti marinara. Things she loves. Things lovingly and hopefully prepared. She didn't eat them. It's like she's rejecting their best gifts, and rejecting them. Mum and Anna shouting at each other. Dad shouting at both of them. She informed me that her mother had said that they would look after her till she was 18, and thereafter she was on her own, something like that.

I couldn't help feeling that a certain kind of normal adolescent/parent battle was being fought out, but in an exaggerated, distressing form.

I said to her that I was feeling I and the two of us together had failed her, and that perhaps I needed to learn that the changes had to come in her, from her, and that they would come gradually.

I encouraged her to tell me the story of the weekend again, from three points of view: her mother's, her father's, and finally her own. At the end of the session I invited her over the next few days to pay attention to one or two other people in the hospital and try to get alongside them, attune to them, and try to sense what was going on for them, from their point of view.

4 May

Today I checked with Anna to find out whether she knew that her remaining time in the hospital is limited. She does know. I said I thought it might be helpful if we focussed on her feelings and thoughts around eating in the hospital. I reminded her that the felt need for control seemed to be one of her key themes.

She launched straight in with great self-awareness. When she feels hungry, she deliberately controls her eating behaviour, because otherwise she is afraid she will eat uncontrollably. When she doesn't feel hungry, for example at snack time in mid-morning, but she has to eat (that is, when control is taken out of her hands) she feels angry. The anger starts in her vagina, and then goes upwards through her body, making her feel an urge to hit the food, or throw it, or yell. She also wants to leave out, not eat, defined bits of her meals, for example, there is a snack bar which was 114 calories and is now 118, so she cuts off a four calorie bit and won't eat that.

10 May

The feeling in my vagina is coming back more and more frequently. CK asked: what's it like? It's like a tingling, but then a big rush of anger just runs through me and I feel like screaming or shouting. I just want to hit something when it comes, throw my plate across the room, or squeeze the food. It happened at the weekend and I squeezed a milky way and threw it on the floor. It was during the meal. I was meant to get half a yoghurt, and it looked to me closer to a full yoghurt. They said it was half a yoghurt and you've got to trust Mary (the weekend cook). I don't trust her at all, cos she always gets it wrong. Other people complain about her too. So I ran out and took my milky way with me and just wanted to sit and eat it on my own and get the anger out of my body. The tingling came when I initially tried to eat my yoghurt. It's like I'm either going to cry or get angry, and I can't cry, so I get angry instead. They followed me, and I squeezed the milky way onto the floor. I used to get this feeling in my vagina when it was (that is, when we had to eat – CK) something runny like beans, or when cereal had got all soggy with milk.

I asked her what she felt about leaving the hospital in two weeks' time. She replied: I'm quite looking forward to leaving. I'll eat properly. Everything will be all right. I want to go on holiday, go back to school, start playing football for fun again. Her parents have said that she will go on holiday only if she puts on weight.

Here is Anna's summary, written by her, for her patient progress review:
– Drive to get better has stopped
– Drive to stay at this weight has increased
– Feel I've matured a bit in here
– Feel more confident talking to adults
– Feel more embarrassed now about the way I look – feel self-conscious about looking so thin
– I can eat some things I've never eaten before without feeling as guilty
– Eating more than I ever was before without feeling guilty
– I eat it and struggle with guilt afterwards.

I asked Anna again about sexual feelings and sexual relations: was she interested in such things? Not specifically. Curious? Not really. How do you feel about me asking? Slightly embarrassed. She wanted to know if you can have sex without having periods. She's curious but in no hurry. Other girls have done some things with each other, but she hasn't.

Anna has never had periods and has no development of breasts, buttocks, curves. She says she has little or no curiosity about sexual matters, but I cannot help feeling that these bodily sensations she is experiencing point in the direction of growing up: it is almost as if she is experiencing aggression and libido intertwined.

The other thing that struck me, as we came to the end of our face-to-face meetings, was the power of anorexia within her, anorexia as an autonomous agency, almost as a part-personality in its own right, a kind of control freak with which her self was sometimes identified. And yet her intelligence was obvious, as was her growing capacity for mentalising, reasoning and dialogue with another person (me) who was not herself. Feeling that our collaboration was perhaps not totally unproductive, although we had failed to dent her refusal to put on any weight, I invited her to write to me at the hospital if she would like to do so. I was sad to see her go.

ANNA'S LETTERS

About four months later, I was surprised and delighted to receive the following letter from her, which is so evidently a continuation, by her, of our dialogue:

Anna's first letter

Hi Colin – it's Anna,

I wrote to Dana about three or four weeks ago and have meant to reply to her following letter but I've been quite busy.

She mentioned that you asked after me, which is very thoughtful and very kind of you.

How are you? Hope you are well! Can't believe it's a year ago since I first came to Huntercombe!

I'm currently at XYZ, an adolescent unit which helps people with a wide range of mental illness. I was an outpatient and attended weekly counselling on a Friday before I came to Huntercombe, but having had four years, initially progressing and then three or so years on, regressing, my parents decided to try elsewhere to see if I could find someone I could connect with. That's when Dr M referred me to Huntercombe. When I left Huntercombe admittedly I was in no position to stay at home, but I tried my hardest to avoid XYZ. Eventually, however, after things had got progressively worse, I was sectioned in July (I think – so long ago I can't remember!).

The first few months were particularly hard and emotional. The diet initially is small (well to me it was hardly small) and then you move onto large portions. OH MY GOSH! I've never seen this amount of food, let alone have to eat it!! When I was shown the diet sheet I was adamant I was not going to eat it. However if you didn't eat something you would sit there for a half hour, then another half hour 'rest', then another half hour in which to be re-presented and then half 'rest' again. To me this was harder than eating the food. So I just ate it within the first half hour period (as quick as I could because I couldn't bear to sit down longer than necessary!) After you'd eaten you then have to have a half hour "rest" period in which you have to sit completely still in order to prevent exercise straight after meals (or for some people stop them being able to be sick).

The rest periods happen after every meal, so that's six times a day. At first I tried to avoid them but soon was forced to endure them. Now I am able to sit for long periods as well as the rest periods.

I'm still on the larger diet which is a set meal plan for each patient, but I'm the only one currently on it. I feel it is much better being with patients with other mental illnesses as it gives you an insight into what other people go through. There are 12 patients in total, four of whom have anorexia. I have put on 12 kg now and am going home Friday to Monday. My section has been lifted and I'm due to go back to school gradually in January. I'm so much happier and never want to return to how I looked before, it is horrible! I've got about 2 kg to go until I'm the minimum weight I should be, but I'm aiming to be 3 or 4 kg more than I am now.

Obviously I'm still having trouble with eating. The volume of food and butter is definitely an issue as well as exercise, but I'm not pacing at all any more and can go two or three days without exercise (although that is anxiety provoking) and I'm not in the best of moods).

I'm hoping things will get better though because I feel things have gone on too long and I hate this place and the people are quite draining.

Sorry to drone on, I just thought I'd tell you how I'm getting on.

I hope you have a great Christmas and I do appreciate all the work you did with me, you are very kind and caring, thank you.

Love Anna X

I was struck by two features of Anna's letter: first, how important it seems to have been for her to have a really tough, personally focussed, tailored regime to help her change her destructive eating and exercise habits. It was as if she was a moon orbiting the planet anorexia, and only such a regime would enable her to escape its powerful gravitational pull. A behavioural approach seemed fully justified. Second, I was struck by her appreciation of our relationship, and her wish to communicate in detail to me what was being done in her new setting to help her to free herself from anorexia, and how that felt to her: a tough behavioural approach on the one hand, and a caring, dialogical/reflective, personal relationship on the other.

I replied to Anna's letter, but did not keep a copy of my reply. Two months later, I received a second letter from her, enclosing also a third letter addressed not to me but to anorexia.

Anna's second letter

Hiya Colin,

Hope you had a lovely Christmas and New Year. It seemed to come and go so quickly. Thank you so much for your letter. It was really quite touching and the quotes will help at times when motivation is hard to find.

I've just been shopping today as I'm going back to school the day after tomorrow. I'm excited but slightly nervous as it has been a long time since I attended, though my friends have been particularly encouraging and have put me more at ease.

I'm also hoping to start football practice again, gradually building towards playing for my club again as I feel my perspective on life and my values have changed during the past year, and being away from football has shown me what else there is to enjoy in life.

Since I last wrote things were beginning to slip back. My section got lifted and I began to get more time at home and out with my friends so I began to get into the mind frame that I've got everything back that I wanted so I felt the reasons for eating had all been achieved so I put less emphasis on it and old habits began to emerge. I began to lose some weight and kept just walking out of XYZ to meet friends until rest periods were over. XYZ were conscious that I was aiming to get back to school and were sick of me absconding from the unit and eventually gave me an ultimatum. I either stay and comply or I leave for good. I knew without them I was going to keep regressing and I was conscious of school not being far away in terms of the start of the new term, so I decided to stay in a desperate attempt not to slip back into old ways. During this time I wrote a letter to anorexia which describes my feelings about the past years. I've given you a copy if you are interested in reading it.

Over the past couple of weeks I have made more progress and complied with everything they have asked of me. I have kept my anger under control and eaten everything which I had begun to refuse. Having to comply has been hard as I've had to cancel many social occasions such as shopping trips with friends, parties and going out with guys. This has made me so determined to move on, not just to put the weight on required to be allowed out again (only to just then maintain an under weight). No, I want to mature physically like a 16-year-old because I feel embarrassed when I go out that I look much younger than I should and I recognise that I do need to put weight on still in some areas. I feel it is more habit that has kept me this way for the past few months, and now I'm only just recognising that if I don't just react on my initial thought, if I sit back and rationalise the situation and remind myself of what I truly want, I can go ahead and eat the food and feel pleased that I am one step closer to achieving the life/ lifestyle I want. Never before have I thought and felt this way. Never before have I actually put the fact that I know I can't get fat into the forefront of my mind. I want my life back so badly and to be able to go out with guys whenever I want, instead of having to put them on hold because I've got to be back to eat. I hope my motivation continues to increase like it is.

You're right it did and still does have a grip of me, but when I look back to when you knew me it makes me embarrassed to have gone around looking that way and to think that's all you remember me as. Now I can identify behaviours which I need to break and to an extent have and can't understand why I ever believed they were right!

It's funny actually I was laughing with one of the nurses at XYZ about all of the bizarre things I did and said when I first came. It makes me cringe and embarrassed to recognise how weird I must have looked and how oblivious to reality I was. I hope I can look back in another four or five months and laugh at the way I still think.

Sorry, I did start this letter two days ago but to be honest have been a bit busy to finish. So it is now Monday night and I've just had my first day back at school. It was so good because since coming home I've re-established all my friendships. My friends were really cool about it and just talked to me normally. I'm so excited about going tomorrow! I wish I'd realised how much fun I could be having with friends sooner!

I don't really mean to sound disrespectful but I don't really think about Huntercombe much at all now because I feel my life and priorities with trying to get my friendships back to where they were are my focus. But (this is weird and embarrassing) occasionally I'll hear a song which was released at the time when I was there and I'll start to remember things and people who I really did, I suppose, idolise at a time when I was not looking or dressing the way I wanted and I feel embarrassed to think that they only know me as that. I can't really explain what I mean but I kind of hate to be thought and remembered as that 'anorexic girl'. I hate being generalized by every other stereotypical 'anorexic' person especially people I really respected and wanted to be liked by.

I don't like to be pitied or thought of as a sad case (that might be my perception of other anorexic people who I resent being 'like'). I don't want to sound horrible and others may not see it as I do, but I just wish I didn't have to be remembered that way when I write to you. Obviously people don't really give a second thought about me because it's ages since I left, but I still can't help feeling embarrassed and wanting to prove I'm no longer like that (visually I mean, obviously I still am mentally).

Sorry about all of the scribbles!

In some ways I wish I could just see you once again just to see how you are! Because this letter seems to be all about me! Hope you're able to continue to help someone in the kind way you helped me.

Anna.

Anna's Letter to Anorexia

Dear that part of me (aka Anorexia),

I know that some people feel you have befriended them. They see you as a friend, a companion, even a soulmate, as if in some fictional world you're a person inside their head. A person who has invested a lot of time in them and someone they can rely upon when they feel upset, anxious or worried.

But to me you are not.

If only it was that simple. If only you were a person maybe then I would be able to differentiate my logical thoughts from your distorted ones to which I succumb in order to cure my own deep-rooted unhappiness and insecurity.

However there is no other person. No you and me. Me and you. It has now become that I am it and it is me. It is me who has invested my time in it. It is me who has placed it at the peak of my priorities and it is me who follows its rigid lifestyle.

Anorexia, you are much more than a person to me. You are a need, a craving, an addiction. You are a way of life. I called for a solution and you came. Now that solution defines me. I don't know who I am or where I'm heading. I'm mixed up in a world of doubt, confusion and fear.

Why do people tell me you are wrong when you feel so right, and why does something which feels so right lead me somewhere that is so wrong?

When I fell into your clutches, Anorexia, it, myself, whatever and whoever you are, I gave up my pride, my dignity, and my soul was frozen. To feel no feelings, to have no shame, to be driven somewhere you fundamentally know is wrong, isn't just frustrating, it destroys you as a person. You no longer feel, look, act or get treated as a person. I had become my illness and my illness had become me.

When I stopped football the realisation of something I had known all along became unavoidable. Anorexia had become me. In my mind there was no divide between me and every stereotypical anorexic. The ones who get recognised and branded in the street, the lonely emaciated waifs who have no interest other than the preoccupation with food nor the ones who pick at their food in order to prevent them getting fat, when in actual fact it's plain to see they're barely alive.

Some of those characteristics no longer exist in me but a lot of what I see in them, I see in myself. It shatters my pride, Anorexia. It makes me angry. I resent being associated with them.

Why have I let you control me so much that I have driven myself to become something I detest?

I want to be free yet I still hold on. So many people have tried to help loosen my grip but I won't surrender. To lose all control is my fear and fear is my hindrance.

There is so much I want to say to you, Anorexia, but can't express. So many emotions I feel towards you.

Life as it is now is not what I want and as you know, it never was.

In hindsight we should have left me to develop naturally, but I know it was not that simple. I know we feared I wouldn't be the best I could be. We wanted to be one better than everyone else. We wanted to look, perform and be the best.

But why haven't we learned after all we've been through that perhaps I will never be that person? Our dream has led me to become the total opposite yet still we persevere.

We want me to look the best I can yet we've destroyed my looks. We made me become thin and gaunt and even now when the gauntness is gone the dream of a curvier figure is yet to be achieved.

We thought we were maintaining and progressing my physical performance. We were striving for excellence yet when I reached as far as anyone could go we still doubted my ability. Instead of believing I had reached that status we pushed further, we took it too far and as a result let it all slip away in a false belief that we were building towards it.

Why don't we ever listen to anyone, Anorexia? Why do we think we're so right when all the evidence suggests and proves we are not?

Look, Anorexia, I know your intentions were and are good and you are trying to help me fulfil my dream, but I think one day we'll have to put the trust we have in each other and our solution into someone else and their solution.

Because the irony is, Anorexia, our fear of failure and rejection and our extreme desire to be perfect, in actual fact is driving us further away from achieving this. It is only when we let go and accept me as I am and believe that that is acceptable we will be nearer to achieving success, success in the form of happiness. We need to realise my self worth should not be dependent on my achievements.

I know that it is not as simple as to part with you, Anorexia, but perhaps one day we could become two. That way we will no longer be in unison, with your thoughts being mine and my thoughts being yours. Then when we've established independence, we might feel more confident with you going your way and me going mine, because I'm not sure there is any place for you in the life I want, and I've been mistaken to think there ever was.

Anna's letter to Anorexia ends here.

CONCLUSION

I have decided to let Anna's letters speak for themselves, rather than add many further reflections. It seems to me that they illustrate David Tait's argument that psychotherapy goes on working long after the actual meetings between therapist and client have ended. They underline the importance of attunement, respect for persons and the building of trust: these are the conditions that enable the client to open herself increasingly to the therapist's contributions, and begin to trust her self again. They also illustrate the notion that psychotherapy really is a dialogue, set in a socially and culturally supportive environment, and that – however much the therapist's comments contribute, and they do contribute a lot - the thinking and meanings that matter most in the end are those of the client. Finally, they illustrate the vital importance of the client's exercise of her own capacity for reflective agency. Anna bravely takes on the battle with anorexia, challenging anorexia's thinking and practices as they have become installed inside her self, struggling to differentiate her self from her adversary and to set her self again on the path of growing up and rejoining the world.

REFLECTIONS

By Dr David Tait

Colin has kindly asked me to reflect upon this narrative. My perspective is that of having been the Medical Director in Huntercombe Hospital when Anna was there. Prior to that I had been a consultant psychiatrist in the NHS. In my own psychotherapy practice my home bases are Winnicott for individual work (if only one name is allowed), and systems theory for family and organisational work.

Colin's paper is fascinating on three counts: the place of psychotherapy in in-patient care, the challenge for the therapist in adapting practice to become a team player in an institutional setting, and how both the patient and the institution evaluate the psychotherapy contribution, particularly when the dividend from that investment may not be realised until later.

For those unfamiliar with NHS psychiatry, psychotherapy is almost unheard of as a component of treatment in adult wards, where patients' difficulties are seen (mistakenly in my opinion) as unlikely to benefit from psychological interventions. At the same time, however, psychotherapists have colluded in this, preferring out-patient work with less disturbed individuals over pushing for a place on the ward. Units for adolescents are perhaps more psychologically orientated, and more likely to have trained therapists on their staff (particularly family therapists).

Treatment for individuals with eating disorders is immensely labour-intensive and requires psychotherapy as part of the approach. Such patients do poorly in general psychiatric wards if indeed they are admitted. This explains why specialist units have been developed, primarily in the independent sector. By contrast adolescents with eating disorders are usually treated in NHS adolescent units, but bed shortages for this age group generate a spill-over into independent units.

One of the difficulties in treating eating disorders is a relative lack of 'scientific' evidence (in the sense it is used in medicine generally) for what works, and this is likely to continue because of low numbers of patients, the complexities of treatment, the frequent co-existence of other psychiatric disorders, and the ethics of clinical trials involving patients with life-threatening illnesses. So we rely on what seems to work in practice, backed up where possible by research.

This leads to a consensus of a mix of psychological treatments addressing putative underlying problems, and a symptomatic approach confronting the emotional, cognitive, and behavioural components of the eating disorder. Freud suggested that if underlying problems are resolved symptoms will simply disappear, but this is by no means always the case. Equally, only addressing symptoms may leave the patient free of her eating disorder, but still disturbed, disabled, and distressed. These extremes are therefore not adopted, but each hospital has to make a choice as to where a balance should lie.

We at Huntercombe decided in favour of psychotherapy having a slightly greater emphasis than symptomatic treatment (the pendulum has since swung in the opposite direction, but still with a robust psychotherapeutic contribution). Within the psychotherapy team further choices had to be made and this was to some extent an act of both personal preference and of faith on my part. My NHS out-patient psychotherapy team comprised psychoanalytic psychotherapists, cognitive-behavioural psychotherapists, and an art therapist, and I imported this model into Huntercombe. I also took the view that experienced therapists without group-analytic or equivalent training could facilitate group work, and that family work, as opposed to routine liaison or more formal therapy, could be provided by experienced therapists without formal family therapy training.

This was the set-up which Colin joined, and I was extremely fortunate to be able to appoint someone of Colin's calibre to the team. A difficulty with individual psychoanalytic psychotherapy in a hospital setting is its inherent privacy. Whilst not understating the complexities of other therapies, it is both relatively easy, and clinically obligatory, to feed in to the ward round family issues which inevitably resonate within the 'family' of a small hospital. At the very least we must avoid re-enacting dysfunctional relationships, and strive to model more appropriate ones. Likewise with CBT interventions, all staff need to know when and how to challenge (and when and why not to!) behaviour in particular, but also the emotions and cognitions surrounding this. Art therapy may reveal what a patient has been unable to put directly into words, but the therapist can translate this into a language which other staff, and the patient, can productively use, whilst the patient can also continue to use the medium of art. And finally groups, as well as their explicit task, are a microcosm of the hospital, so what arises in the group has great importance in identifying whole-system issues, essential if the institution itself is to be therapeutic in the broadest sense.

But the content of individual work, as laid out so clearly in Colin's narrative, does not lend itself to brief feedback, and may not have immediate implications for how the team should approach the patient. Confounding this is the tradition in psychoanalytic psychotherapy that the content of sessions must remain absolutely confidential. Colin's training with the Scottish Institute of Human Relations largely embraced this, and also outlined a model of technique for the therapist to employ. Colin came to Huntercombe already having to reconcile this with his personal Weltanschauung (a systems theory conception akin to world view), which, as the reader will appreciate from the rest of the book, is exceptionally broad. But arriving in Huntercombe put this into even sharper relief.

Colin gives a very open account of how his practice evolved, or perhaps was re-invented, to meet the needs of Anna (and his other patients). I am tempted to suggest that his experience in Huntercombe was an essential piece of the jigsaw that makes him the therapist he is now. Gone are the days when the patient has to fit into the treatment: it is the therapist's job to mould his treatment to fit the patient, keeping true to his theoretical stance in understanding her difficulties, but not letting theory dictate how they embark on their joint therapeutic journey.

In addition, an institutional setting shines a spotlight on the interpersonal, which of course is the intrapersonal made flesh. This also informs the persons-in-community theme of persons-in-relation which Colin describes elsewhere. Colin's part in the dialogical narrative is an object lesson for therapists in how to achieve a unique therapeutic partnership grounded in whatever community the therapist and patient find themselves.

I leave Anna till last because my comments on her part of the narrative are inevitably speculative. In Huntercombe all medical staff have a working knowledge of all patients whether or not they are their designated doctor. This allows for cross-cover at times when an issue arises which cannot wait, and, of course, is crucial for on-call duties when responding to crises. I was therefore fairly well-informed about Anna's treatment and progress: I had no direct role in this but would, on occasion, ask a question or float an idea in the ward round or in staff supervision.

Colin has mentioned my view that the benefit of psychotherapy may not be realised at the time – seeds may be sown, they germinate in therapy, but may not flower until conditions allow. Sometimes the flower does not appear, and a second round of therapy may be a necessary condition for blossom. This takes us on to how things changed for Anna before, during and after a second in-patient stay, on this occasion in the local unit, which accommodates adolescents with a variety of difficulties, and with a more rigid approach to eating disorders. Yet extended out-patient treatment from this unit prior to Huntercombe had not resolved her difficulties.

Anna left Huntercombe no heavier than when she had been admitted, and she describes her clear initial reluctance and continuing ambivalence about further treatment in the local unit. Colin does not mention the current situation, which is that Anna has returned to health and has successfully established herself at university.

What sense can we make of this with regard to the work she undertook with Colin? This leads to another well-worn mantra of mine, that to move successfully from family to independence demands that we are more or less at ease with our family's idiosyncrasies, foibles and, for some, failures. Anna's family, like all families, was unique in its configuration, and it is clear from the narrative that she found it difficult to make sense of it, her role in it, and hence the who, what, and why of her self.

Much of the work done by Colin and Anna was about family and self, and in due course Anna made more sense of the who, what and why, but also the how – her account of her determination to leave anorexia behind; the when – acknowledging the opportunity for maturation as opposed to remaining frozen in time which is one possible consequence of anorexia; and the where – leaving for university with anticipation and confidence. It is clear to me that individual psychotherapy in Huntercombe laid the necessary groundwork for all that followed. This includes not only leaving anorexia behind, but also leaving therapy and the therapist behind.

Two legacies of therapy are noteworthy however. Firstly Anna's lucidity and eloquence in describing her difficulties surely arise from the dialogue, having found both a voice and a language to express herself to another and so begin to understand herself. Secondly she addresses Colin in a very tender and moving way. A traditional view would be to ascribe this to positive transference towards a good-enough mother and a father-figure whose encouragement does not stray into demands or expectations. My reading is of two persons-in-relation, with Anna expressing her gratitude to the real Colin for his work, his wisdom and most importantly his care.

Finally, what lessons do we learn from this narrative? For an institution which aims high, that is, at healing not simply symptom relief, the default position should be that psychotherapy provision is part of what is on offer, patients opting out only if they or staff feel it not to be relevant. For a therapist in an institutional or any other setting, the default position should be that of routinely adapting practice to meet patient need – a patient behaving as patients are supposed to should be the exception. And for the patient? It would be arrogant for the clinician to define her default position, but if the institution is ambitious in what it offers, and has therapists who can tailor that offer to the patient, then her emergent default position might commonly be: *to engage.*

Dr David Tait
First Medical Director,
Huntercombe Hospital
Edinburgh

NOTES

[1] The great religions emerged partly in response to the failure of the states or empires of those days to deal effectively with widespread violence, rape, looting and destruction, through means of law-making and enforcement. The religions, in contrast, sought to instil fundamental values and ways of living through regular communal gatherings, organised around key rituals and practices. Through such enactments, persons and communities internalised these values in their consciousness and behaviour.

The religions thus made significant contributions to the development of human personality and culture: conscience, morality, social norms, respect for persons. They did not aim to suppress, repress or dissociate the aggressive and sexual drives, but to guide, channel and sublimate them in personally, socially and culturally creative ways.

Such efforts, however, are not always successful in their outcomes. In men, this can sometimes take the form of personalities organised primarily around aggression, and in women it can sometimes take the form of personalities organised around attempts to avoid aggression altogether, or to use it indirectly, or turn it against the self.

It is against this background that I sometimes ask the question: what do you do with your aggression?

REFERENCES/BIBLIOGRAPHY

Armstrong, K. (1993). *A history of God.* London: Heinemann.

Armstrong, K. (2006). *The great transformation: The world in the time of Buddha, Socrates, Confucius and Jeremiah.* London: Atlantic Books.

Claude-Pierre, P. (1997). *The secret language of eating disorders.* Canada: Random House.

Coleridge, S. T. (1994). *The works of Samuel Taylor Coleridge.* Ware: Wordsworth Editions.

Donne, J. (1624). *Devotions upon emergent occasions,* Meditation no. 24.

Freud, S. (trans. Strachey, J.) (1980). *The interpretation of dreams.* London: Hogarth Press and The Institute of Psychoanalysis.

Gardner, W. H. (1953). *Gerard Manley Hopkins: A selection of his poems and prose.* Harmondsworth: Penguin.

Jeffares, A. N. (Ed.) (1962). *W. B. Yeats: Selected poetry.* London: MacMillan.

Lask, B. & Bryant-Waugh, R. (2007). *Eating disorders in childhood and adolescence*, 3rd edition. London: Routledge.

Leonard, T. (1973). This Island Now. In *Poems*. Dublin: E. & T. O'Brien.

Leonard, T. (2009). *Outside the narrative: Poems 1965-2009*. Exbourne/ Edinburgh: Etruscan Books/ Word Power Books.

Mahler, M. (1972). On the first three sub-phases of the separation-individuation process. *International Journal of Psychoanalysis, 53*, 333–338.

Mitchell, J. (Ed.) (1986). *The selected Melanie Klein*. Harmondsworth: Penguin.

Ogden, T. (1992). *The primitive edge of experience*. London: Karnac Books.

Skynner, R. & Cleese, J. (1984). *Families and how to survive them*. New York: Oxford University Press.

Suttie, I. D. (1988) (first published 1935). *The origins of love and hate*. London: Free Association Books.

CHAPTER 7

COUNSELLING AS PERSONAL AND SOCIAL ACTION

Key words and themes: personal therapy, individual or social action, privatisation of care, the good society, sympathy, interinanimation, the intrapersonal, the interpersonal, the socio-cultural, values, persons in relation.

This paper was first presented at a conference organised by the Counselling and Society Research Team of the University of Edinburgh, in Edinburgh, in June 2003. It begins with a thematic summary of my personal therapy, as an illustration of the case I go on to make for counselling as a form of personal and social action.

PERSONAL ILLUSTRATION

I come from a west of Scotland/Northern Irish presbyterian family. My father was a minister of the Church of Scotland: his life and work have had a major impact on me. As a young man, I was drawn in two directions: on the one hand towards personal creativity through writing poetry; and on the other, to an involvement with working class people, feeling both a sense of guilt, an identification with their life situations, and a challenge to contribute to the fundamental democratisation of society. I became committed to certain forms of community action and adult education, and was for several years an active member of the Communist Party, whose working class members I admired. I had, and retain, a dislike for the Labour Party which I saw (and still see) as a paternalistic and immobilising 'mechanism for the election of Labour MPs' (the quotation is from Harold Wilson). This dislike is not directed at members of the Labour Party, but at many of their leaders and MPs and at what I would describe as the Party's general orientation.

As the 1970s continued, the experience of the impact of the community action we were engaged in, together with a growing awareness of its marginality in terms of power politics, in the context of the insistent oppositionalism and (as I saw it) wrong-headedness of many of the activities of the political left, both old and new, led me into a relatively depressed and politically isolated position. I saw both the Marxist and social democratic left as using people as means towards the realisation of the ends prescribed by their various political analyses and programmes. The personal lives and the creativity of persons and their communities were regarded by both traditions as largely irrelevant to their unending sloganising and supposedly progressive struggles. It was partly this that took me into psychoanalysis at the end of the 1970s, and I was lucky enough to be introduced to a psychoanalytic psychotherapist who consistently cared about me, came to understand me, and had a way of working which combined unobtrusiveness with a kind, interested presence. Psychotherapy enabled me to slow down a bit, clarify and develop my understanding of myself and my relationships in the context of family and society, opening the way to a very creative period in my working and political life. I was able to collaborate with others in developing a Freirean perspective in adult education through the Workers Educational Assocation (WEA) with outcomes in the writers' workshop movement, education for unemployed men and women, and the Adult Learning Project (ALP) in Edinburgh. At the same time I was rediscovering my voice as a writer, and my writing had some influence on those I wanted to address: practitioners, managers, students, and academics who had a real relationship with the world of practice.

There were other equally important sides to my therapy, one of which had to do with close personal relationships, and the tender and sensual side of life. I can see in retrospect that I was quite an inhibited person whose senses and feelings had, until then, been 'potentials unevoked in the facilitating environment', to use Harry Guntrip's sensitive phrase.

A third dimension of my therapy was more broadly cultural. It had to do with getting to grips with a number of 'outsider' and 'boundary' themes and contradictions to do with coming from Northern Ireland, but being born and living in Scotland; being a middle class child in rural, and later urban environments; being poor and cultured (in the sense of having access to books and music) in settings where most people were better off, had TV sets, and read popular newspapers; going to church, but not believing in God; inheriting a value system stressing altrusim, discipline, and personal and social responsibility, in a context which was becoming increasingly self-interested, expressive, and hedonistic, in which the idea of social responsibility was taken to mean that the structures of the state were responsible for providing what was required.

Some years later I realised that I wanted to help others as I myself had been helped. I trained as a counsellor and psychoanalytic psychotherapist, and have been practising ever since, as well as continuing direct involvement in adult learning and community-making. The changes resulting from therapy consisted, for me, not in becoming something dramatically different from what I had previously been, but in becoming more confidently myself with deeper self-other understanding, and an increased capacity for openness and collaboration with others. Let me try to summarise here how I think these processes happen: they are slow, interpersonally-supported processes involving introspection, sympathy (in the Adam Smith sense), re-experiencing, telling and re-telling, receiving feedback, pondering, connection-making, re-evaluating, and returning to the social, educational and political fray. I emphasise their interpersonal character, and the socio-cultural as well as more narrowly personal nature of their process and context.

I turn now, having offered this personal illustration, to address the question: is counselling a form of individual or social action, or is it both?

IS COUNSELLING A FORM OF INDIVIDUAL OR SOCIAL ACTION?

I hope you can see from the implications of my contributions so far that this is, for me, an easy question to answer. So much so, that it makes me wonder: why is it being asked? Who is asking it? My answer is that we as counsellors are asking it because we feel the need to challenge aspects of the view of counselling that is held by three broad groups. The first group is those with serious political and institutional power. The second is the collectivist left. And the third is sections of the media. Significant voices in each of these groups have negative views of counselling and psychotherapy. Many of those with institutional and political power do not wish to acknowledge the existence or significance of personal difficulties or vulnerabilities, especially as far as they themselves are concerned. They would regard such an admission of perceived weakness as tantamount to political or institutional suicide, rightly anticipating that sections of the media would savage them. Many senior politicians, chief executives, top managers and respected commentators seek and benefit from counselling or psychotherapy, but they, and we, keep quiet about it. It will not be known until they come to write their autobiographies, if it is ever known at all.

Many – not all – of those on the collectivist left dislike counselling because they see it as the privatisation and individualisation of care. It is, from their point of view, a threat to and diversion from collective provision by the state. For them, collective provision by the state is fundamental. It undergirds and secures social life on a universal and equitable basis. They see the personal as either irrelevant or strictly subordinate to the collective. In my view, there are important elements of truth, as well as large dollops of distortion, in their position. If counselling and psychotherapy are really of value, then their funding, and manner of provision is vitally important so that they can be made available to all those who seek and could benefit from them. There is a role for pressure on the state, and action by the state and other big resource holders, to fund counselling and psychotherapy so that those who need it but cannot afford it can get it.

There is another valid point in the collectivist critique, which can be acknowledged briefly by stating that counselling and psychotherapy are not cure-alls. They will not of themselves bring about a socially just society, but I would argue that the right kinds of counselling and psychotherapy are indispensable contributory elements which are constitutive of the good society. A third concession must also be made to the collectivist argument. Every social practice takes on to some degree the colour, the quality, of its socio-cultural environment. This is true of counselling and psychotherapy and there are some trends in therapy which embody the contemporary values of consumer sovereignty, hedonism and self-centredness, which can be summed up in a sentence such as the following: 'I should want whatever I want, and as much as I want; my wishes should all be fulfilled; and other people should mirror my desires back to me uncritically and affirmatively'. I emphasise that I dissociate myself wholly from these trends since they represent a derogation from personal and social responsibility both to and for the other.

The third source of negative representations of counselling and psychotherapy is the media. Counselling's honeymoon with the media ended about ten years ago. Journalists are rightly suspicious of the fact that anyone can set themselves up as a counsellor, without training or competence, and almost any ritualised sequence of activities can be represented as therapeutic: hence the pressure for regulation, and the growth of credentialism. And, insofar as the media reflects and amplifies the views of conflicting interests in society, there has been plenty of scope for hostile attacks on counselling in the media from other professions which perceive the growth of popular interest in counselling as a threat to their expertise and their jobs.

It is because of the influence of such critiques that we need to ask the question: is counselling a form of individual or social action? I turn now to answer it. One aspect of the question we can deal with straight away. Setting aside for a moment our work with couples, families and groups, we should acknowledge that most counselling is work done with individuals. From the standpoint of Adam Smith's dispassionate observer, that is a descriptive fact. It amounts to an acknowledgement that it is single human beings who press the bell at the door of the Scottish Institute of Human Relations, or Person Centred Therapy, or Wellspring, or Cruse, or Alcohol Focus Scotland. They are individuals: they cannot be further divided physically without pain or death, although they are often painfully divided psychologically. But to concede this point is to concede little or nothing, for two reasons. First, the fact that individuals seek out counsellors to work with is an affirmation that counselling places a high value on the person and the personal. Second, once we move from the point of view of the dispassionate outside observer to the points of view of those emotionally and relationally engaged inside participants, the client and the counsellor, we instantly enter the realm of the social.

DIMENSIONS OF COUNSELLING

I will now list the principal dimensions of counselling, discussing them in terms of their sources, processes, referential content and impact. The implication of each item on the list will be that counselling is social and cultural as well as personal in the narrow sense. Indeed, the conclusion is inescapable that, contra Thatcher, there is no such thing as an individual, only persons in socio-cultural relations extending spatially and temporally in every direction. To express this insight imaginatively, I would like to quote from a meditation by the English poet, John Donne:

No man is an Island, entire of it self; every man is
a piece of the Continent, a part of the main;
(Devotions upon Emergent Occasions, Meditation 24. 1624)

Here the phrase, 'a part of the main' means a part of the continent, and the island and continent Donne has in mind could well be the island of Britain and the continent of Europe. The Scottish poet Tom Leonard turns Donne's point round with a witty apercu relevant to our work as counsellors:

No man – or woman –
is an island.

Oceanography, however,
is not a science to be despised.

What I think Leonard is saying here is, yes, Donne is right, we are all parts of the main, but we manage quite often to get ourselves helluva isolated: there are plenty of human islands out there in the ocean of life.

Okay, now here is my list.

Item one: The relationship and the reasons for it

The counselling relationship is social in that a person who is enmeshed in society by virtue of having been born of woman into a family or other social care situation, with current relations of friendship or hostility or alienation in home, work or unemployment, in cultural and recreational settings, and with unavoidable relations with the state in terms of education, tax, health and social security even if he or she hates, resents or feels invaded by the whole bloody lot of them – such a person seeks help from another human being who is likewise enmeshed.

Why seek counselling help? There are always a thousand unique reasons but they usually include some degree of feeling at odds with others in family, work or society, and strained or disturbed within oneself. They often include being overwhelmed or torn apart by anxiety and a host of emotions, and unable to cope with one's social situation and roles as a result. There is often a dimension of value dissonance, value conflict, within the person and/or between them and others, something we don't emphasise enough. There is often a dimension of trauma, past, present or anticipated. All the presenting troubles of the client have interpersonal and socio-cultural dimensions as well as being uniquely personal. And contrary to the myth of the dispassionate therapist, the so-called blank screen, this social turmoil in the client immediately makes a new social impact. It stirs things up in the world of the counsellor, it generates sympathy in the strict sense in which Adam Smith uses that term: when you pluck a string on a violin, the next string begins to vibrate at the same frequency. The client stimulates all sorts of resonances, physical sensations, feelings, fantasies, thoughts, evaluations, and memories in the counsellor. The counsellor's own present and past world of relationships is *animated* by the impact of the client. I use the word animated because it allows me to introduce the precisely appropriate word from John Donne: the word *interinanimation*. The relation of love, says Donne in his poem *The Extasie*, 'interinanimates two soules'. Of course it does, and so do the relations of hate, resentment, confusion, misunderstanding, and alienation. It is a version of this kind of interinanimation which goes on in the counselling relationship. The counsellor has been trained to cultivate his or her knowledge of self and other, so that s/he can use herself as a sort of human barometer in experiencing and reflecting upon the impact of the client on herself: this is what she draws on in enabling the client in his or her explorations.

That was item one: the socio-culturally interinanimating character of the client-counsellor relationship.

Item two: What the client brings intrapersonally

It might be imagined that some aspects of what the client brings have to do with their relationships with other people and some have to do with themselves as individuals. This looks as if it ought to be true, but it is largely a misconception. Let's focus for a minute on what the client brings in terms of himself as an individual, his inner, private world, what we call the intrapersonal. None of this is purely individual. Even genetically, the client brings a unique constellation of genes drawn from two generative sources and via these two, from a tree endlessly branching and subdividing backwards in time. The particular mix is unique, but the sources are social. And once we take into account the human and physical environment in which this individual has been nurtured and with which he has interacted from the moment of conception onwards, even in the intrapersonal domain we are in the realm of the interpersonal and social-cultural. Such therapists as Ian Suttie, Harry Stack Sullivan, and Susie Orbach have emphasised how deeply and pervasively personal identity is also interpersonal and cultural. I have argued elsewhere that the TV in the living room is a factor of personal identity. I had a male client whose parents were mentally ill who convinced me that the TV in the living room played a significant part in bringing him up. The same can be said of the part played by his father's reading of the family bible or the folk tales his mother told him in the development of the identity of Robert Burns. The Burns example illustrates how interpersonal and cultural factors interweave in the development of the intrapersonal identity of the person: just how interpersonal the intrapersonal is.

Setting aside for a moment these under-acknowledged cultural factors, the Scottish psychoanalyst Ronald Fairbairn's great contribution to our understanding has been his outline of how, in the development of the inner world of each of us, there are at least three interpersonal pairings: first, there is a conscious self, relating to a conscious sense of the other often construed as an ideal; then there are two repressed or dissociated self-other pairs operating out of conscious awareness. One of these pairs operates around experiences of need, longing and vulnerability: the needy, longing self seeking the exciting, promising other. The other pair operates around experiences of rejection or punishment: the rejecting or punishing other relating to the internal saboteur in the self which in turn attacks the needy, longing part of the self. And along comes Harry Guntrip, confirming Fairbairn's picture and adding his own account of how the needy self, so vulnerably exposed, its needs unmet and subject to attack, withdraws into a protective citadel and refuses to come out. Oceanography, or perhaps we should call it fortressology, is not a science to be despised. And along comes Harry Stack Sullivan to illustrate how the conflicting social class affiliations and cultural aspirations of his catholic mother and protestant father entered his little soul at an early age and contributed to his own social withdrawal and also to the development of his capacity to empathise with deeply withdrawn clients. And this is just the intrapersonal bit!

Item three: The present interpersonal

The client brings his present interpersonal concerns at home, at work or in unemployment, intertwined with his engagements in social situations and institutions and with his cultural interests. Usually these concerns are the primary focus of the client's work in therapy, often with particular emphases on intense feelings, or difficulties in relation to significant others, tasks and aspirations. Particularly when counselling relationships continue for longer periods, however, counsellors are aware of the need to be sensitive to the simultaneity, the close interweave, between the present interpersonal, the intrapersonal and the socio-cultural dimensions of the person, to the last of which I now turn.

Item four: The specifically socio-cultural concerns of the client

Theoretical and practice-related accounts of counselling have always tended to underplay these preoccupations in both client and counsellor, or acknowledge them merely as social context, a kind of backcloth or set to introduce a theatrical metaphor, which we will elaborate in a moment. My line of argument here is that these preoccupations are vital and central to the work of counselling. As Bob Tait, when he was editor of *Scottish International Review* 40 years ago, wrote to me once in the language of the time: 'where I dig, it's all happening'. I agree with that assertion. The individual person is part of the main. He or she is not only a spectator, but is also part of the stage and the set, several of the actors and one of the scriptwriters of the socio-cultural dramas in which we partake. In a very real sense, the socio-cultural is me. It happens in us as well as outside of us, whether we are willing, unwilling or unconscious actors. Bertrand Russell was making an analogous point when he wrote: 'the stars are in my mind'. There is nothing mystical about this, although it is complicated and constantly changing. Why do you think contemporary politics, on one dimension, has resolved itself into a constant investigation by means of increasingly sophisticated forms of social research, of the preferences and opinions of ordinary people? The politicians need to know how we are construing what is happening, so that they can change their tack and adjust their sails.

I want here to crystallise one particular aspect of the socio-cultural dimension of client concerns. My colleague Siobhan Canavan emphasises the importance of the exploration of values in counselling training, an area on which she feels we place insufficient emphasis. I think she is right, and I'm arguing that there is a huge values dimension in the lives of both client and counsellor, and in their relationship. Normal counselling training discourse sometimes tends to reduce values to concerns about codes of ethics and practice. In my experience, clients are concerned – often tormented – about how to live their lives in a way that is right for them. This is actually a philosophical, universal, and personal concern. Traditionally, institutional religion claimed to do a lot of that for us, but now that most of us have chucked religion out of the window, we find ourselves living in an ethical forest, the *selva oscura* of Dante's *Inferno,* in which competing ethics and anti-ethics swarm and battle to possess us.

To summarise this point: we do not sufficiently recognise that the counselling dialogue of listening and attuning, following and responding, is a dialogue about how to live this particular life, how to conduct these particular relationships, in this particular family, in this particular workplace, with these particular health and money problems, in this society, culture and world about which both client and counsellor have such strong and sometimes conflicting views, and in relation to which they have such hopes and fears.

CONCLUSION

I want now to come to my conclusion, which I hope will already be apparent to you. Counselling is a form of individual action, and we need not be ashamed of that. A senior counselling trainer in the USA, embarrassed by his relatively privileged position and wishing (or so I imagine) to dissociate himself from the individualistic culture of the United States, told me recently that he and his colleagues had now completely given up training for one-to-one work and were concentrating exclusively on social interventions. I nearly fell off my seat. As if work with an individual was not a social intervention! This American trainer's view represents a conception of the individual as isolate, as island, as solitary victim or solitary predator. The view of the individual person which I am proposing is inherently social, but not in the crude, coercive, collectivist sense. We are, in John Macmurray's beautiful phrase 'persons in relation'. Persons, Macmurray argues, are actually constituted by their relations with other persons. Counselling individuals is no more individualistic or anti-social than hearing the confession of an individual penitent before communion. Of course, there are major differences, the principal one being that the institutional church held out an integrated vision of values and rules for living, directing the person as to how they should act in their lives. Our culture, certainly for the time being, has thrown over the traces of what it perceives as the authoritarian church with its commandments. But we cannot so easily get rid of the problems the churches were trying to address: how am I to live this life in this society, in such a way as to pursue and constitute my own good and contribute to that of society? Here I am borrowing the language of another Scottish philosopher, Alasdair MacIntyre.

Counselling, according to this perspective, represents the re-emergence, in an increasingly atomising, devil-take-the-hindmost, post-scarcity culture, of a personalist and communalist perspective of the kind defined by John Macmurray. It consists of the offering of the self of the counsellor to the self of the client, in an act of supportive care, an act of *agape,* in an attempt, together, to create an interpersonal environment in which the client can be safely vulnerable, re-experience themselves in terms of their genetic givens, their intrapersonal world, and their interpersonal and socio-cultural world, with the hopeful aim of re-evaluation, restoration and return to the relational fray: *reculer pour mieux sauter.* Counselling, to quote John Macmurray again, is 'consciously behaving in terms of the nature of the other'. It is not, by itself alone, the means of creating the good society, but it makes a worthwhile contribution to that end, through interpersonal actions that are constitutive of it. In a culture which has overvalorised a conception of society as consisting of large-scale policies and structures managing atomised individuals, it reaffirms the centrality of the practice of the personal.

REFERENCES/BIBLIOGRAPHY

Donne, J. (1624). *Devotions upon emergent occasions*, Meditation 24.

Fairbairn, W. R. D. (1952). *Psychoanalytic studies of the personality*. London: Tavistock Publications/ Routledge and Kegan Paul.

Guntrip, H. (1977). *Psychoanalytic theory, therapy and the self*. London: Karnac.

Leonard, T. (1973). This Island Now. In *Poems*. Dublin: E. & T. O'Brien.

Leonard, T. (2009). *Outside the narrative: Poems 1965–2009*. Exbourne/Edinburgh: Etruscan Books/ Word Power Books.

MacIntyre, A. (1985). *After virtue*. London: Duckworth.

Macmurray, J. (1961). *Persons in relation*. London: Faber and Faber.

Russell, B. (1959). *The problems of philosophy*. London: Oxford University Press.

Sisson, C. H. (1980). (trans.) *Dante: The divine comedy: A new verse translation*. Manchester: Carcanet New Press.

Smith, A. (1759). *The theory of moral sentiments*.

SECTION IV

APPLYING THE PERSONS IN RELATION PERSPECTIVE BEYOND THE COUCH

BEYOND THE COUCH

An Introduction to the Work of John D. Sutherland

Key words and themes: the self in society, persons in relation, personal relations theory, the autonomous and relational self, the self as agent, closed and open systems, the best form of welfare is development, spreading psychoanalytic insights beyond the couch, disturbance at the core of the person, continuity of self, self-system, self-other relational matrix, governing centre or system, the sense of self, the self as actor and chooser.

John D. Sutherland, known to his friends and colleagues as Jock, played a very significant part in the development and wider application of psychoanalysis in the years during and after the second world war, in England, Scotland, and the USA, up until his death in 1991.

In recent years, the Scottish Institute of Human Relations and the Sutherland Trust have contributed to supporting the work of Jill and David Scharff in their scholarly investigations and celebration of the writings and work of both Ronald Fairbairn and Jock Sutherland.

We owe a debt of gratitude to Jill Savege Scharff for her edited collection *The Autonomous Self: the work of John D. Sutherland* (Jason Aronson, 1994), to David E. Scharff and Ellinor Fairbairn Birtles for their edited volumes *From Instinct to Self: Selected Papers of W. R. D. Fairbairn*, vols. 1 and 2 (Jason Aronson, 1994), and to Jill Savege Scharff and David E. Scharff for their edited volume *The Legacy of Fairbairn and Sutherland: Psychotherapeutic Applications* (Routledge, 2005).

In 2007 the Trust and the Institute organised the launch in Edinburgh of Jill Scharff's selection of Sutherland's major papers, entitled *The Psychodynamic Image: John D. Sutherland on Self in Society* (Routledge, 2007). Later that same year the Trust and the Institute collaborated with the Centre for Counselling and Psychotherapy Studies of the University of Edinburgh to run a successful course, entitled *Beyond the Couch*, to spread knowledge of Sutherland's work among a younger generation.

The two pieces which follow do not claim to give a comprehensive account of Sutherland's contributions, but to summarise and highlight, within the context of the aim of the present book, which is to define and demonstrate the persons in relation perspective. It is my contention that Sutherland in his person, his work and his writings illustrates aspects of that perspective.

These two pieces were prepared for the Beyond the Couch course. The first is a set of teaching notes distributed to course members, and the second is a close reading of a recently rediscovered short paper written by Sutherland for a seminar he gave in 1978.

In all of what follows, I acknowledge my indebtedness to Janet Hassan, Alan Harrow, Mona Macdonald, Judith Brearley, Neville Singh, Chris Holland, Elinor Fairbairn Birtles, Graham Clarke, Jill Savege Scharff, David E. Scharff and to two extended conversations with Sutherland himself.

THE WORK OF JOHN D. SUTHERLAND

Sutherland's key themes:

- object relations/personal relations theory: his engagement with and promotion of the work of such key figures as Ronald Fairbairn, Harry Guntrip, Michael Balint, and Donald Winnicott
- at the core of this engagement, his exposition, promotion and further development of Ronald Fairbairn's conceptualisation of the basic inner situation in each person, conceived in relational (self/other) terms
- his emphasis on the autonomous and relational self-in-society, in families, groups, communities, workplaces, and the corollary of that emphasis – the need to apply psychoanalysis and develop psychodynamic perspectives beyond the couch, in group relations, organisational consultancy, counselling and community development; and also in our thinking about current and future developments in society as a whole, for example his reflections on welfare, on the need to integrate health, education and social care, and his interesting observations on the post-industrial society
- his perception of the vital role of the caring professions: social workers, GPs, nurses, psychiatrists, teachers, the clergy, occupational therapists, adult educators and so on; his concept of community mental health; and his promotion of community development (most notably in the Craigmillar housing scheme in Edinburgh) and of counselling services such as the then Scottish Marriage Guidance Council
- his own key area of intellectual innovation: the conceptualisation of the self, imagined as autonomous, grounded in relationships, present from the start of life, first whole, then divided, developing and changing throughout life; the self as an evolving structure-in-process; the hologram as an image of this dynamic self; the self as a supra-ordinate system, capable of reflecting upon itself; the self as an agent, with the ego or 'I' imagined as a kind of executive director of the self, managing both internal and external reality; the self developing not in isolation but in family, society and culture; the key role of affects as a monitoring system for the self in all of its encounters in the world; the self as forming part of a larger system; the self as a (relatively) closed or open system; the self as a person-in-relationships; and the need for a developmental view of the self
- his view of psychoanalytic psychotherapy as a warm, responsive, personal relationship; the patient or client's need to be valued for him- or herself as a

person, involving Sutherland in a groundbreaking departure from the blank screen, self-withholding model of the psychotherapist
- his downplaying of the use of abstract psychoanalytic jargon in favour of what he calls 'four-letter words like love, milk and bits'.

Some wider themes of the epoch relevant to Sutherland's work

- Scottish Christian idealism
- the influence on Sutherland of the personalism of John Macmurray (there is recurrent use of 'persons in relation' and 'self as agent' language and assumptions throughout Sutherland's work, which he integrates with psychoanalytic language and assumptions)
- the post-war growth of the welfare state in Britain; his emphasis on the need to integrate health, education and social care, and his stated view that 'the best form of welfare is development'
- the development of computers and computer studies, then called cybernetics, from which Sutherland borrows the idea of open and closed systems, arguing that the aim of psychoanalysis is to enable the client to become more of an open system
- the emergence of the post-industrial society, and his view of the need for people as citizens to take increasing responsibility within it
- spreading the application of psychoanalytic ideas throughout society, through the professions, communities, institutions, the arts and religion.

Key periods and roles in Sutherland's life

- growing up in Scotland 1905–1920s
- university studies and junior posts 1920s/30s
- analysis with Fairbairn
- training as a psychoanalyst
- Second World War: his leading role in the War Office Officer Selection Boards, promoted to Lieutenant-Colonel
- chairman of the Tavistock Clinic and role in the Tavistock Institute of Human Relations 1947-68
- British and international editorships *(The International Journal of Psychoanalysis, The British Journal of Medical Psychology)*
- Co-founder of the Scottish Institute of Human Relations
- Visiting Professor at the Menninger Institute; influence on psychoanalytic developments in the USA
- Sutherland the author: *The Psychodynamic Image of Man; Fairbairn's Journey into the Interior; An Object Relations View of the Great Man; The Autonomous Self.* For a full list see *The Autonomous Self* (Jason Aronson, 1994) and *The Psychodynamic Image* (Routledge, 2007), both edited by Jill Savege Scharff.

Some of Sutherland's personal, social and intellectual qualities

- enabling
- institution-building
- administration
- bridge-building
- collaboration with colleagues
- managing prima donnas
- courtesy and curiosity
- respect for and interest in other persons
- capacity to make connections across disciplinary boundaries
- capacity to think things through at the level of fundamental assumptions/ underlying theses
- ability to communicate with all levels of society.

FROM EGO TO SELF-IN-SOCIETY: JOCK SUTHERLAND'S CREATIVE STEP

Introduction

In her selection of Jock Sutherland's major papers for her edited volume *The Psychodynamic Image: John D Sutherland on Self in Society* (Routledge, 2007), Jill Savege Scharff includes a paper entitled *The self in personal relations*, dated February 1978, which she describes as 'a remarkable synthesis of the writings of those whose views he valued.'

It seems likely, in the light of its contents, that this paper was written for discussion with members of a seminar which Jock was giving, and that this seminar formed part of one of the early training courses in what was then called Analytical Psychotherapy (now Psychoanalytic Psychotherapy) at the Scottish Institute of Human Relations. Sutherland himself says of it:

this paper represents working notes, my gropings in a very complex area,

with which he has been concerned for fifteen years and which involves

trying to understand the problems that have not responded to psychoanalysis.

The paper represents Jock the bridge-builder, the integrater of disparate lines of thought, the carrier-forward of a respected tradition, and the innovator concerned with locating the whole person in his or her interpersonal and socio-cultural context.

What historical contexts are relevant to this work? I would suggest the following, and you may wish to add others:

- institutionally, the context of the relatively newly established Scottish Institute of Human Relations, its training courses, and its contributions to Scottish society;

- growing dissatisfaction with the Strachey translations of Freud's works, and specifically with his rendering of ich, uber ich, and es as ego, super ego, and id rather than I, over I (or above I), and it;
- awareness that in the Jungian, Rogerian/person-centred, and existentialist worlds (and in the work of the widely influential psychiatrist Harry Stack Sullivan), the terms self, self concept, self-structure and self-system had been in use for many years;
- significant shifts in the philosophy of science away from mechanical and energic conceptions of human biology and psychology
- the influence of the work of the Scottish philosopher of religion John Macmurray, whose personalist perspective had been given its most comprehensive expression in the published versions of his two series of Gifford lectures: *The Self as Agent* (1957) and *Persons in Relation* (1961)(both Faber and Faber);
- the recent interest in the possibility of analysing those diagnosed as 'borderline';
- the disaster for psychoanalysis of the meltdown of the careers of R. D. Laing and Masud Khan;
- I have a sense, in addition, that Jock was also responding to the emergence of the 'me' generation, with its culture of self-centredness and narcissism.

Turning now to an exposition and discussion of the paper itself, I plan to do this by highlighting and commenting on key points in the text.

In line one, Jock signals that he is trying to innovate, to push ahead in terms of psychoanalytic theory, which he characterises as being 'manifestly in the melting pot'. He refers to the concept of the self as being relevant to understanding what he calls disturbances of the total personality, in which a person's commitment to living is compromised. He locates this focus of interest in the work of his colleagues Michael Balint, Donald Winnicott, Ronald Fairbairn, and Harry Guntrip, members like him of the middle or independent group of psychoanalysts. He refers again to disturbance at the core of the person, something deeper than what is encountered at more superficial levels: deeper, for example, than the phenomena associated with traditional Freudian conceptions of the Oedipus complex.

Early in the paper, we note that three or four key words or concepts are jostling for the limelight: the self, the person, the ego or I. And we see that he is also concerned with the notion of a free agent or actor. These terms are closely related in the text: it is clear that he is aware that they overlap. He discusses the Rogerian notion of self concept, largely I think misrepresenting it, and then drops it.

He says that he is concerned, crucially and centrally, with what he calls the key referents of self. What, in other words, does the term self actually refer to? Jock proceeds to list these referents:

- continuity of self, linking past, present and future self-identity
- self as close to but not identical with ego: self as the subject or focal point of motives, some of which, he reminds us, are outwith the ego and to be located in the superego or the id

- Jock now swings back to the earlier term, ego, reminding seminar members of its referents. Here, I think, like his mentor Ronald Fairbairn, Jock is demonstrating his respect for psychoanalytic tradition. He lists the following as key ego functions:
  - organising and controlling
  - maintaining adaptedness
  - mapping the person's world
  - the ego as the system (the first appearance of another new term) which considers options and makes decisions
- then, turning to the work of the humanistic psychologist, Chein, he adds: 'a central integrative function seems to have been given to the self'
- self-preservation, self-enhancement, and self determination, 'all the syntonic behaviours of the actor emanate from the self'
- then he asks: so, how are we to understand cases of multiple personalities? Are these all, as he puts it, 'constituent systems of the person'? Here we note a significant shift from the term self to the term person; and again that word system. Clearly, it is not the Jungian concept of person he is using here, a concept influenced by the Latin word persona, which means mask. Sutherland seems to be using the word person in the same sense that John Macmurray had done.

Now, having assembled this pretty comprehensive list of referents of the term self, Jock comes out and speaks for himself. He characterises the self as what he calls 'a supra-ordinate system'. And again, his account contains echoes of Macmurray:

> a supra-ordinate self-as-agent which can be explored as a natural phenomenon.

A few lines further on we come to the next terminological shift. From self as supra-ordinate system we move to matrix:

> the dynamic whole of living organisms whose activities are integrated within a matrix.

This matrix is coherent, persistent, self-sustaining, self-propagating and 'such a vital matrix is an agent'. This self, says Jock,

> is not knowable directly, (but) its structure can be investigated through self-representations.

This is stirring stuff: I can imagine contemporary neuroscientists like Antonio Damasio pricking up their ears.

Now Jock, having as it were bridge-built his way towards a view we recognise as his own, refers back to his heroic predecessor, the trail-blazer for the complex self-system he is hypothesising, Ronald Fairbairn. But we recall immediately Fairbairn's almost exaggerated respect for the traditional terminology of psychoanalysis. Fairbairn postulated, Jock reminds us, 'a unified ego from birth'; and Fairbairn was recognised by Ernest Jones, Freud's first biographer, as starting from the core of the personality rather than its periphery. Jock-as-Fairbairn presses on, conceptualising a process of

> differentiation within an overall dynamic integrative matrix which is the carrier of the experience of the infant, and within which structuring takes place.

He moves now towards a concept of the self-matrix, an evolving system concerned at the beginning of life simply with making relations with mother/caregiver, and from then on complexifying in reaction to frustrations experienced in that relationship. This is another Fairbairnian shift: we are moving towards a concept of the self-matrix as relational, as constituted by internalised self-other relationships. Macmurray meets Fairbairn inside Sutherland, so to speak. As well as being a joke, that is my attempt to capture a significant moment in Scottish and international psychoanalytic history, because here we have a synthesis, a point of meeting, of philosophical, religious and psychoanalytic perspectives. This essay is one of the places where it happens.

I am not going to follow Jock into his detailed exposition of Fairbairn's theory of the basic endopsychic (internal) situation, but I will summarise it briefly. It is a matrix of four relationships:
- the conscious relationship between the central ego and the ideal object or other;
- the split-off and repressed relationship between the rejecting/anti-libidinal object, and the rejected/anti-libidinal ego or internal saboteur;
- the split-off and repressed relationship between the libidinal ego or longing needy self, and the libidinal object, the exciting, excessively stimulating but ultimately unsatisfying other;
- the anti-libidinal ego or internal saboteur fiercely and relentlessly attacks the libidinal ego, as if to say: don't be pathetic, don't be needy, don't long for love! Be separate, be tough, stand on your own two feet!

Now Jock, ever the bridge-builder, links this essentially Fairbairnian picture with the interpersonal thinking of Sullivan, Klein, Mahler, Bowlby, and Erikson.

What is innovative in this paper by Jock Sutherland is not the Fairbairnian picture of the basic inner situation summarised above, though that is hugely innovative in its own right. That was Fairbairn's innovation. No: the new move here is Sutherland's transition from the language of ego, superego and id to his own new emerging concept of a dynamically differentiating self-system or self-matrix, which is in fact a self-other system, a self-other relational matrix.

Now, having declared his position, he proceeds to highlight this quality of relationality. At its earliest stage, he repeats,

> the patterning of the system (is) in terms of a self-pole at one end of the dynamic relation-seeking system, with an image of a mother at the other end.

And he explicitly jettisons what he calls the impersonal term ego. He goes on to locate what he calls the sense of self as pervading the whole system. This is another vital step. The sense of self is in everything: bodily sensations, perceptions of the world, both external and internal, facts and fantasies, self-presentation, self-concept (now I think more accurately understood).

As he spins the threads and weaves the web of his new conception, Jock continues to bridge-build, to make links with the work of colleagues who use different concepts. He says, for example, that Lichtenstein's concept of 'identity theme' is 'virtually the same as the basic patterning of the self-matrix in a relations-making system'. We move, he says, from a simple early self-mother system (the relatively unstructured matrix, he calls it) to an increasingly structured complexifying system. At this stage in the paper, we begin to hear echoes of systems theory and cybernetics making their way into the picture. This is a distinctively Sutherlandian strand: you will not find it in Fairbairn, or in Macmurray. Jock talks about

a governing centre required by any complex hierarchically ordered system.

The self, I feel, begins to sound like a business, a large and complex organisation. He adds:

a person needs a governing system, a system whose task is to plan, to make decisions, and to act for the whole.

It is almost as if, having thrown the ego overboard and replaced it with the self-matrix, Jock now pulls the ego back on board and installs it in the driving seat. I feel that his formulation here is less than totally clear: but his intention is clear enough:

The ego ... is the organisation of the transactions with the environment under the 'direction' of the self-matrix.

Is that ambiguous, or am I just tired? Exactly which bit of the system is doing the directing: the ego, or the self-matrix? Later on in the day on which I wrote the first version of this chapter, I was reminded by a colleague that the Jungians, too, have been struggling for many years to bring into relationship their distinctive uses of the terms self and ego. That night I dreamt that Jock was wrestling here with how to achieve a satisfactory integration of different aspects of his new conception: on the one hand the sheer complexity of the self-other system and the all-pervading quality of the sense of self; and on the other hand how to locate and conceptualise the executive functioning within this complex self. Jock realises that the system is a dynamically differentiating whole and that it is a gestalt, a whole which is more than the sum of its parts. Where then is its executive core, and how does it work? It is to name this governing dimension of the self-system that he wants to bring back the concept of ego. I find myself wanting to use words 'I' or 'core self' rather than 'ego.'

In view of much more recent, post-Sutherland, and post-modern conceptions of the self, it is fascinating that at this point in the paper Jock starts to consider the psychoanalytic phenomena of splitting, touching on versions of it associated with Fairbairn, Guntrip, and Winnicott, but not Klein (a curious omission in this context). He makes a valuable distinction between the adapted self (which he equates with the false self) and the adaptive self (which is able to read and respond appropriately to a changing environment). Then he hauls himself back from any further consideration of splitting, reminding himself that his aim has been

> to advocate the replacement of impersonal terms like ego with self as actor and chooser,

and turns again to the bridge-building task of reconciling various existing elements of the psychoanalytic tradition with his new conception.

The self-matrix, he has demonstrated, following Fairbairn, has a central system and subsystems. Within this total matrix, Jock locates the processes of repression and instinctual drives and their derivatives, such as sexual fantasies. All the phenomena we associate with ego, superego and id, he argues, can find a place in the new model. And it enables us to have a much better understanding of the role of deprivation in the early structuring of the self.

It also, for Jock, permits a departure from impersonal and distancing psychotherapeutic styles: analytical psychotherapists, he asserts, can adopt a warmer, more spontaneous attitude (shades of Kohut and Rogers), stigmatised by those who oppose it as 'kindly'. Ever the bridge-builder, he argues that this difference of view can be settled by more research! No wonder they valued him so much. Jock's intellectual style prefigures the contemporary notion of social inclusion, and his personal practice exemplified it.

He returns again to his innovator mode, emphasising the impact that such demanding therapeutic work (engaging as it does with disturbances at the heart of the self) can have on the self of the therapist. He quotes with approval the existentialist view of psychotherapy as a sequence of interpersonal encounters. While arguing that continuing analysis of the self of the psychotherapist might be too painful (a view with which I strongly disagree), he suggests that groups of analysts might work together on what he calls 'problems of self-object differentiation'; and they could publish their findings. He acknowledges the existence of difficult cases, blocks and failures. In these he sees new opportunities to advance our understanding of self, and concludes with a summons to us all to continue to study the phenomena of the self.

Wider reflections

In moving toward a conclusion, I found myself left with an uneasy feeling of having missed a vital theme. I found a clue to my unease in a sudden realisation that, in the paper under consideration, Sutherland's new concept of the self was beginning to sound like a job description for a managing director or chief executive: a governing centre indeed, and a very masculine one at that. What seemed to be missing from his list of functions were those qualities associated stereotypically with the feminine: to receive, to give, to feed, to nurture, to comfort, to tune in, to accompany. Yet I was aware from the accounts of those who knew him and from my own encounters with him that Sutherland had these receptive and attuning qualities, alongside the governing, monitoring and adaptive qualities, at the core of his personality. I remembered also that, although the Scotland to which he returned in the later 1960s to co-found the Scottish Institute of Human Relations (SIHR) was still in many respects a patriarchal society, his collaborators in that task included a number of very creative, authoritative women, people like Janet Hassan, Megan Brown, Una Armour, Jill Savege Scharff, Judith Brearley, and Mona Macdonald. Throughout the development of the Institute, Sutherland encouraged and supported these women in the creation, for example, of the Human Relations and Counselling Course, unquestionably the most successful project of the first 25 years of the life of the SIHR, and the one which has had the most widespread impact in Scottish society.

These are complex themes whose full unfolding must await an authoritative history of the Institute which will I hope be undertaken in the future. At this stage, I think we have enough evidence to argue that Sutherland, as well as being himself an instance of the great man archetype, like Freud and Fairbairn, and Buchan and Ghandi (about whom he wrote in precisely those terms), was also a very significant transitional figure in Scottish society, who helped to make space for the emergence of women as leaders in the field of human relations, and was an example of the interweaving of masculine and feminine qualities in the conduct of public affairs and the leadership of institutions.

CONCLUSION

I regard this paper as especially significant within the corpus of Sutherland's work. It interweaves bold innovation with respect for tradition, bridge-building and interdisciplinary connection-making. We hear one of the outstanding psychoanalytic minds of the 20th century wrestling with the task of re-conceptualising phenomena which are inherently difficult to grasp. He tries one metaphor, then another, then another. He moves back and forward from the old concepts to the new. We see the new synthesis taking shape before our eyes. That is the advantage of having access to his working notes: he hasn't yet closed down the options in favour of one single account. Finally, it helps us to locate the occurrence of these shifts in psychoanalytic thinking in time: the middle to late 1970s. Of course, the concept of self, which is at least as old as the Germanic languages, and is one of those four letter words he preferred to pseudo-scientific abstractions, has continued to develop further in the years since his contributions were made.

REFERENCES/BIBLIOGRAPHY

Jones, E. (1952). Preface. In W. R. D. Fairbairn, *Psychoanalytic studies of the personality.* London: Tavistock Publications and Routledge and Kegan Paul.

Macmurray, J. (1961). *The persons in relation perspective.* London: Faber and Faber.

Macmurray, J. (1957). *The self as agent.* London: Faber and Faber.

Scharff, D. E. & Fairbairn Birtles, E. (Eds.) (1994). *From instinct to self: Selected papers of W. R. D. Fairbairn,* vols. 1 and 2. London: Jason Aronson.

Scharff, J. S. (Ed.) (1994). *The autonomous self: The work of John D. Sutherland*. London: Jason Aronson.

Scharff, J. S. (Ed.) (2007). *The psychodynamic image: John D. Sutherland on self-in-society*. London: Routledge.

Scharff, J. S. & Scharff, D. E. (Eds.) (2005). *The legacy of Fairbairn and Sutherland: Psychoanalytic applications*. London: Routledge.

Sutherland, J. D. (1989). *Fairbairn's journey into the interior*. London: Free Association Books.

Sutherland, J. D. (1994). An object relations view of the great man. In *The autonomous self: The work of John D. Sutherland*, op. cit.

Sutherland, J. D. (1994). John Buchan's 'sick heart'. In *The autonomous self: The work of John D. Sutherland*, op. cit.

Sutherland, J. D. (1994). The autonomous self. In *The autonomous self: The work of John D. Sutherland*, op. cit.

Sutherland, J. D. (1994). The psychodynamic image of man. In *The autonomous self: The work of John D. Sutherland*, op. cit.

Sutherland, J. D. (2007). The self in personal relations. In *The psychodynamic image: John D. Sutherland on self-in-society*, op. cit.

CHAPTER 9

ROBERT BURNS IN THE COUNSELLOR'S CHAIR

A Psycho-Socio-Cultural Analysis of the Burns Myth

Key words and themes: idealisation, *Scottish stereotypes, sentimentalising, identification, censorship, respectabilification, contradictions, conflicts, pride, shame, humiliation, exploitation, dissociation of sensibility, hypocritical Puritanism.*

This paper was first presented as *The Immortal Memory of Robert Burns* at the Moray House Institute of Education Burns Supper, 25 January 2000. It was first published in the November 2000 issue of *Psychodynamic Counselling.*

INTRODUCTION

It is no small matter to be invited to toast the immortal memory of Robert Burns: it is an honour which gives rise to a certain amount of anxiety. What will I say, and how will it be received? My sense of anxiety is increased by virtue of the fact that, while I take great pleasure in Burns suppers and the public performance of his work, I have strong views about the Burns cult as it has developed in the last 200 years. I want to pose three related questions: which memory or memories are we talking about? Who is Robert Burns and what does he represent? And what is the nature and meaning of our interest in him?

I shall not conceal from my brothers and sisters here assembled that I have been most cruelly treated in relation to this invitation. I assumed that I could expect to speak for perhaps an hour and a half, in line with hallowed tradition, and you can imagine how chagrined I felt when I was informed by the Grand Mistress of Ceremonies that I had a mere 15 minutes. I had managed to bargain her back up to 30 minutes when the Grand Master himself entered the room, and ruled that I had a maximum of 25 minutes. I am sure you will share my view that there is no point in battling against force majeure. You have to be strategic. But I tell you in confidence that I intend to get my revenge by making a number of wild and unsubstantiated assertions. Furthermore, there will be no footnotes (well, just the one), no references, and listeners should not be surprised if a certain amount of plagiarism creeps in. What you are about to hear will not raise the quality of the Faculty's submission for the research assessment exercise, and is unlikely to grace the pages of a refereed journal, although it might make it into the *Mauchline Farmers Gazette.*

I did give some thought to a title, and came up with *Robert Burns in the counsellor's chair,* but that is not quite right. It is closer to *The myth of Robert Burns in the socio-culturally orientated analyst's chair.* But that does not have the same ring. So I gave up on titles.

But – as the narrator of Tam O'Shanter would have said – to our tale.

The idealisation of Robert Burns

My first theme is the idealisation of Robert Burns. What we get at school, and often at Burns suppers, is not Robert Burns the complicated man he was, but a selective, distorted, and simplified version of him. We get the idealised version, we get the myth, or what Carol McGuirk calls the wishful reconstruction. What characteristics are ascribed to Burns in this representation? Let me list a few: he is presented as warm, genial, a lover of freedom, a man of the people, a patriot, a drinker. He is gentle and tender, tall and handsome, and consumed with love for his fellow men, and particularly for women. He has native common sense, but on the whole he is presented as a man of feeling rather than as a thinker. 'He had a heart that was light and full of joy.' 'He never allowed his troubles to extinguish the flame of joy that burned in him and his work.' Just a wee hint of plagiarism there.

It is not only Robert Burns himself who is idealised and simplified. It is also his parents. I quote:

His father was an honest and godfearing man who worked on the land from dawn to dusk, his body bowed with labour, his spirit erect with native dignity and firm integrity.

We can see that certain key Scottish stereotypes have been formed around Robert Burns. This representation of his father, William Burnes, describes him as concealing

a wealth of affection beneath a craggy exterior, [he] brought up his family of boys and girls in reverence for God, respect for the law, desire for education and love of independence.

Now I am not denying that Burns and his folks may indeed have possessed some of these qualities, but I am saying that they have been exaggerated and sentimentalised. Anything negative, difficult, unacceptable, or contradictory tends to be finessed out.

What attitudes are embodied in these representations of Burns? Briefly, attitudes of gratitude, respect, admiration, honour, even reverence, and certainly an attitude of powerful identification.

Sentimentalising tendencies

What is the general atmosphere of these representations? Again, briefly, it is an atmosphere heavy with affection, approval, and sentiment. Burns is 'a poet to touch the heart'. Incidentally, I am no stranger to this atmosphere myself nor do I deny that there is a dimension of Burns that evokes it. At the weekend I reread 'The Cotter's Saturday Night', a poem redolent of these idealising and sentimentalising tendencies, and when I came to the last three stanzas I was so deeply touched that I started to cry. Let me not mock this response, but let me not fail, either, to wonder what it means.

Incidentally, I shall just throw in here what Carol McGuirk says about Burns's own contribution to this idealising process:

> Burns is always Scotland's poet ... the Immortal Memory is a recollection of a vanished Scotland that never was ... a selective and nostalgic construction of the poet's powerful imagination.

Cheeky besom, eh?

Moving on, then, what is the method used in these representations? In brief: eloquence, eulogy, extravagant praise, stereotyping, as I have already said, but also censorship, or, to put it less negatively, intentional selective systematic omission of certain facts and features of Burns's life and work. And, because of the shortness of time, this indignity that has been visited upon me, I shall tell you now that the main things that are omitted are sex, politics, and personality. Sex is the easy one to remember and we shall return to it soon. As markers for the other two, you might like to hold in mind this quotation from Walt Whitman:

> Do I contradict myself?/Very well then I contradict myself,/I am large, I contain multitudes.

That applies to Burns too. And this from G. Ross Roy:

> Censorship applied to passages which might give offence either for political or social reasons ... cleansing literature of passages which were obscene or sexually descriptive.

Before we go on to look at some of these contradictions, let us briefly ask why the myth has been created and sustained and let me put a hypothesis to you. I cannot prove this, or, rather, I am not right now in a position to assemble the evidence, but believe me, there is plenty of it. As one intellectual friend said to another: 'What's your evidence for that?' And the other replied: 'Who needs evidence?' Quite right too. We must not let empiricism get in the way of serious thinking. But I digress. The hypothesis is this. Burns hated hypocrisy. He hated respectability. As Catherine Carswell said in her biography of him,

> He was hemmed in by gentility, and it nearly drove him mad.

Respectabilification

Yet the poor sod had hardly breathed his last when the process of sanitising and respectabilification got under way. You may puzzle over this word respectabilification. You will not find it in any dictionary. I confess that it is a Kirkwoodian neologism. I have been forced into inventing it by this outrageous pressure of time which has been visited upon me. But to our tale and to cut a long hypothesis short, the whole of the 19th century was basically devoted to creating a respectable version of Robert Burns. The irony of it: the holy beagles, the lads in black and all their running dogs whom he had so mercilessly satirised in his lifetime got hold of his story and reinvented it. To put it prosaically, in the words of G. Ross Roy:

> The 19th and 20th century editor saw no impropriety in cleansing the mouth of Scotia's bard.

In fact, it is a bit more complex than that. It is a bit like Freud's theorisation of dreams, when he argues that the manifest dream is a compromise formation, partly representing and partly concealing the latent dream thoughts, which are, of course, entirely about sex. For manifest dream here, read the Burns myth as it has developed.

Now – talk about the return of the repressed – I know that you really want to get on to the sex bit, but I ask you to restrain your impulses in that direction, because I want to say something about these contradictions in Burns that I was talking about.

And one thing I forgot: the very appearance of Burns has been misrepresented. The Nasmyth and Skirving portraits show him as tall, strikingly handsome and elegantly dressed. His head is fine, and he is really rather dishy. But this is how his servant Willie Clark, who worked for Burns around 1789–90, when Burns was 31, described him:

> a working man, with his broad blue bonnet, drab, old-fashioned long-tailed coat, corduroy breeks, dark blue stockings and woollen leggings to keep the mud off his shoes, and in winter, his black and white checked plaid.

And here is Walter Scott's observation of him:

> His person was strong and robust: his manners rustic … a sort of dignified plainness and simplicity. His countenance was more massive than it looks in many of the portraits. I would have taken the poet for a very sagacious country farmer … There was a strong expression of sense and shrewdness. The eye … was large, of dark cast, and glowed … when he spoke with feeling or interest.

Others used words like coarse, rough, and black to describe him.

External contradictions

Now, we shall get to the sex in a minute. You really do need to cultivate a capacity to restrain and sublimate these drives that are pressing towards instant gratification. Contradiction, conflicts, tensions, this is what I am on about. And not just contradictions within Burns, though there were plenty of those, but also the dialectics of the outer world and how they interacted with his own internal tensions. Let us list some of these external contradictions.

First, the old unindustrialised countryside, the runrig system, dominated by the weather, with shortages recurrent and famine always a possibility. All of that, versus the new improved farming, with the enclosure of fields, building of roads and dykes, and growing of hedges, the liming and draining of the land, the growing of crops for the beasts so that they would not die in winter. Burns and his father William and his brother Gilbert were 100 per cent supporters of the new methods. Burns's lifetime was the period of implementation of this agricultural revolution. But the land they worked, on the farms of which they were tenants, in every instance remained poor. You were lucky to leave the tenancy of such a farm without substantial debt.

Second, the dialectic of local rural life, industrialisation and urbanisation. Burns really exemplifies in his own life an early version of this process out of which modern Scottish urban society was born: the moves from farming at Lochlie, to Mossgiel and finally to Ellisland, before the transition to the vennels of urban Dumfries to be a gauger, or excise officer, which was a sort of 18th century VAT man, whose job was to go round and gauge or measure how much value certain workers had added to the raw materials by their efforts. By no means a popular role.

Third, an important socio-cultural contradiction deeply entrenched in Scottish society at least since the Reformation. Calvinist Puritanism versus peasant earthiness. It is wrong to polarise Burns excessively in relation to this theme. I have this feeling that he really loved Holy Willie. He could not have portrayed him so accurately if he had not empathised with him so deeply, particularly with his need for concealment. If I were ever writing a play about Burns, I would have him address Holy Willie in the following terms, in French of course: 'hypocrite fornicateur, mon semblable, mon frère.' In fact we know that by Burns's day the intensity and dominance of Calvinism had lessened somewhat: the 18th century had seen a great revival in dancing, and the old peasant practices of cohabitation and bundling had never altogether disappeared. This conflict, of course, lives on in Scottish life, right now. It has deep roots and is full of contradictions. It is not a matter of good versus evil.

Contradictions within Burns

Turning our attention now to the contradictions in Burns himself, let him speak first:

> My worst enemy is moi-meme. I lie so miserably open to the inroads and incursions of a mischievous, light-armed, well-mounted banditti, under the banners of Imagination, Whim, Caprice and Passion; and the heavy-armed veteran regulars of Wisdom, Prudence and Forethought move so very, very slow that I am almost in a state of perpetual warfare, and alas! frequent defeat.

Let me quote here the last stanza of a beautiful song, 'The winter it is past':

> Oh ye that are in love and cannot it remove,
> I pity you the pains you endure;
> For experience makes me know that your hearts are full of woe,
> A woe that no mortal can cure.

The persona addressing lovers here is strikingly different from that of the ram-stam boy, or the narrator of Tam O'Shanter.

Thomas Crawford puts it like this:

> a mind in motion, giving itself over at different times to conflicting principles and feelings: they mirror that mind as it grapples with a complex world. Burns had to be, in himself, and not simply in play, both Calvinist and anti-Calvinist, both fornicator and champion of chastity, both Jacobite and Jacobin, both local and national, both British and European, both anarchist and sober calculator, both philistine and anti-philistine.

Kenneth Simpson sums it up as 'complexity and even multiplicity of self', drawing our attention to manic, depressive, and anxious trends in Burns's character. He goes on to argue that it was this feature of Burns that made him master of voice and persona:

> Burns lived in various worlds simultaneously. His chameleon nature and charismatic personality made this possible ... Burns became trapped behind the personae which he had so readily created.

And Simpson concludes on a national note:

> If since 1707 Scots have been uncertain as to their identity, then it is understandable that they should worship a poet who had such a gift for creating voices and personae. But the poet himself paid a price.

I want to link together a small number of conflicts in Burns's nature and behaviour:
- the tension between terse, concrete and sometimes deflating language, and inflating verbose pomposity
- the tension between the satisfaction of sexual urges and the development of sustained personal relationships
- the tension between sublimation and uninhibitedness
- the tension between puritanism and libertarianism
- the tension between social responsibility and its opposite, represented by, for example, 'The jolly beggars'
- the tension between friendship and ferocious flyting
- the tension between intense sociability, and enjoyment of solitude.

We tend to think of Burns as extroverted, gregarious and assertive, but Edwin Morgan writes:

> There is another Burns, not the extravert, but something more strange, more mysterious, more secret.

Shame and pride

Finally, I want to draw attention to what seems to me a core underlying tension in Burns: between pride and daring assertiveness, on the one hand, and concealed shame, on the other. You may think this surprising, and even want to deny it. So I think did Burns. He found it difficult to cope with. But he was to some degree aware of it, and it not only underlies some of his difficulties but also is one of the key factors in explaining our identification with him.

A sense of shame is a pervasive human experience. It goes with culture, in the anthropological sense: it is linked with humiliation, for example, the humiliation of poverty. Gavin Sprott, in his monograph entitled *Robert Burns: Farmer*, gives us a clue as to the possible origins of this feature in his picture of the Burns family living on the farm at Mount Oliphant when Robert was aged 6 to 18 years old, which Sprott describes as probably the hardest period of Burns's life. The land was wretched. It was unimproved. They had no servants. The boys, Robert and Gilbert, were doing men's work. Burns captures an aspect of the humiliations involved in *The twa dogs: a tale:*

Poor tenant-bodies, scant o cash
How they maun thole a factor's snash.
He'll stamp and threaten, curse and swear
He'll apprehend them, poind their gear,
While they maun stand, wi aspect humble
An hear it a', and fear and tremble.

I hypothesise that this concealed and largely denied sense of shame is what fires Burns's pride, his independent-mindedness, the spirited bravery of 'a man's a man for a' that', and his recurrent need to make risky statements that got him into trouble. It had another effect which was self-destructive. His pride frequently led him to conceal his financial difficulties, even from close friends. The simplest illustration of this theme relates to his collaboration with George Thomson. Burns played a pivotal part in the creation of three important collections of Scottish songs. The first, in collaboration with James Johnson, produced *A Scots Musical Museum.* The second, with George Thomson, produced *A Select Collection of Original Scottish Airs.* The point I want to make is this: Burns did a huge amount of creative work. He discovered tunes and words, or else Thomson would send them to him. He wrote new verses or improved on the verses he found. Lesser poets than Burns were paid well for their writing. It is said that an Irish songster of the same period was paid 100 guineas per song. Thomson volunteered at the outset of their collaboration to pay Burns 'any reasonable price you shall be pleased to demand'. Burns replied:

in the honest enthusiasm with which I embark in your undertaking, to talk of money, wages, fee, hire, etc would be downright Sodomy of the Soul!

He disdained even to discuss payment. Yet he was frequently in debt, anxious about money and in increasingly ill-health. Here was a man, of peasant origin, with no inherited wealth, who earned what income he had by hard work, was never comfortably off, and too proud, independent, and, I suppose I would say, grandiose, to look realistically at his financial position and seek payment for the astonishing contribution he was making. All Burns got for these seminal collections of songs was a few free copies of the books when they came out.

Censorship and eroticism

Now you will want to know what the third collection of songs was. It was not published in his lifetime, but the songs were mostly written or rewritten by Robert Burns. I started by mentioning that the sanitising of Burns began as soon as he died. His exploitation began sooner. A rascally banker managed to persuade the dying Burns, who was anxious to provide for his wife and family, to sell him his third collection of songs for £50. The document then disappeared, surfacing about 20 years later when it was published as the first of many versions of *The Merry Muses of Caledonia.* This was not Burns's title, but it is the one that has stuck. His first biographer, Dr James Currie, began this particular bit of misrepresentation by inserting a misleading sentence into a letter from Burns in which he says of these songs: 'A very few of them are my own.' If you read *The Merry Muses,* you will see that, to adapt a suitable phrase, the hands of Robert Burns are all over them.

The omission of these songs from the published collections of his works throughout the 19th century, and even into the 20th century is the main instance of censorship and misrepresentation. And believe me it is major. Even now, for example, if you look through James Mackay's bicentenary edition of *The Complete Poetical Works,* you will find that the erotic versions of *Green grow the rushes o* and *Duncan Gray* are still omitted.

Catherine Carswell says:

> Burns fought the stultifying influence of anti-sexual protestantism in Scotland by collecting and improving the bawdy songs of the peasants he loved and of whom he was one.

If you have not read them, I encourage you to start tomorrow. A new edition has recently been published. Many of the great Burns songs you know have parallel erotic versions. Frequently both are equally good: *Green grow the rushes o, The ploughman, John Anderson my jo, Coming thro' the rye,* and *Duncan Gray.* Other works in *The Merry Muses* which have no parallel version but are still outstanding are *The court of equity, Nine inch will please a lady, Ode to spring,* and *Madgie cam to my bed stock.* They are all stimulating, bouncing with vitality, joyful and sexually explicit. Burns's recurring preoccupations are with the male and female genitals and (I have chosen this phrase with care) the interpersonal actions involved in intercourse. He wrote a short preamble to the collection, which goes like this:

> Say, Puritan, can it be wrong
> To dress plain truth in pretty song?

What honest Nature says we should do
And every lady does, or would do.

He has a rich store of words for the male organ: pintle, pillie, plenipotentiary, solemn league and covenant, staunin graith, tail-tree, and cutty gun. He tends to exaggerate the length of this particular member: he clearly wants to establish nine inches as the norm, and when he gets carried away he adds 'twa thumb-breadths' and concludes: 'and that's a sonsie pintle!'

The female organ rejoices in such names as maukin, tirlie whirlie, yellow yorlin, needle ee, canister, nest, gyvel, and tail.

The verbs for intercourse are to roger, to mowe, to nidge, to ding, and to dunt. The noun, of course, is houghmagandie.

It is impossible to read these poems and songs without delight and a realisation that they form a core part of Robert Burns's contribution to the rehumanising, indeed the re-embodiment, of human culture.

CONCLUSION: THE DISSOCIATION OF SENSIBILITY

In conclusion, I want to refer to T. S. Eliot's idea of the dissociation of sensibility, and suggest a new slant on it. You will remember that Eliot argued in *The Sacred Wood* that a dissociation occurred in British culture in the 17th and 18th centuries, separating thinking from feeling. He thought it happened some time after the work of John Donne, who, according to Eliot, felt his thought like the odour of a rose. I have always found this idea to have a profound resonance. Edwin Muir, in *Scott and Scotland,* tried to develop a specifically Scottish application of it, arguing that the Scots are crippled because they think in English and feel in Scots. I think Muir was onto something important, but did not get it quite right. I am suggesting that we bring this idea of the dissociation of sensibility to bear both on the work of Robert Burns and on the subsequent idealization and misrepresentation of it.

My view is that Burns at his best struggles to sense, feel, think and speak in an integrated way, in a way that is true both to himself and to the thematics of his society as he perceived it. But he has subsequently been represented, and to be fair, sometimes represented himself, as a man of feeling, a notion he got from Henry Mackenzie, author of the book of that name. Thus he got caught up in the Scottish version of this British dissociation of sensibility which ended up a hundred years later in the couthy, sanitised, desexualised sentimentality of the kailyard.

The really important dissociation or split in which Burns was trammeled up and with which he wrestled, was the split between socially acceptable sentiment combined with common-sense or practical wisdom, on the one hand, and earthy, vital, bawdy eroticism married to irreverent, pugnacious and very thoughtful challenges to the excesses of hypocritical Puritanism, on the other. Burns fought Scottish respectability to the death. To his own death. He also, unintentionally, helped to give birth to the 19th century version of it. Certainly, as soon as he died, it reasserted its supremacy. But other libertarian puritans rose up internationally to follow Burns and fight the Burns myth: William Blake, Walt Whitman, Sigmund

Freud, D.H. Lawrence, Carl Rogers, and now our younger generation of Scottish writers: Jackie Kay, Christopher Whyte and James Robertson.

I invite you, then, to toast the memory of our great bawdy poet, our great poet of the body: what he celebrated really is immortal, in the sense that it survives repeated attempts to conceal or even bury it.

The immortal memory of Robert Burns!

NOTES

[1] The plagiarised passages describing Robert Burns's father, William Burnes, are taken from Jack Masterton's undated booklet, *Speaking of Burns*, published by Macdonald.

[2] The quotations from Carol McGuirk, G. Ross Roy, Kenneth Simpson and Edwin Morgan are all taken from Kenneth Simpson's book *Burns Now*, cited below.

REFERENCES/BIBLIOGRAPHY

Carswell, C. (1930). *The life of Robert Burns.* London: Chatto & Windus.

Crawford, T. (1960). *Burns: A study of the poems and songs.* Harlow: Oliver & Boyd.

Eliot, T. S. (1960). *The sacred wood: Essays on poetry.* London: Methuen. New York: Barnes & Noble.

Freud, S. (1976). *The interpretation of dreams, Pelican Freud Library 4.* London: Penguin.

Harkin, M. (Ed.) (2005). *The man of feeling: Henry McKenzie.* Toronto: Broadway Editions.

Mackay, J. (Ed.) (1993). *Robert Burns: The complete poetical works.* Darvel: Alloway.

Masterton, J. (undated). *Speaking of Burns.* Macdonald (source of the plagiarised passages describing Burns's father William Burnes).

McIntyre, I. (1996). *Dirt and deity: A life of Robert Burns.* London: Flamingo.

Muir, E. (1936). *Scott and Scotland.* London: Routledge & Kegan Paul.

Randall, E. (Fd.) (1966). *The merry muses and other Burnsian frolics.* London: Luxor Press.

Simpson, K. (Ed.) (1994). *Burns now.* Edinburgh: Canongate Academic.

Sprott, G. (1990). *Robert Burns: Farmer.* Edinburgh: National Museums of Scotland.

Whitman, W. (1960). *Leaves of grass.* New York: Signet, New American Library of World Literature.

CHAPTER 10

SCOTLAND AS A LEARNING SOCIETY

Identity, Difference, and Relatedness

Key words and themes: learning society, relatedness, paranoid schizoid position, depressive position, splitting, projection, introjection, idealisation, intellectualisation, mass projections, socio-cultural factors of identity, being part of a learning project wider than ourselves, dependence, independence, interdependence, difference, partnership between equal nations, self-government, learning relations.

This paper was first presented as a contribution to the conference Scotland as a Learning Society: Issues of Culture and Identity, at the University of Edinburgh in February 1995. It was first published as *Occasional Papers Series: No. 9* by the Centre for Continuing Education, University of Edinburgh in 1996.

INTRODUCTION

Ever since I was asked to contribute to this conference, I have struggled over how to link the theme of identity, difference and relatedness to Scotland as a learning society. Much as I would like to shift the blame on to the conference organisers, I am not in a strong position to do so, since I suggested the theme myself. In that moment of insight, identity difference and relatedness seemed, and still seem, to me at any rate, the key to a whole range of concerns.

I should say in my own defence that I am a practising counsellor and psychotherapist working with individuals, couples and groups, and involved also in the training of counsellors and the use of counselling approaches in other settings. The orientation to which I adhere is known as personal relations theory. It takes the view that we can best understand or help people by attending to the multiplicity of relationships they, and we, have experienced and internalised throughout their, and our, lives.

But first, back to the learning society. Like many colleagues here today, I have worked as an organiser of adult learning throughout my adult life. 30 years ago, adult learning barely figured in the broad canvas of education. We had schools full of children, and colleges and universities full of people in their late teens and early twenties. Only a small number of adults engaged in learning in any visible way through extra mural departments, or the WEA, or night school classes. The mature student was a rarely sighted breed.

Now all that has changed. Popular demand and central government intervention have ensured that colleges, universities, and even some schools welcome adult students of all ages. I want to refer briefly to one or two accompanying changes. There has taken place over the past 30 years a shift from the high valuation of the role of the teacher as teacher to a position where, while the importance of that role and task is not denied, the role is now increasingly conceptualised as the manager of learning resources or the facilitator of learning.

From teaching to learning

At the same time there has been a shift away from an emphasis on imbibing knowledge – books, papers, research reports, lectures – to a greater valuation of active learning and reflection upon experience, both structured and unstructured. There has been a related shift from valuing cognition alone to the acknowledgement that emotions, feelings and even relationships have something to do with the process of knowing. All of this – which has been neither smooth nor uncontested – has contributed to a gradual shift of emphasis from teaching to learning.

The notion of the learning society dovetails with and has given succinct expression to some of these changes.

In order to establish the link with the theme of identity, difference, and relatedness, I must refer also to a shift that occurred for me personally somewhere in the mid 1970s. It had to do with becoming increasingly dissatisfied with the impersonal, large-scale and narrowly economistic thinking that had come to dominate politics. It seemed to me – and I know to many others – that human beings, their dignity, their perceptions, their consciences, their feelings, their capacity for both self-reliance and mutual aid, their very existence as persons in relation to other persons, had largely got lost sight of. It was this that led me in the direction of the work of Paulo Freire. He had developed, in Brazil and Chile, what he called his psycho-social method. This emphasised that people should be treated as subjects, not objects, that they had important things to say about the situations in which they lived their lives, and could have key roles in co-determining their own learning programmes and naming and investigating their own themes. And, of course, as you know, Freire regarded himself as a personalist.

But this only takes me a little further forward towards my theme. I am still struggling to make the link.

Knowing yourself and your country

Well, two quotations have been coming into my mind, or rather one quote and one motto. I recalled from the 2nd year English class at Glasgow University in 1962 the injunction 'cognosce teipsum': know yourself. I remembered I had come across it in a book called *Silver Poets of the 16th Century*. So I dug it out and there it was: a poem called *Nosce Teipsum* by Sir John Davies. After reading the first 20 lines I realised it was not quite what I was after. Its line was: why did my parents send me to school to gain knowledge since knowledge corrupted humanity. God originally wrote the rules about being good in the minds of Adam and Eve, and they'd have done so well if they'd only stuck to those rules, but the Spirit of Lies corrupted them. He told them that when they had found out about being good, they only knew the half of it. There was an exciting something else called evil, and they didn't know anything about that! This immediately made them curious, and they found out about evil – and that was their downfall.

So I thought: that is not really the note I want to strike at all.

The other quote was from Shakespeare's *Macbeth:* Act 4, Scene 3. Malcolm and Macduff are kicking their heels outside the English court, waiting for the king to decide to give them some troops so they can go back up to Scotland and finish off Macbeth. Again they get into a deep discussion about good and evil. And they very nearly fall out when Malcolm pretends to be just as bad as Macbeth, and Macduff despairs and tells him to get lost. Malcolm then protests: I was only kidding you on, I was testing your integrity. In fact I'm totally innocent. I've never had sex, I've never told a lie in my life, I'm totally on your side. So please stay and help me to become King. At this point, in walks Ross, the messenger. In a couple of minutes he's going to tell Macduff that Macbeth has murdered his wife and children. But before he gets there, he says hello, and Macduff asks him:

Stands Scotland where it did?

and Ross replies:

Alas, poor country,
Almost afraid to know itself! It cannot
Be call'd our mother, but our grave: where nothing,
But who knows nothing, is once seen to smile;
Where sighs and groans, and shrieks, that rent the air,
Are made, not marked; where violent sorrow seems
A modern ecstasy

And so on. You get the general drift. It's good and evil again, and Scotland seems to have more than its fair share of evil. An unworthy thought crossed my mind: why did they have to go and get help from England? And a paranoid thought rapidly followed it: is this Shakespeare's unconscious anti-Scottish prejudice? And then I reminded myself: you're just trying to establish the connection between the issues of identity and difference, and the idea of a learning society, and you'd better hurry up.

What I want to say is simply this: that some of the most important learning or knowing we can do is about our own identity. And learning about identity does indeed connect with issues of good and evil.

What I want to do now, in order to ground my contribution, is to give a brief outline of the development of some psychodynamic thinking about personal identity, and then to suggest by way of examples how it has a bearing on human living and relating not only at personal and interpersonal levels, but at institutional, national, and international levels as well. So I'm putting forward some propositions about knowing yourself at a personal level, and also at societal levels.

Let me enter one caveat. I'm not implying people ought to go for counselling or psychotherapy, nor, if they do, that they ought to seek out a therapist with a particular orientation. There are a number of schools of counselling, each with its own theory and practice. Research evidence suggests they are all equally effective. And there are other ways of approaching self-knowledge. I am simply offering one set of insights.

Self and relatedness

Our thinking about the self starts off from the baby's inheritance from two sets of genes, which gives it a particular endowment, a unique constellation of qualities and potentials. But already as it develops in the womb it is impacted upon and begins to interact with its environment: its physical environment, which then is also its human environment, the living body of its mother.

Following the experience of birth, the infant is now in a different situation of physical separation from the environment that so recently contained it. There is now a physical environment, a human environment of caregivers, and there is space all round. The baby becomes aware of caregivers handling and holding and feeding and comforting it. And sometimes, of course, they're not there, and it doesn't get held or fed or comforted.

The experiences of relationships the baby has over the next few years have been characterised in various ways:
- Margaret Mahler talks about a slow process of separation and individuation.
- John Bowlby talks about the formation of attachments, and bonding, and also about what happens when these attachments aren't secure, or are broken.
- Donald Winnicott talks about what he calls the holding environment, and then about the transitional space between baby and caregiver, in which the baby begins to explore out and return to safety. He talks also about the baby's discovery or creation of a transitional object, perhaps a sheet or soft toy, which for Winnicott symbolizes the caregiver.
- Wilfred Bion talks about the caregiver, and the psychotherapist, as a container.

Daniel Stern, in his book *The Interpersonal World of the Infant*, traces the baby's progress through the first 18 months of life, starting off with an initial sense of an emergent self in a domain of emergent relatedness. There follows a sense of core self, involving awareness of being a body, with feelings and some sort of history, in a domain of core relatedness with a caregiver now experienced as a separate person, who has different feelings and a different history. Then there develops a sense of a subjective self, with awareness of mental states such as feelings, motives, and intentions, in a domain of inter-subjective relatedness. The baby can now share a focus of attention with the caregiver, can pick up other people's feelings and motives, and have a sense of being in tune or out of tune with them. Finally, there's a sense of a verbal self, from about nine months on, in a domain of verbal relatedness. The baby can now store up knowledge of self and others, and symbolise and communicate through language.

Inner and outer

Melanie Klein's (much earlier) contribution drew on her therapeutic work with adults and young children. She led the way in developing our understanding that a person's early growth, psychologically, involves a complex interaction between what goes on 'outside' and what goes on 'inside', particularly where painful, intolerable experiences are concerned. She described two positions she believed we all experience in the first year of life, positions involving feelings, anxieties, thoughts, and relationships.

The first of these she called *the paranoid schizoid position.* These strange words mean, literally, persecuted split. Klein held that in the first three to four months of life the baby was not able to be aware of the caregiver as a whole separate person. The baby, she believed, coped with bad, unbearable experiences by getting rid of them – by projecting them out of itself, and onto or into the caregiver. In doing so, it had also effectively split its bad experiences from its good experiences. That is, it kept the good experiences inside, and expelled the bad ones. But this defensive manoeuvre caused more problems than it solved. Because it had put the bad feelings out into the caregiver, the baby now experienced the caregiver as bad, and by, as it were, taking in or experiencing the caregiver as bad, got the bad experiences back inside anyway. So, in a sense, things just went from bad to worse.

Whenever I try to explain Klein's ideas they come across as speculative, fantastic, and highly improbable. However, what I'd ask you to try and hold on to here is the picture of a recently born baby literally not knowing what's going on, lacking language, having had some very unpleasant experiences, for example with wind or hunger or thirst or other distress, trying to cope with these experiences, and using psychological processes of projection and introjection in its relationship with its caregiver as ways of somehow coping or managing.

The second position Klein describes belongs more to the second six months of life. She thinks the baby can now recognise the caregiver as a whole, separate, other person. It is still, of course, pretty helpless and dependent on its caregiver, and may still have a whole range of painful, distressing experiences. She believes the baby now realizes that the caregiver, who sometimes feeds when feeding is needed or comforts when comforting is needed, who 'tunes in', is the same person as the one who fails to feed, or fails to comfort, who is missing or who doesn't 'tune in' accurately with where the baby is at. And the baby now can experience ambivalent feelings towards the caregiver. She calls this *the depressive position.*

Klein believed that these two basic positions in some sense continue to be available to us throughout our lives and that we move back and forward from one to the other, sometimes processing our current relationships and experiences in a paranoid schizoid sort of way, sometimes in a depressive sort of way.

Defensive processes in personal development

Enough of Melanie Klein! Anna Freud, on the other hand, gives us a much simpler account of how the growing child coped with painful experiences whether these were traumas originating from the outside, being assaulted or abandoned for example, or internal experiences, like having feelings and wishes which were so unacceptable to the child that its anxiety went through the roof.

She describes what she calls mechanisms of defence, which we might nowadays be more comfortable calling ways of coping with unbearable situations. These defences involve denying the existence of all or part of our intolerable experiences, and often repressing them, that is, involuntarily pushing them out of our awareness and keeping them there.

The specific defences she describes include *splitting, projection, introjection, idealisation, turning against the self, intellectualisation, reaction formation, undoing*, and so on.

Before giving some examples of these defensive processes, let me add that we think of them not only as defensive, but also sometimes as positively developmental, specific ways in which we, as individuals, organise our selves, structure our identities. Our identities are formed in the ways we shape our responses to both internal and external events and to the significant others in our lives.

Let's take splitting first. Splitting is an early, fundamental, and pretty universal process. Splitting is a way, for example, of dealing with the intolerable experience of hating the person you also need and love. You need to keep the loved person good, so you split off the bad bit and see it in somebody else. Now you've got one wholly good person and another dreadfully bad person (who may be you), and this way of seeing can override any evidence that the truth about either person is more complex. Or it may involve splitting the self, for example, into one bit that can manage life okay and get along, and another bit that is desperately hurt and vulnerable and mustn't be seen.

Or maybe there's a split-off bit of yourself that is very rejecting and punishing which again you may need to conceal or may not be aware of at all, till it jumps out and hits somebody.

We think of splitting as involving repression, but it can also sometimes be a dissociative process in which there are two distinct, but conscious characters or sub-selves: and the person seems to switch from one to another.

Projection and introjection

Projection is also very early and universal. Here the bad or unwanted quality is put into a significant other person and, as it were, disowned. I was thinking about this a few weeks ago, reading about the death of the playwright John Osborne. We learned from the obituaries that Osborne, who presented himself as heterosexual, had a continuing homosexual relationship with a male friend throughout his life, which he kept secret. But he made periodic vitriolic public attacks on homosexuality. He split it off, projecting it out into others where he proceeded to attack it.

Introjection is another basic process that has been insufficiently acknowledged as central to the growth of our identities. In this process we take in qualities, atmospheres, states of feeling, injunctions, and ways of relating, from our caregivers and make them parts of ourselves. Let me give you an example from my son Paul's development when he was about a year old. We were living in Italy and while I was out teaching my wife used to go across the landing with Paul and spend time with the old lady and her two daughters in the next flat. She had potted plants all round the walls in her living room, on the floor. On the first occasion – I wasn't present – Paul must have gone up to one of the plants, or maybe more, and picked it up by the leaves. The next time I was there I watched him going up to several of the plants one after the other – and we have a photograph to prove this – bending forwards and with a serious and forbidding expression on his face, shaking his finger at it.

What he had done was very significant. He had taken in or introjected the experience of an older person – Signora Marcuzzo or my wife – wagging her finger at him and forbidding him verbally to touch the plants. He had got the message, and identified with her telling him off, and then proceeded to tell off the plants. So, he introjected and identified with the authority figure, and projected the victim experience into the plants. This can also be taken as an example of what Anna Freud described as identification with the aggressor.

You will have recognised by now that these defensive processes cannot really be examined in isolation. They tend to be interconnected. A pattern unique to the individual person is established in each of us.

A brief word about some of the other defences. The process of idealisation of someone is well known to us, as is its opposite: rubbishing and denigrating someone. Turning against the self is a way of protecting a loved or needed person from one's angry feelings towards them. Reaction formation is experiencing, often in an exaggerated form, a feeling opposite to the one it conceals. You may have had the experience of expressing gratitude towards someone to whom you don't feel grateful at all, deep down. Undoing is about washing the blood from your hands.

Intellectualisation is very common in universities as you might expect. It is a defence against experiencing feelings or vulnerabilities or at least against letting other people know you have them.

I could go on. The point is we all do these things. If we didn't have our defences, our ways of coping, we would be quivering wrecks. Each person's identity comprises a unique and complex building-up over the years, from birth to the present, of an entire structure comprising their personality.

Socio-cultural factors in identity

So far, we have discussed identity as if it were a purely personal thing, or more precisely, an intra- and inter-personal thing. And so, in its early origin, it is. For

139

me, there is no denying the significance of those early patterns of relating, feeling, and coping laid down in the first few years of life. But it is essential to acknowledge also the impact of other wider sets of interactions with brothers and sisters, uncles and aunts, grannies and grandpas, the peer group, teacher, the school class, adult friends, workmates, mentors and partners, and the impact of the wider environment, physical, cultural, and social. It's clear that issues of language, for example, are very significant for personal identity because language, although personally learned, is culturally shared. Again the impact of the physical environment, whether built or natural, is considerable, and interacts with the impact of the common culture of the locality in which we live and the wider cultures of social class, gender, ethnic group, region, the nation, continent, and world, as these are mediated both in direct interpersonal, group, and institutional ways, and through the media: the TV in the living room is a factor in shaping personal identity.

I also take the view that our identity is impacted upon, not only by the totality of our present cultural context, but also that of the historic past, which is alive and active in the present in a host of ways. Clearly matters now begin to get extremely complex. The task of tracing and understanding one's own identity if one is, for example, a working class woman growing up in a housing scheme in Dundee, whose parents have lived in Dundee all their lives, is complicated enough, given the unique interactive vagaries of the individual psyche. But tracing and understanding one's identity is maybe an even more daunting undertaking if one has complex, multiple roots. Or is that a mistaken assumption?

Take a fictional example of a 30 year old woman, brought up in London, whose parents were Ugandan Asians driven out by Idi Amin, and whose grandparents came from India. Suppose this woman goes to university in Coleraine and marries a working class Ulster protestant whose parents have disowned him? Is it going to be harder or easier for her to get a steady sense of herself, than it is for him? Maybe she is, in fact, a relatively simple person.

Where and what is home?

Or what if you are like me, a middle class child born and living in Scotland whose parents always went 'home', as they put it, to Belfast every summer, and you were left wondering exactly where 'home' is, and exactly what 'home' means? Where do you fit in, what language is really yours, which class, tribe, or group do you really belong to? Do you belong at all? Or are you an outsider looking in at everybody else's feast? Do you belong to a culture because it claims you, because you find yourself immersed and saturated in it? I was talking recently with a woman colleague at work and I was speaking with some feeling about the importance of the rock from whence you were hewn – meaning your family and culture of origin – when she rounded on me, again with strong feeling, and said: and what if the rock from whence you were hewn is lying on top of you, crushing the life out of you? I really had no answer for that. There is a connection to be made here with what Donald Winnicott calls the 'true self' – that secret person I really am, deriving from my potential self – and its relationship to the false self which I present to the world for protective purposes. We all have a false self, to some degree, but the question is perhaps how it connects with our true self. Everybody has to decide for themselves whether or not they want to 'take on' their life, to interrogate it, investigate it, trace their roots and evaluate them, work on themselves – and if so, how they do it. This is entirely a matter for each of us.

What I am arguing is that whether we are looking at our personal selves, or our relationships – marriages, personal partnerships, work relationships – or our history; or whether we are looking at a nation, a whole country and the history of its relations with neighbouring countries; or the desirability of thinking of Scotland now as a learning society – this Scotland, the Scotland that is trying to figure out whether to continue in the present Union with England, or go for devolution, or go for political independence either inside or outside the European Union – the Scotland that is trying to figure out what is going on in Ireland right now, or what is going on in England right now; when we are carrying out *any* of these identity-related[1] enquiries, I am arguing that we will find it useful to identify ways in which the defensive, coping processes involved in the early formation of an individual person's identity are at work, in amplified, exaggerated, large-scale, and potentially very dangerous ways.

From a closed to a more open system

In counselling and psychotherapeutic work, whether with individuals, couples or groups, the therapist works in a facilitative and largely non-directive way in order to help people explore the painful feelings, inner conflicts and relationships they are experiencing. The hope is that by staying with and working through the painful experiences and the defences they have constructed to manage them, they will be able to accept and integrate some of the split-off, projected and repressed parts of themselves. We can call it making the unconscious conscious, we can call it taking back the projections, we can call it the integrative process. We can emphasise the therapeutic effect of the relationship. Jock Sutherland speaks of the person moving from being a relatively closed system to being more of an open system, capable of receiving feedback and adapting. And of course Sutherland believed that these insights should not be confined to the relatively narrow world of psychoanalysis, but should be made available throughout society, through counselling, couple work, community psychiatry, through the professional training of social workers and nurses, through organisational consultancy, and so on. He believed that we all need to be part of a learning project that is larger than ourselves.

If we become able to take back some of our projections, and accept and reintegrate some of the disowned parts of ourselves, we are, in that very process, becoming more aware of our own identity, and have a more rooted sense of ourselves. This has two incidental effects. One is that we are more able to *experience* significant other persons as they are in themselves, as other real unique complex persons, and less as screens or coathangers for our own projections, our split-off bits that can't be tolerated. The other is that we are more able to *relate* to

141

others as they are. We are less suspicious, less withdrawn, less defensively covered-up.

This kind of self-knowledge can be thought of as internally freeing or liberating, but also as reconciling since it is about resolving conflicts. Sutherland gives the example of Mahatma Ghandi as a man who struggled with his own severe inner conflicts and with those of his society, India, both in terms of its anti-imperialist struggle with Great Britain, and the endemic conflict between Muslim and Hindu.

Taking back the projections

Let me now try and give some examples of how these human relations insights might have a bearing on our wider society. I don't need to remind you that whole nations tend to project certain negative qualities on to other nations. You know about Irish jokes in Britain, about Newfie jokes in Canada, and jokes about catholics in Ayrshire. I heard recently that the Germans make jokes about Norwegians. These jokes involve socially shared projections, and it is easy to identify which qualities are usually projected: stupidity, animality, ugliness, dirtiness, laziness, sexuality, incompetence, unreliability, badness, incapacity for self-government, lack of responsibility, and so on.

It is interesting how almost all of them involve some sense of comparison, of ranking, higher and lower, superior and inferior, how they involve getting rid of what are felt to be unacceptable qualities, and in general involve the creation of *included* and *excluded* groups.

Nor do I need to remind you of the most horrific mass projection of the 20th century and possibly of all time: the projection of all the negative human qualities onto or into the Jews in particular, and what that led to. And how, incidentally, we would all prefer to think it was the Germans and specifically the Nazis who projected these qualities into the Jews. Of course it was the Nazis who organised the so-called final solution, but a cursory glance at most literature written before 1940 shows that it was a widespread, almost a universal, projection.

When I address myself now to the respective situations of Scotland and Northern Ireland, as potential learning societies, I am full of hope, and an equal amount of anxiety.

Let's take the Irish situation first. Coming as I do from Ulster Protestant folk, and being married to a woman from Donegal Catholic folk, I regard the current initiative as the most hopeful and significant political development of my adult life. I recognize the therapeutic work of the reconciler, John Hume, and I only wish he could have some secret talks with Ian Paisley and David Trimble. I know at a personal level the projections involved here: Catholics are different, dirty, they breed like rabbits, are lazy, untrustworthy, lacking in what is called gumption, and live off the state. As a child I sometimes did believe you could tell a Catholic by the look in their eyes, a view that was universally shared in Ayrshire in the 1950s among Protestant children. Now as an adult I puzzle and listen for clues, I wonder about the meaning of words, I notice the contradictions. I hear Protestants insisting they are British, and I know that they mean it. How ironic it is that fewer and fewer people in Scotland, where many of them originated, feel British now. I hear the words Sinn Fein, ourselves alone, and the Protestant motto, quis separabit. I think – yes, this sense that I can be totally independent, we can do it ourselves, we don't need the treacherous Brits. And quis separabit I suppose comes from who will separate us from the love of God which is in Christ Jesus – but it must also mean, who will separate us from mainland Britain. We're British. And then I remember these same British Ulstermen and women singing Irish rebel songs in the 1950s and 60s when I was a boy. And I puzzle again over the fact that their voices and their home and hearth values are the same as those of the Catholics we know in Donegal. I remember my Northern Irish Methodist granny talking about going up to Dublin, up to the capital, and making it clear that she had no difficulty with the idea of Ireland being one country. I remember that my father left partly because he hated the sectarianism. And I remember hearing about the heresy trial in the 30s, when the liberal Presbyterian Principal Davey was tried for heresy in an ecclesiastical court by the fundamentalists, and whose son Ray (my father's best friend at university) founded the Corymeela Community which is dedicated to reconciliation.

Dependence, independence, interdependence

And I think about Tom Leonard's attempts to get to grips with this intractable difference. He spoke about insistent dependence that he linked with the catholic pole and insistent independence linked with the protestant pole. And I remember his poem in which the Glasgow woman says

ahm thaht depehhhhndint
hingoanti ma vowwwwulz
hingoanti ma maaaammi

howz thi time

ma manz thaht diffffrint
awfa shoart vowwwwulz
hizthaht indipehhhhndint

ahl bettr away

And I think about Tom Lovett saying: you know, that's true, this thing about dependence and independence, but it's also the opposite: in practice, the protestant working class is very dependent on authority figures, and relatively less likely to think for themselves, and organise themselves independently, and on the other hand catholic working class people, subjected though they are to the patriarchal authoritarian structure of Irish Catholicism, are much more willing and able to think for themselves, for example, on contraception, and much freer to organise independently at community level.

143

There are massive processes of splitting and mutual projection going on here, with deep-seated accompanying fear and mistrust. I am hoping, perhaps naively, that the up-and-coming generation will begin to be able to take back some of these projections and see themselves as – on both sides – vulnerable and dependent creatures capable of growing together towards a mature interdependence, with increased capacity for communication and an acknowledgement of the virtues and values – the difference – of both sides.

I see a different version of the same conflict going on in Scotland. Here we have seen, in the last 20 years, the cultural fruits of efforts to be true to ourselves, to home in on our roots, and have the courage and confidence to innovate, in Scottish music, painting, poetry, drama, short stories, novels, films, the recognition and valuing of Gaelic, and urban working class Scots, the courageous abolition of the self-inflicted pain of belting – an obvious example surely of giving up one crucial identification with the aggressor.

Autonomy, relatedness and self-government

We can acknowledge also the efforts that have been made to throw off the bogus identity of Britishness that has been foisted on us, and that we participated in creating. Lesley Riddoch wrote recently in *The Scotsman* about how there seemed to be no way of getting out of the bullying game of British bulldogs in her Ulster protestant playground. I myself have a recollection of a similar kind. Perhaps others here today can remember the book *Geordie* that circulated in the 1950s, with its innocent Scottish/British hero who chanted

> We're the good old British bulldog breed,
> And Sampson will teach us to succeed!

And we should acknowledge the symbolic significance of the work that has gone into seeking 50/50 representation of men and women in the Scottish parliament that is so heartening and really does go to the core of one of the deepest and most painful splits of all – the over-simple combing out of two sets of human characteristics and allocating one lot to women and the other lot to men, in a way that distorts the true identities of both. And may I say that, in my view, men and women really do have quite different identities: but the traditional culturally and economically imposed polarisation of qualities that involves all sorts of mutual projections and misunderstandings, misrepresents our actual identities by stereotyping them. You can't see the other as the other is, nor can you see your need for relatedness to them, in their difference, until you have taken back some of the projections, integrated some of the split-off parts and seen yourself for what you are, including your neediness and dependence.

Finally, I would like to say that I am unhappy about the emotional and relational terms in which the current debate about Scotland's political future is couched by most of our politicians. Independence versus devolution is another mutually projective system. Devolution implies a paternalistic granting of power downwards by Westminster. I don't want to be handed out our own wee Scottish bit of the myth of the crown-in-parliament to play with in Edinburgh while Daddy and Mummy do their own august and mysterious thing down there in Westminster. Nor on the other hand do I want a velvet divorce. I don't want to saw England off at Berwick. That really is a farce: pretending to be independent when everyone knows we are interdependent and becoming more interdependent with every month that passes. Fletcher of Saltoun was not opposed to some sort of union with England. The Kirk was in favour of some sort of union with England. What very few Scots wanted was an incorporating Union in which the autonomy and self-government of the one country was swallowed up in the aggrandisement of the other.

I make no apology for seeing the matter in marriage counselling terms. What is needed is not an increase in the housekeeping money, nor the patriarchal granting of the right to decide for yourself what you spend it on, and not a velvet divorce either. Once you get rid of some of the projections, and begin to get the lost bits of yourself back, you find that you don't hate them that much after all. You even begin to recognise that they're beginning to realise they've got problems of their own. What we want, what we need, is a renegotiated contract, a marriage or partnership agreement between equal nations who recognise each other as different and recognize their need for each other. A new partnership based on autonomy and relatedness is required. And we should be consulting ourselves in some detail about what bits we want to manage for ourselves and what we want to manage jointly. Let's ask your actual citizens out there what sort of self-determination and self-government they want, as if we really believed we *were* citizens.

SUMMARY

In summary, a learning society is one in which people are encouraged to engage in knowing themselves, each other and the world. It is an engagement that is both personal and interpersonal *and* societal and historical. Knowing involves not only cognition, but also emotion and relating. It is an intersubjective process that may be imagined, following Sister Doreen Grant, as involving 'learning relations'. An implication of the notion of a learning society is that learning is, somehow or other, integrated with responsible participation in society. A specific focus is proposed on learning about identity, difference and relatedness, as touching the heart of the most difficult challenge facing us as human beings: how to know our selves and our own culture, with its values and roots, yet also become a more open system, capable of knowing, communicating and collaborating with other people from other cultures, and valuing them. A parallel is suggested with marriage counselling. Contemporary examples of attempts to take on (and evade) this challenge are current developments in the relationships between the catholic and protestant communities in Northern Ireland, and between Scotland and England. The development of the capacity to be reflectively rooted in one's own culture and reciprocally open to other cultures is posed against rootless cosmopolitanism. Such inter-culturalism is seen as a necessary condition for meaningful multi-culturalism.

NOTES

[1] The term 'identity-related inquiries' is used here as shorthand for the kinds of adult learning and research involved, for example, in undertaking counselling training or personal therapy; investigations of one's own or other people's roots; studies of inter-communal and inter-cultural relationships; exploration of the factors involved in the development of self-confidence; exploration of the roles of feelings and relationships in perception, cognition and memory throughout the life cycle; investigations of how such factors as child-rearing practices, attitudes to old people, stereotyping or scapegoating interact with economic and technological factors to shape and give texture to a culture; studies of the potential contribution of psychotherapy and counselling to politics; the revitalised study of moral philosophy and literature as tools for living; and the study of transference, counter-transference, and intersubjective attunement (and lack of it) as pervasive factors in human society. In such forms of learning and enquiry there is an acknowledgement of the interplay of inner and outer worlds, and both introspection and sympathy are valued as legitimate and reliable modes of knowing, though by no means the only ones.

REFERENCES/BIBLIOGRAPHY

Alexander, P. (Ed.) (1962). *William Shakespeare: The complete works.* Everyman.
Bowlby, J. (1977). The Making and Breaking of Affectional Bonds, 1 and 2. *The British Journal of Psychiatry, 130.*
Brown, D. & Pedder, J. (1979). *Introduction to psychotherapy.* Tavistock Publications.
Bullet, G. (Ed.) (1962). *Silver poets of the sixteenth century.* Everyman.
Grant, D. (1989). *Learning relations.* Routledge.
Guntrip, H. (1971). *Psychoanalytic theory, therapy and the self.* Basic Books.
Kirkwood, G. & Kirkwood, C. (2011). *Living adult education: Freire in Scotland,* 2nd edition. Rotterdam: Sense Publishers.
Leonard, T. (1984). *Intimate voices.* Galloping Dog Press.
Mahler, M. (1972). On the first three sub-phases of the separation-individuation process. *The International Journal of Psychoanalysis, 53.*
Patrick, F., Schuller, T., et al. (1995). *Scotland as a learning society: Myth, reality and challenge.* Scottish Community Education Council.
Scharff, J. S. (1994). *The autonomous self: The work of John D. Sutherland.* Jason Aronson.
Segal, H. (1978). *Introduction to the work of Melanie Klein.* Hogarth Press.
Stern, D. (1985). *The interpersonal world of the infant: A view from psychoanalysis and developmental psychology.* Basic Books.
Sutherland, J. D. (1989). *Fairbairn's journey into the interior.* Free Association Books.
Winnicott, D. (1988). *Playing and reality.* Penguin.

SECTION V

APPLYING THE PERSONS IN RELATION PERSPECTIVE IN ADULT EDUCATION AND ADULT LEARNING

CHAPTER 11

CHALLENGING EDUCATION, CREATING ALLIANCES

The Legacy of Paulo Freire in the 21ˢᵗ Century

Key words and themes: the limits of empiricism, communication as dialogue, the culture of silence, gender and subjectivity, the high-modernising paradigm, identification with the aggressor, the community high school movement, codification and decoding, democracy and the possibility of multiculturalism, race and racism, the experience of ambiguity, anti-dialogical sectarianism, educacao popular, saper popular, poder popular, transforming the school system, integration or self-determination, citizens or degraded consumers.

This report and critical reflections on the 1991 New York conference in honour of Paulo Freire's 70ᵗʰ birthday was first published in *The Scottish Journal of Community Work and Development, Volume 3, Spring 1998.*

INTRODUCTION

When Alex Downie invited me to contribute a retrospective piece on Paulo Freire for this edition of *The Scottish Journal of Community Work and Development,* I was glad of the opportunity to reflect again on the significance of Freire's life and work. The immediate context is, of course, his death on 2 May 1997, at the age of 75. He is no longer with us in the flesh, and in that sense his work is completed. I can think of people who will be glad he is gone, and others for whom his departure, like his earlier presence, will be a matter of indifference. A prominent British professor of education once asked me why we should pay attention to a Latin American theorist. I was so astonished that I was unable to formulate a reply.

We in Britain now live in a post-imperial society recently dubbed (with unintended irony) 'Cool Britannia', in a technocratic period in which empiricism has come to dominate not only the physical sciences, where it is an appropriate orientation, but also the social sciences, where it has largely succeeded in displacing the perspectives offered by philosophy, ethics, theology, literature, history, psychoanalysis, feminism and the more imaginative versions of sociology, as a means of understanding human society and the human situation.

Not that Paulo Freire devalues the significance of empirical evidence. On the contrary, he refers repeatedly to the empirical dimensions of reality, which he regards as real and knowable through inter-subjective investigation. Freire is no subjectivist, no mystic, and no post-modernist either. He differs from the still dominant empiricist paradigm by virtue of his old-fashioned belief that there are dimensions of being human – ideas, values, cultural practices, feelings, ways of being, ways of relating – that are not reducible to empirical considerations alone.

Receipt of Alex's letter and subsequent conversations with him reminded me of an important international event which, to the best of my knowledge, went unreported in the academic journals of Cooling Britannia. This was the Institute, or Conference, held in honour of Paulo Freire's 70th birthday at the New School for Social Research in New York in December 1991. This event, to which my wife Gerri Kirkwood and I contributed, was illuminating cross-culturally and intellectually, and it had been my intention to write an account of it for publication. Pressure of other tasks had led me to set this project aside in an unfinished state, and it lay in a folder together with the original records of the event itself, until conversations with ALP workers Stan Reeves and Vernon Galloway shortly after Paulo Freire's death reminded me of its existence.

It was suggested by Stan that we should hold a wake for Freire. We agreed that a forward-looking celebration of his work might be more fitting, but the idea of a wake was not entirely inappropriate, if it could be managed in such a way as to convey the sense of a creative rising from the dead, like that of Tim in *The Ballad of Finnegan's Wake*. In Freire's case, it would be his ideas, values, and methods that would rise, into the new millennium, surviving his own mortality, just as he himself gave new life to the ideas of Aristotle, Christ, Hegel, Marx, de Chardin, Fromm, Buber, Mounier, and Kosik.

The title of the present paper incorporates that of the 1991 conference, which was *Challenging education, creating alliances.*

REPORT AND REFLECTIONS

Gerri and I were met on arrival in Manhattan by a representative of the conference steering committee who helped us make contact with our hosts Nancy Mohr and John Dichter. Nancy and Alan made our visit a pleasure, providing enjoyable meals, taking us for walks, and discussing the difficulties and achievements of the alternative high school movement, which forms an integral part of public school provision in New York. Alan and Nancy both worked as principals of these schools and we were fortunate enough to visit one of them.

We learned that Freire events had been arranged throughout the week in the New School for Social Research, in the City University of New York (CUNY) and in the private houses of senior academics. Our friend Ira Shor had arranged invitations for us to attend these events. It was good to meet Ira after corresponding with him for many years. It was also a pleasure to meet Paulo and Nita again: they had stayed with us in Edinburgh in the late 1980s during Freire's visit to the Adult Learning Projects in Edinburgh and Dundee organised by Fraser Patrick.

Dialogue or monologue?

The first event, under the title *Extension or communication revisited* (referring to the second part of Freire's early book *Education the Practice of Freedom,* first published in Chile in 1969) got the week off to a good start. Clifford Christians, who described himself as a first-generation Freirian, spoke eloquently on the theme of dialogue and the culture of silence. He outlined Freire's theory of communication, which combined elements of logic, empirical observation, consciousness of history, and dialogical relation. He emphasised that, for Freire, communication implied reciprocity: it was the encounter of subjects in dialogue. 'In the beginning was the relation,' Clifford argued, defining Freire's conception of the personal as essentially interpersonal, as opposed to the Lockean view of the self as an isolate. He reminded us of the contrast between dialogical (I – thou) and monological (I – it) communication, which Freire had taken from the work of Martin Buber. Monological communication was a feature of cultural invasion, in which the invaders imposed their ways of seeing the world on the invaded. The outcomes of such antidialogical communication were dehumanisation and the culture of silence. He emphasised that the culture of silence also existed in societies like the USA that were information-rich. Monological tools, he argued, could not break the culture of silence, and he questioned whether big media could ever be other than monological. He appeared to assume that only small-scale alternative media had the potential to be genuinely dialogical.

In his conclusion, Clifford Christians put a challenging question to Freire. In Clifford's view, only non-violent action was dialogical. The only defensible revolution was one nurtured by dialogical action and dialogical relations. Violence was morally reprehensible. Where – he wanted to know – did Paulo stand on that issue?

In his reply, Paulo commented that in the 1970s some people had argued that his ideas only applied to the third world. The Paulo Freire method had been perceived as 'a third world extravagance'. Behind this attitude, he argued, lay a sense of the superiority of the first world over the third, as well as certain feelings of guilt. There would always be cultures of silence. 'I fought with love and hate against the culture of silence. My utopia was much too utopian.'

Gender and the complexities of dialogue

The next paper was uncompromisingly entitled *The dialogics of negation: gender and subjectivity*. I thought it was one of the outstanding contributions of the week. Given by two postgraduate students of the New School for Social Research, Tracy Essoglou and Angel Shaw, it represented a profound challenge to Freire's concept of dialogue and his dualities of subject versus object, speech versus silence, and extension versus communication. According to Tracy and Angel, these dualities failed to do justice to the experience of women, which was characterised by ambiguity, self-doubt, bitterness, and self-censorship. They spoke of the complexity of that which is unspoken and that which is uncertain. We had to recognise that what we say often silences what we don't say. Women, they asserted, inhabit the domain of the mess, the inchoate, the epistemologically inadmissible. For dialogue to be more that mere rhetoric, there had to be a place for consciousness of the unsayable.

151

In women's experience, the empowerment of one person was often achieved at a considerable cost to another. Their experience was of unconscious servility: unspeakable, unthinkable, and lacking authority. For women, naming the world was not without danger. A dialogical situation was difficult to achieve.

Focusing then on subjectivity, which is central to Freire's notion of dialogue, they argued that it was partial. Individuals inhabited many subjective positions. There was a tension between identification with the 'I' (the subject/person/self) and the tenuousness of that identification. The implication of their position was that whole dimensions of subjectivity could be negated in dialogue. Nevertheless they acknowledged that among one's own kind naming the world could be empowering.

Turning to Freire's ideas about consciousness and language, and with specific reference to his concepts of naïve consciousness (Aristotle's doxa, or unsubstantiated opinion) and critical consciousness (Aristotle's logos, true knowledge, involving intentionality, investigation, and the capacity to deliberate), they argued that in the absence of the validation of a multiplicity of languages, women were obliged to speak the master's language. Language was a locus of power and servility, and subjectivity a battleground between doxa and logos. The realm of the senses (and, they might have added, of the emotions, relationships and the inner world) was rendered suspect by the triumph of rationality. In conclusion, they argued, there had to be a recognition of the validity of many languages, and an acknowledgement that women were in a constant state of defining themselves.

This remarkable paper generated enormous excitement. My only point of difference with its authors was that, in my view, their observations applied to men as well as to women.

Challenge to modernism

Manthia Diawara's paper, entitled *High-modernising and anti-modernism in African cinema,* represented another challenge to a set of ideas and political practices with which Freire has been associated, if only through his admiration for Frantz Fanon and Amilcar Cabral. Manthia's point of departure was African subjectivities, the impact of the independence achieved by African countries during the 1960s and 70s, the accompanying ideologies, and alternative ways of understanding subsequent political and cultural developments. This cluster of themes was explored with specific reference to African cinema and the politics of representation. The decolonising struggles led by such charismatic figures as Patrice Lumumba, Sekou Toure, Amilcar Cabral, and Kwame Nkrumah, were conceptualised in terms of development, autonomy, nationalism, modernisation and enlightenment.

Their strategies involved nationalisation, large-scale planning, the emancipation of women, and mass literacy projects. Such movements used popular culture to transmit their ideology and enthusiasm, mobilizing 'the people' for the objectives of 'the struggle'. Their leaders tended to subordinate means to ends, often ruthlessly, and could be characterised as elitist, authoritarian, and chauvinistic. This is what Manthia characterised as the high-modernising or modernist paradigm. The failure (or corruption) of these movements had led to the emergence of an alternative paradigm that he characterised as both anti- and post-modernist. This alternative perspective was nostalgic, stressing African subjectivity, valorising desire and the aesthetic, and emphasising indigenous self-reliance against dependence on foreign remedies. It turned away from the failure to modernise the African city towards a rather romantic view of rural development based on a rediscovery of the virtues of traditional village culture.

There was no doubting the pain communicated by Manthia as he recounted the emotional impact on himself of viewing the film *Allah Tanto,* which revealed his hero Sekou Toure as a ruthless murderer.

For me, it was illuminating to observe how the disappointment of expectations of emancipation following the success of anti-colonialist struggles might lead some intellectuals to question ideologies associated with modernism and turn in the direction of post-modernism, and to wonder if there were parallels in the first world.

I myself contributed to the discussion following these two papers, arguing that the psychoanalytic concepts of identification with the aggressor and identification with the corrupt might be relevant to understanding post-colonial societies, and that Christopher Bollas's concept of the unthought known could be linked with the feminist critique of Freire's dualisms.

These papers generated a sense of promise and got the week off to a great start. During the next couple of days we attended two social events: first a reception for Paulo and Nita hosted by the Principal of the New School, and second a gathering of activists and educators associated with Highlander, the internationally acclaimed institution for workers' education founded and led by Myles Horton, with whom Paulo had recently written a talking book, *We Make the Road by Walking* (Temple University Press, 1990). The atmosphere was cordial. It was a deliberate attempt to facilitate dialogue between community-based, academic, and literacy orientated Freireans on the one hand, and labour movement organisers and educators on the other.

VISITS OF OBSERVATION

Community High Schools are schools for teenagers who drop out of conventional secondary schools or are expelled from them. They accounted, so we were told, for one fifth of all high school graduates in New York City. These schools represent a very different approach from that based on separate subjects of study, competition, and individual high achievement. We visited the Bronx Community High School along with its Principal, Dr Nancy Mohr, and sat in on a staff meeting. It was characterised by informality of style, and an emphasis on collective projects. Nancy gave out her daily 'Mohr notes' that touched on most aspects of the life of the school. Her role was not that of authoritative figurehead, but rather responsive group co-ordinator with her finger on the pulse of the life of the school.

For an hour we sat in on one of the family groups. Each student joins a family group on arrival in the school and stays with it until she leaves. Each day starts in family group. It isn't group therapy, but owes something to it, with children expressing some of their feelings and thoughts about their lives. The teacher who facilitated the group we visited was on the receiving end of a considerable amount of anger. All the students in the group were black or Hispanic. We were impressed by the way they were able to use the group, and the resilience of the teacher who led it. Nevertheless, as an educator who is also a psychotherapist, I had some doubts about the effectiveness of such an approach. It seemed to invite some initial expression of personal themes and tensions without providing a sufficiently sustaining and containing context for extended exploration of them. Maybe the aim was more modest: to allow enough release of tension at the start of the day to lessen the chances of explosions later.

Our next visit was to a University Settlement House on the Lower East Side of Manhattan. This was home to a literacy project for Hispanic women who were single parents on welfare. It was called the mothers' reading programme. Here again we were welcomed and allowed to sit in on a remarkable teaching/learning situation. Maritza Arrastia, the teacher, was a journalist who was bilingual in English and Spanish, and knew about Paulo Freire's methods. She co-ordinated the work of two learning groups in different rooms at the same time. If you think this is impossible, I assure you that we saw and heard it, and it seemed to work. She used an adaptation of Freire's method of codification and decoding, presenting a picture of a situation easily recognisable to the women as their own. They worked in pairs to comment on it, and she led them in working it up from the visually perceived situation into a story by the use of stimulating questions. As the collective story emerged, she wrote it phrase by phrase on the blackboard, and it became the women's text. She led them through reading it aloud several times, and then each person wrote it down for herself. When her work with one group had reached a point where they could get on with a particular task on their own, she would go through to the next group in the other room, and pick up the next stage of their work.

It was shocking to see how under-resourced the project was, but we were impressed by the energy, skill, and commitment of this young teacher, the response of the women and the trust they placed in her.

Our next and final visit was to a project in Brooklyn called the *Open Book*. Again the students were mostly black or Hispanic. The group was led by a male teacher whose style differed significantly from that of the mothers' programme tutor. Although operating in a circular group format, he worked quite a lot with individuals during the session. Again the group had confidence in him. They had been together for quite a time, and we were struck by the trust existing between the members. This project specialised in publishing members' writing and was reminiscent of work done at Centreprise in London and the WEA in Edinburgh in the 1970s and 80s.

DEMOCRACY AND THE POSSIBILITY OF MULTICULTURALISM

The next event of the conference introduced us to one of the key dynamics of the contemporary North American situation. It was a big set piece session on multiculturalism in education, with a middle-class male senior official, a Hispanic working for the city's education department, pitted (or so it seemed) against a passionate black female academic who was dean of faculty of one of the universities.

The issue was the inequality of schooling for blacks and Hispanics as compared with whites, and what to do about it. Was the concept of multiculturalism useful or not? The problem, one speaker said, was that the concept of multiculturalism did not deal satisfactorily with bias against excluded groups: native Americans, Latinos, Asians, and African Americans. They got the least experienced teachers, had the largest teacher turnover, and the lowest funding. It was pointed out that 80% of the prisoners in the country's jails had experienced school failure. Multiculturalism was disuniting. Affirmative action was not about coming together, and singing and dancing and eating different meals, but about confronting the past, which means experiencing discomfort, guilt, and pain.

Paulo, in his response, spoke about his idea of democracy. There was no democracy without risks. It involved danger, adventure, creation, and the establishing of limits. Multiculturalism was not the juxtaposition of different cultures, nor the superimposition of one culture upon another. On the contrary, democracy was the source of the possibility of multiculturalism. Democracy was the courage to be different, to respect the difference and to try to learn from it. He went on:

> I don't believe in unanimity. Democracy is the confrontation of difference and the necessity to overcome antagonisms ... We cannot wait till God comes to solve this problem. It is not his task. It is our task: to look for justice, not to collapse us all into one ... [We have to discover] how it is possible for us to grow together in the differences, never trying to forget the differences: to get unity in diversity. That is one of the characteristics of democracy ... Changing is difficult, but it is possible and necessary.

BUILDING ALLIANCES, OVERCOMING ANTAGONISMS

The Thursday evening session was entitled *Building a progressive educational alliance*. This reflected the explicit aim of the conference to build an alliance of public school teachers, labour educators, community-based programmes, higher education, and teacher education. We learned at the start how high the level of interest in the conference had been: 620 participants had registered with another 200 applicants having to be turned away.

The first speaker was Jose La Luz, leader of the Amalgamated Clothing and Textile Workers Union. What had led to the breakdown of the alliance, he asked, and what were the lessons for rebuilding it? We are here to listen, and we are going to stay here, he said, encouraging his labour movement followers in the hall.

The next speaker, Rita Tenorio of the Teacher's Union, highlighted issues of racism, sexism, and classism. Helen Lewis of Highlander asked: how do we unlearn the bad habits we learned during our own schooling?

Quickly, it became clear that the explosive issues of race and racism were at the heart of the gathering. What had integration done for the black community? The blacks had lost their own institutions. Integration had benefited the black middle class, not the mass of black people. Speakers declared that they would not let this issue of racism be ignored. They challenged the use of English as the medium of communication at the conference. The reality was that it was blacks and Latinos who were in the poor urban schools. The challenge was to overcome white supremacy.

By now the atmosphere of the session had become tense and conflictual. There was an attempt to dislodge English and install Spanish as the language of the event. Then there was a demand to have each statement translated into Spanish. Was the enemy in here, or out there? Somebody asked: how do we bring society into the classroom? (That night, it was there already!) How are we going to make a correct assessment of things? We are governed by whites, we are governed by males ...

This atmosphere of suspicion and antagonism kept reappearing in different guises: black versus white, Spanish versus English, hard left versus liberals, working class versus middle class. The old 'women versus men' theme was far less intense than it had been in the 1970s. This dimension of the conference could be conceptualised in Fanonian and Freirean language as horizontal violence, though actual physical violence was not involved. The oppressors, wherever they were, could sleep safely in their beds as long as the radicals were at each others' throats in the usual way. It was depressing to experience this degree of factionalism especially where the organisers were trying so hard to create alliances. Who would dominate the alliance seemed to be one of the unspoken issues. Freire's own eloquence of the previous session seemed unequal to the task of acknowledging and accommodating the competing interests and mutual suspicions. I found myself at moments longing nostalgically for the old communist party, and its 'correct analysis' uniting different sections and enabling them to work together for a common end, but I never forget the high price that was paid for such undemocratic centralism.

CONFERENCE WORKSHOPS

The Friday and Saturday were mainly given over to 48 pre-planned workshops and other spontaneously formed caucuses and groups focused around communities of interest or emerging themes. For a selection of these, giving the flavour of the event as well as some sense of the planning that had gone into it, please see Appendix 1. No fewer than 155 workshop contributors, a quarter of the total number of conference participants, are listed in the official programme, testimony to the highly participatory and pluralist nature of the event. In each workshop three or four speakers were nominated together with a moderator or a respondent. Detailed planning was left to the contributors, which meant that there was as much or as little co-ordination of the workshops as they managed to organise.

Along with Pia Moriarty, and Peggy Rivage-Seul, Gerri and I did a workshop on Freire's method of codification. Peggy presented a series of cartoon-style codifications from Brazil and led the group in exploring them. I then outlined the Scottish historical moment, discussing the tension between themes of social justice and national self-determination in the context of the welfarism/Thatcherism dialectic. I emphasised the Scottish experience of double identification with oppressor and oppressed, as an illustration of a theme explored by both Fanon and Freire.

Gerri then presented a selection of the ALP codifications and proposed to co-ordinate a decoding session using a picture of a 1950s classroom in Edinburgh. Carlos Torres attacked the idea of doing a decoding session at all, arguing that it took the codification out of the lived reality that gave it its existence and its validity. He asserted that this reduced Freire's political method to the status of a mere technique. He was supported by a male academic, Herb Kohl, but they were counter-challenged by women members of the workshop who argued that experiencing was more than a technique, and just as valid as academic theorising and accounts of political action elsewhere. The decoding session went ahead, with Carlos joining in and Herb staying out.

Black activists and white liberals

Of the other workshops I attended, I will mention four that illustrate dramatically the key themes of the event. The first was *Critical education and politics in society*. This was striking for the presentation by Stephen Brookfield, and the response he evoked. Stephen offered what might be characterised (with no adverse criticism intended) as an interpersonal, almost Rogerian interpretation of Freire.

He was involved in the training of adult educators, and presented the results of some research he was doing on their training experiences that highlighted the emotional/affective aspects of critical pedagogy. He discussed the following themes: the devaluation of personal experience versus the testimony of experts; the sense of sadness and loss involved in giving up a right/wrong, black/white view of the world in favour of tolerating the experience of ambiguity, which led, he argued, to critical sophistication; the cultural suicide involved in cutting yourself off from your class or sub-culture of origin, and the need for peer-group support; and the complex challenge of the power differential between teacher and student. In summary, he seemed to be saying: don't put me on a pedestal as a teacher, but I do have some important things to teach you. Stephen argued that, while the power differential could lead to students being silenced, teachers could be authoritative without being authoritarian.

The main response came from a black woman activist who accused white academics of liberalism, and evading the real issues. She saw these arising from the systematic exclusion of blacks from power and resources in American society. Her

157

position was a classic restatement of the 'them and us' theme. It was literally a black/white analysis. I commented that one of the underlying themes of the conference, and of this workshop, was that whites (labelled 'liberals') were trying to expiate their guilt by ingratiating themselves, while blacks (labelled 'activists') were trying to humiliate them and force them to accept personal responsibility for black experiences of oppression. The black activist agreed that that was indeed the theme, and for some time members of the workshop began to address it, and look at the complexity of experiences of oppression. Gradually, however, the emphasis drifted back to heavy gunfire from the entrenched black position, while the whites cowered in their liberal redoubt. The theme of the group – and in some ways of the conference – was acted out, repeated in a stuck way, rather than confronted and explored through dialogue.

Popular education, popular knowledge, popular power

The next workshop I attended was *Politics, ideology, and Freirean pedagogy* with Stanley Aronowitz and Augustin Lao. Stanley is an academic teacher of cultural studies, with previous experience as a labour organiser. He gave an account of Freire's ideas which, in my view, overemphasised the dimension of collective political struggle to the detriment of the personal and the psycho-social. I argued that it was wrong to attempt to assimilate Freire's thinking either to old or new left positions or to identify him over-simply with either modernist or post-modernist perspectives. Freire's position was a challenge to all those perspectives that tend to treat people as objects to be mobilised, provided for, or converted. Warming to my theme, I argued that the sectarian left wanted to rescue people from false consciousness, and install in them a new, correct consciousness, while Freire's view involved the invitation of conscientisation, enabling people themselves to move through processes of coinvestigation and dialogue from present to potential consciousness.

These two stances differed fundamentally and were at odds with each other, I argued. An African member of the workshop, whose name I did not catch, asked Stanley where Freire stood on the issue of non-violence (that question again!) and Stanley replied with an account of a strike by women workers that he himself had organised. This struggle was a minority action, he recalled, in which strikers at first sought to persuade the majority of the need for the action, and having failed to do so, went ahead with the strike and picketed the workplace, filling their handbags with stones which they threw at their colleagues as they went to work. Stanley appeared to me to be justifying this action as Freirean, when from my point of view it was a perfect illustration of anti-dialogical sectarianism.

Stanley and other hard left interpreters of Freire are, in my view, engaged in a project aimed at assimilating Freirean concepts and values to an amalgam of old and new left positions. It seems to me that they place less value on particularistic literacy projects, women's projects, and community-based initiatives. These are valued less, I suspect, because they are not usually integrated with large-scale political movements. Freire, they claim, never initiated educational programmes except within a wider political framework. Now it is certainly true that Freire's own educational work has always been linked to political movements, though these were not usually monolithic. But it is also true that Freire has consistently attacked the theory and practice of anti-dialogical sectarianism. It seems to me that Stanley and his like tend to lose sight of the personalist and psycho-social dimensions of Freire's synthesis. In their hands, Freire's approach begins to resemble the old collectivist education for mobilisation around objectives determined by a political elite.

Augustin Lao, who shared this workshop, spoke of Freire's rejection of dogmatic mechanistic Marxism in favour of radical democracy. The key concepts were 'educacao popular', 'saper popular', and 'poder popular'. He explained that in Spanish 'popular' means 'of the people', not populist or massist. Freire's pedagogy was not just a methodology, but a social practice of liberation by and of oppressed people as historical subjects. It was, he said, neither vanguardist not spontaneist, but involved dimensions of autonomy and co-ordination.

Reforming education: Teachers, parents, children, and popular movements

The next workshop I attended focused on the work of education reform that Paulo Freire had recently been leading as Secretary for Education in the City of Sao Paulo, from 1989 till 1991. The main speaker was Carlos Torres. Paulo was a member of the Workers Party, and his selection for this post reflected that political commitment. The aim was to transform the school system. One of the key problems Freire identified was that the status of teachers had been seriously eroded. He began by securing a significant increase in their pay. It was seen as important, Carlos stressed, to respect the teachers: this was itself a generative theme, named as respecting the workers in the school. It was implemented systematically as a policy. Thus, only schools and zones of the city where the teachers voted by a majority to participate were included in the project. Some of Paulo's political supporters were exasperated by this voluntarism of his, which they saw as petty bourgeois liberalism. But Freire's theory that people must be treated as subjects not objects applies also to teachers. They could not be expected to take part in such a project against their will.

School councils were established to run each school, consisting of the principal (elected for two years, then reverting to ordinary teacher status), representatives of the staff including teachers, janitors, cooks, secretaries, and cleaners (50%) and representatives of the parents and children over 10 (50%). All representatives were directly elected. It was interesting to learn that the Teachers Union opposed the principle of direct election of the teacher representatives. Direct elections would, of course, mean weakening the power of the Union's representative structure.

Carlos reported Paulo's own analysis of the difficulties he faced, which arose mainly from within the popular social movements he had involved in the project. The first Paulo calls 'basismo', a tendency deriving from petit-bourgeois intellectuals who go to the base and adopt the position that the base is always right. All wisdom and knowledge are ascribed to the grassroots. The second difficulty, linked to the first, is that as soon as someone is put in a position of power, they are immediately attacked. They become the enemy. We would recognise both of these problems, and particularly the latter, which we would call oppositionalism. Where this influence becomes dominant, such movements really become incapable of taking and exercising power. Other problems Carlos identified were extreme factionalism within the Worker's Party, and overlaps of membership between the party and the popular social movements.

Approximately 30% of the schools took part in the project. There were additional monetary incentives for teacher participation. The aim was to create popular public schooling in which whole communities were involved. It was resisted by the Teachers Union, the state bureaucracy, and the right-wing press. At the time of the workshop, which was about six months after Paulo's resignation, the project was in difficulty, but could not be described as having failed. It would continue under a new leader.

Integration and the struggle for self-determination

The last workshop I attended was entitled 'The crisis in black education'. I found it inspiring, although (or perhaps because) it was confronting great difficulties. It consisted almost entirely of black activists and educators. There was a sense that the great campaigns for integration had achieved much less than had been hoped for. There was an explicit acknowledgement that anti-white rhetoric failed to address the root of the problem. There was a difference of analysis between the older and younger black activists. The older generation continued to value the gains of the integrationist struggle, and looked to further it. The younger members felt that blacks had lost their own institutions as a result of integration, which they saw as a pyrrhic victory. They argued that there was a need to recover the struggle for black self-determination and they were looking with interest at the (then) current dramatic developments in Eastern Europe and the old Soviet Union. Here an old empire, masquerading as a progressive social formation, had been destroyed by resurgent nationalism. It was time, some of them were arguing, for a black nationalist movement at the heart of the biggest empire of them all, the United States of America. It was an electrifying proposition.

I have to say that I tended to agree with the analysis offered by the older heads in the workshop, but the young radicals had a crucial point in their favour. Human beings are not mono-generational, a-cultural abstractions engaged in a theoretical struggle. They are real persons-in-relation, with specific cultural and historical inheritances. The strengths of these inheritances need to be celebrated and built on, just as their weaknesses need to be faced up to. In this sense there is no alternative to self-determination, or – to put it in Paulo Freire's language – cultural action-reflection for freedom.

That night we had a party to celebrate Paulo Freire's 70th birthday. There was beer and food, superb singing from the woman who had challenged Stephen Brookfield, marvelous Brazilian dancing and presents for Paulo and Nita. Greg Tewksbury read an ee cummings poem, and unity broke out all round. We said goodbye to many new friends with feelings of excitement, but also confusion and some despondency which we knew was shared by others.

CONCLUSION

The most painful impression I was left with was an awareness of the position of black Americans in the USA who are experiencing a profound political and psychological crisis. They are now outnumbered by Hispanic immigrants who seem to them to be more effectively organised and more successful in fighting for resources. The blacks fear they are going to lose out yet again and resume their old place at the bottom of the heap. In public they blame the whites and lash out against institutionalised racism, but there is a recognition that there is something deeper that needs to be addressed.

The psychological dimension of this seems to me to be an abasement of the spirit in the under-class, black, Hispanic and white, that needs to be tackled in its own right. I believe that we have overstressed the themes of race and gender, to the detriment of class and culture, in the last 20 years. We need a new and more accurate class analysis addressing the fact that Western societies are now systematically operating economies based on the existence of an under-class that is marginalised in terms of work, hope, and political power, but is integral to the functioning of society in an economic sense. Plato and Aristotle would have recognised members of this class. They are not citizens. They are slave consumers. Their economic function is to consume junk housing, junk food, junk drugs, and junk services. William Blake said that poverty appalled the mind. He was right. We now live in a society that treats up to 30 per cent of our fellow citizens in ways that are appalling. It doesn't need to be like this. It can be tackled. There are those in our political parties and in the media who believe that popular participation is old-fashioned 1960s rhetoric. They imagine that these problems can be addressed by technocratic solutions. I do not deny, for example, that information technology can play some part in increasing democratic engagement and institutional responsiveness. But on its own it will do nothing to prevent the formation and consolidation of an under-class of marginalised and degraded consumers. I believe we can create a society in which citizenship and social justice for all are established as matters of fact, not items of progressive political rhetoric. The basic form of participation is meaningful, useful and decently remunerated work. This is the challenge facing the Scottish people, the new Scottish parliament, and peoples and nations throughout the world struggling for self-determination.

APPENDIX 1

Selection of workshop topics giving a flavour of the conference

Friday morning's programme included workshops on: Freire and teacher transformation; Freire's method of codification; worker education and union organizing; critical maths in the classroom; popular education in building community organisations; the role of the state in influencing the direction and goals of literacy; the mission of labour education; the need for a multicultural approach to worker education; and understanding student leadership and its role in the learning process.

Friday afternoon included: feminism and critical education; critical literacy and community in the classroom; school change; educators, parents, and the community; multiculturalism in the schools; the challenge to teachers; the experience of immigrant children in the public schools; towards empowerment models for teacher education; adult education and community action; women of colour and the pedagogy of life experience; participatory theatre and drama; and disempowerment, alienation, and dropouts.

Saturday morning began with: critical education and politics in society; popular education and critical teaching; union-based train-the-teacher programmes; practical applications of Freirean pedagogy in worker education; school restructuring, language and youth culture; rethinking history, rethinking Columbus; publishing out of the community; and popular education and community organising: addressing the issues of race and gender.

Saturday afternoon included: critical teacher education; popular education from adult esl literacy; the crisis in black education; Latino education and critical pedagogy; politics, ideology, and Freirean pedagogy; community and economic development; principles of popular education in the US context; oral history, narrative and the pedagogy of writing; and – finally – language, pedagogy, and group identity.

REFERENCES/BIBLIOGRAPHY

Brown, C. (1975). *Literacy in 30 hours: Paulo Freire's process in north-east Brazil*. London: Writers and Readers Publishing Co-operative.

Collins, D. (1977). *Paulo Freire: his life, works and thought*. New York: Paulist Press.

Freire, P. (1972). *Cultural action for freedom*. Harmondsworth: Penguin.

Freire, P. (1972). *Pedagogy of the oppressed*. Harmondsworth: Penguin.

Freire, P. (1972). *Education for critical consciousness*. London: Sheed and Ward (also published in 1976 as *Education: the Practice of Freedom*. London, Writers and Readers Publishing Co-operative).

Freire, P. (1978). *Pedagogy in process: The letters to Guinea-Bissau*. New York: Seabury Press.

Freire, P. (1985). *The politics of education: Culture, power and liberation*. London: Macmillan.

Freire, P. & Faundez, A. (1989). *Learning to question: A pedagogy of liberation*. Geneva: WCC Publications.

Freire, P. & Macedo, D. (1987). *Literacy: Reading the word and the world*. London: Routlege and Kegan Paul.

Freire, P. & Shor, I. (1987). *A pedagogy for liberation: Dialogues on transforming education*. London: Macmillan.

Horton, M. & Freire, P. (1990). *We make the road by walking: Conversations on education and social change*. Philadelphia, Temple University Press.

Kane, L. (2001). *Popular education and social change in Latin America*. London: Latin American Bureau.

Kirkwood, G. & Kirkwood, C. (2011). *Living adult education: Freire in Scotland*, 2nd edition. Rotterdam: Sense Publishers.

Mackie, R. (1980). *Literacy and revolution: The pedagogy of Paulo Freire*. London: Pluto Press.

Shor, I. (1987). *Critical teaching and everyday life*. Chicago: University of Chicago Press.

Shor, I. (1987). *Freire for the classroom: A sourcebook for liberatory teaching*. Portsmouth, USA: Boynton Cook.

Shor, I. (1992). *Empowering education: Critical teaching for social change*. Chicago and London: University of Chicago Press.

Taylor, P. (1993). *The texts of Paulo Freire*. Milton Keynes, Open University Press.*

* For a biographical sketch of Paulo Freire's life and work and for a discussion of the intellectual roots of his thinking, Paul Taylor's *The Texts of Paulo Freire* (1993) is particularly recommended.

FREIREAN APPROACHES TO CITIZENSHIP

An Interview with Colin Kirkwood

By Emilio Lucio-Villegas

This interview first appeared in *Citizenship as Politics: International Perspectives from Adult Education* (2009), edited by Emilio Lucio-Villegas and published by Sense Publishers.

How do you explain the Adult Learning Project?

The Adult Learning Project (ALP for short) was founded in 1979 in Gorgie Dalry in Edinburgh, Scotland. It was an initiative of the South West Edinburgh Area Team of the Community Education Service of Lothian Regional Council, led by Fraser Patrick. ALP was initially funded for three years by an urban aid grant from the Scottish Office. As a result of ALP's success, funding via urban aid was extended for a further three years, and funding was later taken over by Lothian Regional Council, and later by the City of Edinburgh Council.

Traditionally adult education in Scotland was (and still is) based on the study of separate subjects or skills. The original idea for an adult learning project in Gorgie Dalry was that people should study the subjects and skills they wanted to study, incorporating a notion of local community control. However, before the urban aid application was submitted to the Scottish Office, Fraser Patrick decided instead to base ALP on a translation and adaptation of the ideas and methods of Paulo Freire. This meant that ALP would involve people living in Gorgie Dalry in identifying the significant situations and concerns of their lives, codifying them in visual, auditory or written form, or some combination of these, decoding the codifications in groups and identifying the emerging themes. Programmes of learning would then be constructed based on these emerging themes, involving as many of the people of the area as possible.

Once ALP was established, this process was indeed undertaken. The key methodological sequence of the approach developed was:
– say your own word
– presentation by expert
– dialogue.
Coordinators led the learning programmes, and out of them came various action outcomes including community action programmes such as Play in the Terraces, and workshops like the Photo Workshop and the Writers Workshop.

This sequence of initial investigation, codification and decoding, identification of themes, creation of learning programmes, leading on to action outcomes has been repeated throughout the life of ALP, and is one of its principal distinguishing features.

In Spain, adult education is usually connected with schools and government. But ALP is linked with community work and does not appear to depend exclusively on the City of Edinburgh Council. How does ALP work?

In Scotland, adult education is provided by a variety of organisations funded directly or indirectly by local and/or central government. These include the Community Education Service (now called Community Learning and Development) of local councils; the Workers' Educational Association (a nationwide voluntary organisation funded by local and central government); the Open University, and the Adult Continuing/Lifelong Learning departments of other Universities; the Colleges of Further Education (probably the biggest single provider in terms of volume); and also some private sector providers.

So in this sense the organisation and funding of adult education in Scotland is not unlike that in Spain.

ALP itself, contrary to to the impression given in your question, was founded by local government (Lothian Regional Council) and now forms a small part of the work of the Children and Families Department of the City of Edinburgh Council.

What makes ALP unique in Scotland as in Britain as a whole is that it is based on the ideas and methods of Paulo Freire. Attempts have been made to adopt a Freirean approach in other areas but they have not been successful in the longer run, although the work of ALP and the ideas of Freire have continued to be widely influential in many domains.

ALP includes a community work or perhaps we should say a community action dimension partly because of ALP's commitment to engaged citizenship and action outcomes arising from learning programmes. And partly because it belongs to a modern tradition in radical adult education in Scotland, England, Wales and Ireland, which links adult education with community work/action/development.

ALP does in fact depend on the City of Edinburgh Council: the salaries of the workers, the office space, the equipment, the rooms and halls used for learning programmes and workshops are all provided by the council. But ALP also enjoys a great deal of autonomy and raises a lot of money through its ceilidhs and other events, which it uses to fund much of its learning and development work. And ALP has a crucial, vibrant dimension of student and teacher democracy: the ALP Association, which runs ALP. Every learning programme, workshop and action group has a representative on the ALP Association, and several times a year the members of all the groups meet, for conference and celebration, in the ALP Gaithrins. In addition, a number of ALP initiatives have led to the creation of independent, self-funding organisations such as the Scots Music Group.

In the ALP book, you devote many pages, including a glossary, to explaining Paulo Freire's thought. What is the influence of Freire's work and his ideas on ALP?

ALP is grounded in the ideas and methods of Paulo Freire: his work is literally fundamental to the life of ALP. The ALP workers recurrently run courses on Freire's ideas and practices, so that new people can continue to learn about his work. When new tutors are invited to lead learning groups in ALP, they are encouraged to read Freire's books and the ALP book, and to work dialogically.

But ALP is not slavishly devoted to a literal reading of Freire. It is constantly trying to adapt his ideas to the evolving context of local, Scottish, British and global society and culture. This involves reinventing his ideas in flexible and imaginative ways, and supporting cultural exchanges with projects in other countries such as South Africa, Ireland, Portugal and Brittany in France.

The best way to understand the influence of Freire on ALP is to read the new Castillian and Valencian translations of the ALP book, including the new chapter seven, written by Vernon Galloway, Stan Reeves and Nancy Somerville, which brings the story of ALP up to date. A second edition of *Living Adult Education: Freire in Scotland* has just been published in English by Sense Publishers, in 2011. It includes a new preface by Jim Crowther and Ian Martin, as well as the updating chapter 7 referred to above.

Sometimes people involved in adult education and community work are unable to move on and make space for new people to come in. How has ALP managed to change and develop in this way?

ALP has generated an unusual combination of continuity and change. In terms of key personnel, of the four original ALP workers, (Stan Reeves, Fiona McCall, Gerri Kirkwood and Joan Bree), Fiona moved on after four years and is now a trainer and supervisor of counsellors. Gerri moved after ten years to become Assistant Principal of a Community High School. Joan moved after twenty years to become an administrator in a larger voluntary organisation.

Stan Reeves has continued to work in ALP from 1979 until today. He has been a constant source of inspiration, reinvention and renewal of ALP, partly because of his charismatic and dialogical personality, partly because he has always sought and welcomed involvement from new people, partly because he generates imaginative new applications of Freire's basic assumptions, and partly because as well as being an outstanding adult educator he is also a practising musician (he plays the accordion and other instruments) and a leading figure in the current revival of Scottish traditional music.

This combination of continuity, change and renewal has encouraged many other creative figures to come in and make their mark in ALP.

Another factor is ALP's commitment to outward looking social and democratic involvement. This applies not only within the project but has enabled ALP to make generative links with the women's movement, the community land and ecological movements, refugee organizations, and contemporary writing, photography, music and political movements.

In Jock Sutherland's sense, ALP is an open system.

Some of the people living in Edinburgh and involved in ALP are immigrants. What work is ALP doing in collaboration with immigrants? What are the challenges for adult education with immigrants?

ALP workers and learner/activists have always been aware that, as Galloway, Reeves and Somerville have argued, the theme of culture would have to take on a multicultural dimension. Throughout the life of ALP they have collaborated with a variety of immigrant groups including people from Asia, the Middle East, the former Soviet Union, Latin America and eastern and middle Europe. They have worked closely with the Scottish Refugee Council, and it was in the course of this collaboration that ALP evolved an effective and popular model of cross-cultural working called *The Welcoming,* which is described in the new chapter of the ALP book.

A key challenge of working with immigrants is to achieve practical and dialogical ways of bridging gaps of language and culture. This is done through weekly encounters between local community learner activists and recently arrived immigrants and asylum seekers, including sharing a meal, discussing contemporary situations in Scotland and in the countries of origin of the asylum seekers and immigrants, language classes in English for speakers of other languages, and celebratory cross-cultural performances of music and dancing.

One of the learning programmes in the ALP book is entitled On Being Scottish. *In a globalising world, what is the role of adult education in helping people to recover, maintain and develop their own identity?*

The acceleration of technological development, whether in the field of information and communication technologies, or technologies of transport, armaments, and the production, packaging and distribution of food, is one of the principal drivers of the globalising trend. Other factors include the widespread adoption of the assumption that economic growth is a permanent necessity, the development of an increasingly reckless global finance industry, and the deliberate encouragement of inequality and the exploitation of low-paid workers in increasingly under-regulated 'free' markets. Setting these socio-techno-economic features against a broader backcloth of the arrogance of some aspects of science and the disparagement of religion helps us to understand why trends of deracination, individualism, narcissism, hedonism and celebritism are running rampant. The distinction between descriptive and normative discourses (that is, between 'is' and 'ought' statements) is being eroded, and – in the higher echelons of society - ethics is being reinvented on the basis of a combination of merely statistical norms on the one hand and power manoeuvres by dominant elites on the other. A view of society as a kind of rational machine driven by wealth creation and the pleasure principle is gaining ground, and the recognition of the significance of the personal, the communal and the traditional is being squeezed out, to be replaced by a combination of George Orwell's *1984* and Aldous Huxley's *Brave New World*.

In such a context it is tempting to conceptualise the task of adult education in terms of the recovery of personal, social and national identity, but while this is part of the task, it is not the whole of it. Identity is vital to human beings, but identity is meaningful as an integral part of a culture in which notions of the personal, of persons in community, and of the just and good society which supports the well-being and flourishing of all its members, are convincingly embedded as practices and aspirations. This is the process of liberation to which Paulo Freire's ideas and practices summon us, the utopia towards which they point, which we reaffirm and seek to constitute in our practice of adult education.

In short, identity has always been a central component of the work of ALP but not the whole of it. Without the affirmation and search for social justice and the denunciation of exploitation and manipulation, locally, nationally and globally, it becomes separated from its roots.

One of the European Union's fetish words is citizenship. How does ALP help people to become citizens? How can adult education in general encourage people to exercise citizenship?

These questions are important and invite an extended essay which we are not in a position to undertake at present! Instead we will attempt to outline briefly what might be a Freirean/personalist position on citizenship. Freire postulates that human beings are persons, to be regarded as subjects who know and act, rather than objects which are known and acted upon. His view of education is that our engagement as subjects with the significant situations and concerns of our lives is fundamental, not incidental. We cannot do this on our own, but together as persons in relation. Freire is aware of the danger of what he calls massification: people are not to be manipulated or treated as stage armies. He takes a very specific view of political leadership. He admires strong, principled, visionary leaders who are fighting to create the good society and who engage with oppressed people as persons involved in a struggle for liberation. He includes among such leaders Antonio Gramsci, Fidel Castro, and Amilcar Cabral. He also admired Mao Tse Tung and Julius Nyerere. With the benefit of hindsight, we can question some of his choices, but the principles underlying his position are clear.

Freire also makes a valuable distinction between the popular and the populist. For him, the term 'popular' means 'of the people' in a genuine sense. He talks about 'popular power' and 'popular knowledge'. The 'populist', on the other hand, is a quality of the attitude and behaviour of leaders who, as Freire puts it, shuttle back and forth between the elites and the people, who use popular images, ideas and values to manipulate people, thus objectifying them.

It is against this background of assumptions that we can approach an understanding of a Freirean view of citizenship. Citizenship derives from the Latin words 'civis', meaning citizen, and 'civitas', meaning the body of citizens in a city

169

or other significant settlement or community. It refers in modern times to the rights and responsibilities of free people in a state. Historically it can be linked to the concept of democracy in the Greek city state, to the experience of citizens of the Roman Republic and the Roman Empire, and more recently those of liberal, social and so-called people's democracies. These considerations encapsulate the potential and also the limitations of the concept of citizenship. Its potential is to value and entrench the contributions of each and every person in a society. Its limitations derive from the extent to which it is associated with the exercise of political power by politicians in any society. Too often in liberal, social and people's democracies, the deployment of the rhetoric of citizenship has been associated with pressures exerted on citizens by politicians or demagogues in relation to objectives of dubious value imposed from above.

It was in response to such considerations that the early Christians tried to formulate ways of combining citizenship with Christianity. The idea of being simultaneously a citizen of Rome and a Christian was intended to enable Christians to withstand political manipulation without becoming merely oppositional. Freire's work can be seen as a modern extension of this tradition. Citizenship is important for Freire, but he sees the citizen as a person, and the 'civitas' as a body of persons in relation or persons in community. This view of citizenship places the role of the person-as-citizen at the heart of Freirean pedagogy, seeking to insulate it (ethically but not experientially) from the impact of manipulation and demagoguery, without devaluing genuine leadership. The emerging themes, the meaningful thematics, of any Freirean learning programme derive not from the current priorities of national governments or the European Union, although these may be powerfully influential. But it is open to all such bodies to align themselves with and resource programmes of education based on a Freirean perspective. It is not a matter of being 'in and against the state' but of being simultaneously inside and beyond the state. It is in this sense that adult education can encourage and support citizenship. ALP programmes of learning encourage citizenship unlimited by, in the sense of going beyond, narrowly political considerations.

For me, one of the most important and interesting aspects of the ALP book is the connection between adult education and community work. What is the key to this connection?

When Scottish readers began to engage with Freire's writings (particularly *Pedagogy of the Oppressed* and *Cultural Action for Freedom*) in the 1970s, we were particularly impressed by Freire's notion that learning programmes were not ends in themselves, for the sake of study alone, but parts of a process of engaging persons as citizens in reflective action in the communities in which they lived and worked. This was what so impressed us about his early work in Recife and Pernambuco in north east Brazil. The educational work had outcomes in terms of cultural action both to celebrate the way of life of the people and to address specific existential problems and injustices in their circumstances through reflective popular action.

In Britain as a whole, and specifically in Scotland, we were familiar with the theory of community development applied in the British Empire as many of its constituent peoples struggled to achieve political independence. Some of us had been employed as community workers on community development projects in so-called areas of deprivation, funded by central and local government or by voluntary agencies. And others had been involved in autonomous community action in inner cities and peripheral housing schemes throughout the UK. One of the major criticisms of community development and community action was that such phenomena confined their concerns to geographically circumscribed areas as if the problems originated and could be solved there. Contrary to this view, it was argued that while community and community action were important values, questions of poverty, deprivation and alienation were not caused by factors originating within circumscribed localities, but were the effects of social and economic relationships and values across society as a whole: local, regional, national and global. Nevertheless there was an acknowledgement that people live and form relationships in communities of place as well as communities of work and interest, and that all of these were appropriate starting points for learning, analysis and action.

In Freire's writing we found explicit confirmation of our view that poverty and exploitation could not be understood with reference to circumscribed localities but in terms of larger totalities; but equally that this did not invalidate starting from where people live and work.

For ALP, community action was a natural outcome of adult learning, and sometimes also, depending on the nature of the problem, an appropriate starting point for adult learning. Throughout the life of ALP, this has been the case, whether the learning and action takes place in a locality, at national level, or in a community of interest.

Some people say that Freire's theory and methodology is only valid in the third world. How do you justify the translation and adaptation of Freire's work in a first world setting by ALP?

Paulo Freire in his writings always respects the particularity and uniqueness of every community, every language, every culture. Simply to carry over a practice from one society or culture into another and implement it there is likely to involve processes of imposition, which he describes as cultural invasion. But that does not mean that he believes in cultural apartheid! Ideas and practices generated in specific socio-cultural contexts have a kind of freedom: they can take off, fly away and land in many other – very different – socio-cultural contexts where they may unexpectedly put down roots and flourish in new forms. What is important in such processes of geographical and cultural translocation is the dimension of translation into other languages, entailing processes of encounter, engagement, dialogue and connection-making. This can happen at both conscious and unconscious levels. In a fascinating interview with Sister Margaret Costigan published by the WEA in Scotland in 1982, Paulo Freire said: 'you have the third world inside you'. In such complex relationships, insights, ideas and practices from one setting undergo adaptation and reinvention in the new setting.

Such were the processes that occurred in the course of the arrival of Freirean ideas in Scotland in the 1970s. We read Freire's books. We struggled with the translation of certain concepts from Romance languages, and specifically from Brazilian Portuguese, into English. We grappled with the application of Freire's ideas and practices in our specific first world setting. In the course of these processes of engagement we realised that the Freirean synthesis was not purely Brazilian. He had drawn together ideas from a whole spectrum of traditions and just about every corner of the globe, integrating and applying them in his own lived reality, his region of origin in the north east of Brazil. We realised also that no socio-cultural context is entirely sui generis or self-contained. Ideas and practices travel, translate, adapt, take root, co-habit, marry. The challenge for us in Scotland was to engage with, understand and adapt Freire in a Scottish situation. We found that it was possible, immensely refreshing, and generated enormous energy. Paradoxically, it highlighted the underdeveloped nature of democracy in Scotland! The ALP book, and its update in chapter seven, tell the story of what happened from there.

The main problem we faced was not popular resistance, but intellectual resistance in certain quarters, a kind of combination of first-world cultural arrogance and unconscious racism. Indeed, one of us was asked in an interview for a job in a Scottish University by a British professor of education: why should we be interested in the ideas of a Brazilian adult educator?

What in your opinion is the significance of adult education and literacy work in so-called developed and developing countries today?

In one sense the power of education and the fundamental importance of literacy, that is, the development of the ability to master and make critical use of a range of languages to name, know and act on the world will continue to be as significant as ever.

What is changing rapidly is the technology of information and communication and other technologies, and their relationships to the exercise of power in the world. Alongside these changes and dynamically interacting with them are changes in the dominant values of society.

To begin with information technology: within the last fifty years we have witnessed the development and spread of such media as television, computers, mobile phones and the internet. These are being used to generate new means of manipulation, control and wealth by power elites everywhere across the globe. To give one important example, they have enabled those wielding political, economic and financial power to know with much greater accuracy what public opinion is and to follow its changes day by day, week by week, month by month. The power elites have learned how to follow the flows and eddies of opinion, and how to channel it, so that they can keep in tune with it and adapt their presentation, policies and practices in order to maximise their power, wealth, and control.

This connects with current changes in dominant values. In the past several thousand years, which we might call the period of organised religion, certain values came to predominance. These included the ideas of love, compassion, forgiveness, cooperation, service, reverence for the whole of creation, the valuing of all forms of life, and respect for others as persons. They were accompanied by specific values associated with thought, language and action. The dominance of the idea of truth and truthfulness had as a universally accepted implication that, so far as practically possible, there should be a correspondence, a consistency, between what people thought, what they said or communicated, and what they did. This assumption has been significantly undermined.

There had, of course, also been other powerful values associated with coercion, deceit, dissimulation, cruelty and violence, but these were held in check to some extent by the countervailing power of the values associated with religion. The obvious example is the dialectical (and dialogical) relationship between Imperial Rome and the Christian religion.

In the 20th century, alongside the gradual decline of religion and the disastrous failure of Soviet and Chinese communism, we have seen the rise in the power of science and the development of the technologies it has generated. The old values promoted by religion have declined as religion itself has declined. Countervailing values have emerged including the notion of society as a rational machine and the dominance of the pleasure principle; the influence of relativism (the notion that, since knowledge and values are determined by circumstances and preferences, with changed circumstances and preferences come changed values); and the influence of nihilism (the notion that since there are no fundamental or foundational values, all values and processes of arriving at values can be undermined: anything goes). The notion of a distinction between 'is' and 'ought' statements is also undermined by the same processes. The specific discourses associated with upholding and following good ways of life, and creating good societies are also undermined and replaced by scientific and technological advances which are held by many to be value-free.

In the face of all this, there is no need to despair, but a need to hope, speak out and act in accordance with one's conscience. We need to reaffirm and also reinvent the values previously associated with religion, and engage in dialogue with science and technology to re-stimulate the recognition of positive and negative values.

It is to this project that Paulo Freire's ideas and practices make an immense contribution. Freire and the other personalist thinkers (John Macmurray, Martin Buber, Emanuel Mounier) are 20th century prophets for the 21st and succeeding centuries. We are entering a new era of encounter between the power of empire and the power of compassion. Freirean adult education and literacy work, conceived as cultural action for freedom, have a vital role to play in the reaffirmation of the good way of life and the struggle to create the good society.

Emilio Lucio-Villegas
Head of the Cátedra Paulo Freire
University of Seville, Spain

TOM STEELE

AFTERWORD

These chapters can be read as an account of a journey of self-discovery Colin has taken over several decades. Fragments of autobiography glint from the page forming a linking, if episodic, narrative from which the author himself emerges. Colin was born a Son of the Manse, his father an Ulster Presbyterian minister who, disturbed by the sectarianism of his native country, resettled in Scotland. Colin was born in Scotland and his childhood from the age of 10 was spent in Ayrshire where he heard from his fellow schoolchildren the many names a Catholic child could be taunted with. Later we find he studied literature at the University of Glasgow which confirmed a lifelong love of language and what Richard Hoggart might have called *the uses of literacy*. This included the Ayrshire poet, Robert Burns, to whom a chapter here is dedicated and who turns out to be a lot muckier than myth allows, Colin revelling in Burns's plural namings of the (private) parts.

He seems not to have been called to the Church, never having believed in the literal existence of a transcendent benevolent deity, though not altogether losing his sense of the value of religion as a source of tradition and communal good. For a while he embraced the Marxism of the Communist Party of Great Britain (CPGB) but found its authoritarianism was no substitute for real authority. He married Gerri, from a Glasgow/Donegal Catholic family, who became his partner working in what was a vocation of adult education. They lived in Italy for a year and formed lifelong friendships there. Perhaps it was this opening up to non Anglo-Saxon cultures that enabled them to embrace the newly translated work of Paulo Freire in the early 1970s. They led the way here and were instrumental, with others, in setting up the Adult Learning Project (ALP) in Edinburgh, one of the most path-breaking projects in Britain – only to be asked by a puzzled Professor of Education what they found of interest in a Brazilian educator. (I heard another Professor remark at a seminar later in the 1970s that there was nothing in Freire that could not be found in the work of R H Tawney.)

At what point Colin decided to make the turn into counselling and psychotherapy is not clear but Freire's 'dialogism' might have provided the fulcrum that tipped him into prioritising the personal. He himself underwent psychoanalysis from 1979–84, and it is tempting to describe Colin's translation into a psychotherapist as a second vocation. But it can also be seen as continuous with, and deepening, his work as an adult educator, an intensification of the personal perhaps but one that was intimately connected with the social and explicitly the 'persons in relation' perspective he adopted. Colin's last full-time post as Head of the Centre for Counselling Studies at Moray House Institute of

Edinburgh University was still nested among adult educators, to whom he was deeply committed.

This takes us to the meat of the book: a series of essays on the founding fathers (some might say Holy Trinity) of this uniquely Scottish approach to psychotherapy, the philosopher John Macmurray, the psychotherapist Ian Suttie and the psychoanalyst Ronald Fairbairn. Jock Sutherland adds further insights.

The persons in relation perspective owes its origin ultimately to the pragmatic philosophy of John Macmurray. During the 1930s Macmurray was, according to his DNB entry, strongly attracted to Marxism and believed that a just socio-economic order and a classless society were necessary conditions of genuine human community. Colin notes that in 2002 he came across his father's copies of two of Macmurray's books complete with marginalia. The benign bomb that 'exploded in his soul' was that belief in God was not necessarily the core of religion. Moreover it appeared that his father had also been deeply touched and confessed to Colin in one of their last conversations that, though he still believed in Jesus, the institutional church and its doctrines held less interest for him than they once had. Macmurray's reputation has suffered from his being lionised by Tony Blair, who clearly had learned little of substance from him but thought that he had. What might have appealed to him was Macmurray's prioritising of action over thought but Macmurray was challenging Cartesian philosophical dualism not advancing neo-liberal imperialism. Macmurray's most significant philosophical works were *The Self as Agent* (1957) and *Persons in Relation* (1961) given as the Gifford lectures in Glasgow in 1953–4. He shows here that personal identities are constructed from social interaction rather than in isolation and thus that society is logically prior to the individual. He was by this time well known as a broadcaster, setting up possibly one of the first attempts at a 'university of the air' and was one of the most respected voices in the post-war debates over the shape and expansion of higher education. Indeed his philosophy of action approach may have foreshadowed the creation of the polytechnics in 1965. So, it seems to me, the links between Scottish philosophy, the question of identity and public education were already well established.

For Colin, the psychotherapist Ian Suttie, a lesser known figure than Macmurray, again shifts the focus away from a sole concern with the individual to their relationships with others. His replacement of Freud's 'instincts' with 'love' implies the primacy of social bonding in identity formation – or at least that's how I read it. Colin claims that Suttie, like Macmurray and Fairbairn, drew on Scottish Christian and philosophical traditions in being able to challenge Freud's thinking with 'confidence and authority'. All this seems highly plausible to me. Learning about the Scottish Enlightenment and its tradition of 'common sense' philosophy has been a personal revelation since my arrival to work in Glasgow in 1996. Suttie's *The Origins of Love and Hate* (1935) seems to have influenced Macmurray and maybe Suttie plays the Father to Macmurray's Holy Ghost here? Suttie's whole thrust seems to emphasise social relationships and the feelings inspired by them: the need for companionship, love, tenderness and fellowship, for example, the denial of which leads to stress, emotional pain and ultimately breakdown. So what Colin calls the 'social disposition' is a key element of Suttie's contribution. His account of how the taboo on tenderness morbidly affects male relationships seems undeniable (as well as being the spur to some men's hostility to feminist perspectives). 'Fear of loss of love' may well trump Freud's 'fear of punishment' as an effective prohibition.

The third figure (Son?) here is the psychoanalyst, Ronald Fairbairn, whose revision of Freud was far- reaching but who did not make the break with Freudian language undertaken by Suttie[1]. Colin focuses on Fairbairn's notion of the 'internal saboteur', the anti-libidinal ego, that basically tells the rejected self to toughen up and don't be needy – how many times have you heard it! It just seems like something we have to do simply to get on with life. But do we? Maybe, but it's worth seeing what the cost of this is as a potentially pathological division of the self, of splitting ourselves in two, of one part of us hating the side of us that needs to be loved and looked after. OK, so perhaps we can live with that, but how does it affect how we live with others? Perhaps we also hate that needful aspect of those who crave our affection, who need us to love them, just as we need to be loved. Is it enough just to say to them pull yourself together, you'll get over it, there's work to be done? Possibly that's how society is forced to tick over, but what is the cost to the individual? A population of divided souls aggressively turning against themselves whenever they can't cope simply doesn't bespeak communal health. It doesn't sound like the *commonwealth* of citizens, neighbours and fellows that we imagine the Good Society to be. Collectively, we need others to be good for all to live in harmony, but to be good they need to be whole people, not internally fissured. Counselling, Colin maintains, can be a contribution to the Good Society by enabling individuals to relate better to each other, find their healthy identity in society, and pursue socially valuable activities.

Colin's discussion of Fairbairn and Macmurray in Chapter 3 includes much of his own personal journey, especially in finding a way of thinking about God without having to believe in his literal existence. God can be seen as the 'good other', a metaphor for how things might be if 'divinely' ordained, without actually being divinely ordained. This is an attractive idea. Although an atheist since early adolescence, I have long thought the idea of 'God' had an important cohesive function in society but was too closely connected to a fear of a punishing supernatural authority – and manipulated by a canny priestly hierarchy to keep each in their place. On the other hand the God/good other equation, freed of the men in black, institutional power (with its concomitant corruption) and magical thinking is worth consideration.

Closer to home for Colin is Jock Sutherland, his analyst's analyst, who held that the self is not directly knowable but that its structure can be investigated through self representations. I took this view to be a form of constructivism, which reminded me of Sartre's small study *The Transcendence of the Ego* (1936) which I studied as an undergraduate in the late 1960s. Sartre also believed the ego was not directly observable but was glimpsed, as it were, from the corner of the eye. He thought it was not so much constitut*ive* but constitut*ed,* made up somewhat after the events of conscious activity, consciousness itself being quite impersonal. It was a liberating phenomenological philosophy, it seemed to me then, that threw off the burden of a determining 'character' which was held responsible for one's activities, and made oneself a true moral agent. One no longer had the get out of saying 'Oh well, I did this because I am such and such a type of person', because one's character/self was continuously being created by the moral choices one made.

Sutherland's approach owes a lot to Fairbairn, expressed in the former's not entirely felicitous phrase 'self matrix' as a relational complex derived, in the first instance, from frustrations with one's mother. I'm not sure I didn't get a bit lost here, knowing that 'mother' is such a deeply intertextual sign in psychoanalysis, with all kinds of dynamic connotations. However, Colin argues that Sutherland was synthesising an important conjunction of Macmurray and Fairbairn's theories, no less than 'a significant moment in Scottish and international psychoanalytic history' because it combined philosophical, religious and psychoanalytic perspectives. Not knowing enough about any of these, I thought I needed more persuading but no doubt it is a debate that will be eagerly continued by professionals. I can see the value of seeing the self as a system, rather than the autonomous ego centre of convention, but I'm still confused as to where individual agency is located. For Sartre it was consciousness and for Nietzsche before him it was *Will*, but how far this is constrained by one's self is not clear to me – another paper Colin!

The latter chapters here concern Scotland as a 'learning society' (a phrase in vogue a few years ago) and Colin's path-breaking work with ALP but a linking chapter might have been useful. Some clues are given by Colin in taking a psychotherapeutic approach to national policy development. Extending Sutherland's perspectives on open and closed systems to think about the 'nation' is very suggestive. Projecting bad qualities onto its admittedly perfidious neighbour, England, has been a traditional Scottish pastime, especially for those of the Braveheart tendency. But the union and the British Empire lined a lot of Scottish pockets too and Scotland can no longer think of itself as the sat-upon poor relation. Getting out from under the Westminster of Tory fundamentalism is a key objective though.

In his final chapter Colin pursues Freire's message of treating the person as a subject in relation to others rather than instrumentally as an object to be manipulated into someone's desired shape. One can also trace Colin's political trajectory here. No longer the high price paid for the authoritarianism of what he calls the CPGB's '*un*democratic centralism' whose analytical clarity he sometimes missed: but how to be the authoritative (rather than the authoritarian) teacher[2]. It's a hard row to hoe as all of us involved in adult education have found. Even the term 'education' is uncomfortable now; policy speaks of 'learning' and 'facilitating' rather than 'teaching'. Freire might well have endorsed some such shift of emphasis but he would still have insisted that 'I am a teacher, not a facilitator', and that the teacher has a (moral) obligation to put a point of view – rationally considered and factually supported – even though it must not claim to be absolute truth. Learners, or students as they were once called, may need to see the teacher as an exemplar, as Ghandi thought, as the good other perhaps. Is this an example of 'Christian' citizenship? I'm uncomfortable with the term since 'citizenship' derives from classical humanism and for me, the values I would most want to draw from Christianity have those deeper roots – the scepticism, the dialogue, the irreverence.

I approached this Afterword as someone whose career has been spent in adult education, as a good friend of Colin and as someone who benefited immensely from a period of psychotherapy. The long reach of the Scots Colin describes here extended down to Leeds by way of Harry Guntrip who influenced the professional training of psychotherapists there and whose teaching WEA classes at the Swarthmore Centre, where I worked, was long remembered as a Good Thing. Guntrip's courses on Psychology and Philosophy during the 1940s and '50s related the major philosophical theories of Plato, Aristotle, Kant, Hegel and Marx to the psychoanalytical theories of Freud, Adler and Jung and attempted to outline a philosophy for everyday life. As his DNB entry notes:

> Guntrip's writings have been influential and have made psychoanalysis, in particular object relations theory, more accessible. They are the writings of a man with a mission to communicate and to convert, and represent his own integration of religion and psychodynamic science.

It seems to me that Colin's own work is a very worthy contribution to this tradition. His prose is lucid and wholly lacks the obscurantism of so much psychological writing. It is a fine example of what the poet Tom Paulin, in another context, has called 'a Presbyterian Grace'.

NOTES

1 Colin has made two highly illuminating comments on my Afterword and I think it is right to include them here as the initial elements of a dialogue. His first is for me, at least, a wonderful clarification of what the idea of the Trinity might mean in practice:

> With reference to Tom's interest in exploring the imaginative or symbolic meaning of the Christian Trinity, I'm not sure how far his ascription of the roles of father, son and holy spirit to Suttie, Fairbairn and Macmurray (in that or any order) will take us, because all three of them offer illuminating ideas and emphases relevant to *all three* persons of the Trinity. For what it is worth, my take on this question is that the three persons of the Trinity represent three clusters of relational positions, experiences, roles and qualities. To summarise:
>
> God the father, and mother, represents those 'good other' relations between persons that are parental, avuncular, grandparental and ancestral;
>
> God the son, and daughter, represents those 'good other' relations between persons that are filial, sibling, cousin-like, collegial and with strangers – relations roughly between people of the same generation;
>
> and God the holy spirit (God with us) represents those 'good other' relations between persons where the good other may or may not be *internally* present (having been internalised and subsequently occluded) in circumstances and at times when he or she may not be *externally* present.

I simply hadn't thought of how the idea of the Trinity might apply to real relationships and this is a very fruitful corrective to my own unlearned thinking about it.

[2] Colin's second response makes it clear that his reasons for joining the CPGB, as I should have realised, owed much more to *actual working relationships* than to signing up to Soviet Marxism.

> ... with reference to my membership of the Communist Party during the first half of the 1970s, let me make clear that is was not Marxism-Leninism, or statism, and certainly not uncritical support for the Soviet Union that drew me in that direction. Having already been inspired by the work-in at the shipyards on the upper Clyde, uniting a disparate workforce and wider communities and led by their own shop stewards around affirmative rather than merely oppositional action, it was my encounters with communist activists in the council tenants' movement in Glasgow which attracted me. I will never forget my admiration for their decency, commitment, often amounting to devotion, and their grasp of social and economic reality. I should add that I equally admired many others: Catholics, Protestants, Labour Party supporters, supporters of the SNP (Scottish National Party), members of the International Socialists, and still more who fought shy of any organisational commitment. I guess I was already something of a personalist even then.

> Having said that, I am intrigued by the idea Tom may be hinting at, namely that in choosing to join the CPGB I was expressing an unconscious search for a church genuinely committed to social justice, and an (equally unconscious) identification with my father as pastor, teacher and community leader. With hindsight, I think that is probably true.

My own attraction to Marxism was much more theoretical and I can see that I have projected this on to Colin. This response makes it clear, as he says, that the reasons for joining the CPGB were quite distinct and stemmed from his human relationships.

Tom Steele
Honorary Senior Research Fellow
School of Education
University of Glasgow

BY THE SAME AUTHOR

Living Adult Education: Freire in Scotland, 2nd edition
(with Gerri Kirkwood, Sense Publishers, 2011)

Voluntary Sector Counselling in Scotland: an Overview
(with Liz Bondi, Judith Fewell and Arnar Arnason, University of Edinburgh, 2003)

The Development of Counselling in Shetland: a Study of Counselling in Society
(COSCA and BACP, 2000)

Vulgar Eloquence: Essays on Education, Community and Politics
(Polygon, 1990)

Directory of Counselling Services and Training for Counselling in Scotland,
(Scottish Association for Counselling and Scottish Health Education Group, 1989)

Adult Education and the Unemployed
(with Sally Griffiths, Workers Educational Association, 1984)

Some Unemployed Adults and Education
(Workers Educational Association, 1981)

BIOGRAPHY

Colin Kirkwood is a psychoanalytic psychotherapist living and working in Edinburgh, Scotland.

From the 1970s onwards, he played leading roles in adult education and community action, promoting the ideas of the radical Brazilian educator, Paulo Freire, and becoming head of the Workers Educational Association (WEA) in south-east Scotland.

While training as a counsellor and psychoanalytic psychotherapist, he researched and edited the first *Directory* of counselling and counselling training services for the Scottish Health Education Group, and later became head of the Centre for Counselling Studies at Moray House School of Education of the University of Edinburgh. He and his colleagues based the counselling studies programme on a dialogue between psychodynamic perspectives and the person-centred approach.

After retiring from the University, he worked for five years as Senior Psychotherapist at the Huntercombe Edinburgh Hospital, with woman and girls suffering from severe eating disorders.

He has written several books including *Adult Education and the Unemployed* (1984), *Vulgar Eloquence: Essays on Education, Community and Politics* (1990) and *Living Adult Education: Freire in Scotland* (second edition, 2011) (with Gerri Kirkwood). He has also published poetry and literary criticism.

He is a devoted husband of Gerri, father of Paul and Anna, and grandfather of Rachel, Peter, David, Sean and Stella.

colinkirkwood@blueyonder.co.uk

Lightning Source UK Ltd.
Milton Keynes UK
UKOW052355170912

199173UK00002B/66/P